PRAISE FOR *HAIL MARY*

"*Hail Mary* tells the definitive story of the National Women's Football League—the touchdowns, the fumbles, the passion, the power. These are stories that nearly vanished—or in some cases, were purposely erased—from football's history, but through D'Arcangelo and de la Cretaz's deep dive, they're brought back to life in the voices of the players. Their truth and identity as Herricanes, Dandelions, Dolls, and Troopers is finally seen, their imprint on the game of football is indisputable."

—Tony Reali, host of ESPN's *Around the Horn*

"All too often, the history of women's sports lies buried beneath the surface, never seeing the light of recognition. D'Arcangelo and de la Cretaz do the historic work of bringing this story to life. In this vivid account of the rise and fall of the NWFL, they give us a much-needed record of the women who helped pave the way so we could all exist today. It's hard to imagine all the stories untold that led to the life I live today—I'm grateful to know these women who blazed the trail I walked upon."

—Layshia Clarendon, WNBA player

"I greatly enjoyed *Hail Mary*. I found it to be not only educational, but also entertaining and uplifting. By forty pages in, I'd begun trying to picture who was going to be cast to play what parts when they turn this thing into a movie."

—Shea Serrano, *New York Times*–bestselling author

"D'Arcangelo and de la Cretaz graciously and painstakingly piece together the story of a rarely remembered league and the women whose love of football made the unlikely possible. Memories from countless players, plus photographs and old memorabilia, tell the story of a fight to play that was both unique to its time and repeated over and over in the decades since. The NWFL is an important part of the history of women's sports, and in telling its story—its successes and failures—the authors offer a throughline from the gridiron gals of yesteryear to the female footballers of today."

—Sarah Spain, host of ESPN's *Spain & Company*

"Sport demands examination of its hidden histories, especially when involving groups of people that have been marginalized. In that vein, you are holding in your hands a book that will be regarded as a classic of the genre. In the hands of Britni de la Cretaz and Lyndsey D'Arcangelo, we are introduced to a world ninety-nine percent of sports fans don't know existed, and we are richer for it. Sports are for everyone, especially when met with fierce societal resistance."

—Dave Zirin, author of *A People's History of Sports in the United States*

HAIL MARY

HAIL MARY

THE RISE AND FALL
OF THE NATIONAL WOMEN'S
FOOTBALL LEAGUE

BRITNI DE LA CRETAZ

& LYNDSEY D'ARCANGELO

BOLD TYPE BOOKS

New York

Bold Type Books
116 East 16th Street, 8th Floor New York, NY 10003
www.boldtypebooks.org
@BoldTypeBooks

Printed in the United States of America

First Edition: November 2021

Published by Bold Type Books, an imprint of Perseus Books, LLC, a subsidiary of Hachette Book Group, Inc. Bold Type Books is a co-publishing venture of the Type Media Center and Perseus Books.

The Hachette Speakers Bureau provides a wide range of authors for speaking events. To find out more, go to www.hachettespeakersbureau.com or call (866) 376-6591.

The publisher is not responsible for websites (or their content) that are not owned by the publisher.

Print book interior design by Amy Quinn

Library of Congress Cataloging-in-Publication Data
Names: De la Cretaz, Britni, author. | D'Arcangelo, Lyndsey, author.
Title: Hail Mary : the rise and fall of the National Women's Football League / Britni de la Cretaz and Lyndsey D'Arcangelo.
Description: First edition. | New York, N.Y. : Bold Type Books, 2021. | Includes bibliographical references and index.
Identifiers: LCCN 2021010467 | ISBN 9781645036623 (hardcover) | ISBN 9781645036616 (ebook)
Subjects: LCSH: National Women's Football League (U.S.)—History. | Women football players—United States—History. | Football—United States—History.
Classification: LCC GV955.5.N37 D4 2021 | DDC 796.330820973—dc23
LC record available at https://lccn.loc.gov/2021010467

ISBNs: 978-1-64503-662-3 (hardcover), 978-1-64503-661-6 (e-book)

LSC-C

Printing 1, 2021

To every single woman who took the field as a member of the National Women's Football League, this book is for you.

CONTENTS

I'm proud of it. It was like I was some kind of pioneer or something. When I grew up there were only three careers we could have: nurse, teacher, or secretary. I never dreamed of playing pro football and yet I did, if only briefly.

—Susan Hoxie, Los Angeles Dandelions

Joyce Johnson, LA Dandelions
Photo provided by Joyce Johnson, LA Dandelions

INTRODUCTION

"John Unitas, Bart Starr, Roman Gabriel, Joe Willie Namath," wrote the infamous, hard-nosed sportswriter Bud Collins in the December 1967 *Boston Globe*. "These are names you know, men you respect for their ability to handle a football as well as several words of English on a TV commercial. They are acceptable quarterbacks but they are sissies when you consider them against Marcella Sanborn, quarterback of the Cleveland Daredevils."

Who—it was fair to imagine all of Collins's readers asking—was this woman, or this team? Collins continued, praising Sanborn while deriding these legendary male football players: "I mean, do they play defense? No. They sit on the bench and try to remember their lines for the next commercial," he wrote. "But Marcella Sanborn has no time off to recover from the bruises and scratches inflicted by predatory linebackers. She plays safety on defense. She is a 60-minute woman, and that is why Mrs. Sanborn, a makeup wearing pro football player, gets my annual Athlete of the Year Award."

Marcella Sanborn was one of the first to try out for a new women's football team, founded in 1967. In between raising her sixteen-year-old daughter, Claudia, and the hours she put in as a supply supervisor at the Ohio Bell Company, the thirty-nine-year-old Clevelander saw an announcement in the paper and thought—as so many women had before her—*Why not?* Having grown up playing football with boys from her hometown of Ury, West Virginia, Sanborn figured she was tough enough to hold her own.

Others, like Sanborn, tried out and made the team, too. Each one was ready and willing to ditch her everyday attire for cleats, pads, and helmets, and gladly take the field.

Originally, the team owner—one Sid Friedman, a fifty-year-old talent agent and promoter—imagined his players wearing tearaway jerseys and miniskirts. For him, the team was "a barnstorming venture more than actually competition." Women like Sanborn and so many others answered Friedman's ad that fall, and the newspapers eagerly announced there was a "gal's team."

But though the Daredevils team was supposed to be a gimmick, something changed along the way. The players made it real.

○————○

American football is considered masculine by nature. It's aggressive, violent, and tough, and requires a high level of endurance, speed, skill, and athleticism. These are all attributes that women are not expected to have—at home, in public, and certainly not on the playing field, if they are allowed on the playing field at all.

It isn't just the concept of women *playing* football or being physical that has confounded men. Since the sport's inception at the end of the nineteenth century, what has troubled men is the *interest* that women have shown in the sport itself.

"What is it? Why is it football takes such a hold on them," asks a 1913 *New York Times* essay, "makes them new people, turns the rules upside down and complicates the woman problem a hundredfold? It's a chapter the psychologists have yet to write." The essay continued, insinuating that women were attracted to the physicality and aggressive nature of football due to innate, primal instincts. "The cave woman watched her man cleave his axe into a head of an animal, yowled and howled, with all the satisfaction of an appetite appeased," it read. Even a hundred years ago, it seems—and despite the author's ludicrous scorn and warped bigotry—women were "hungry" for football.

What men, and society in general, have failed to understand is actually far less complex and analytical. It's rather simple. There's something about the elements of football that appeal to the human psyche,

regardless of gender. It's a team-oriented sport that focuses on both physical and mental capabilities, and yet there's an opportunity for players to
shine in their individual positions. There's a great deal of strategy to every
play call, whether on offense or defense, and the tempo is fast-paced from
start to finish. It's also a lot of fun.

But women weren't given the chance to experience football in all its
glory and immerse themselves in the game. Instead, they were relegated
to the sidelines while they watched their male counterparts take part in
the enjoyment.

At some point, it was only natural that they began to whisper boldly to
themselves, *I want to do that, too.* And in the 1970s and 1980s—against
all the odds, against every prejudice—a league of women did just that.

o———o

In 1970, the *Philadelphia Inquirer* published an "Action Line" column that
featured questions with answers by the editorial staff. One woman from
Lewisburg, Pennsylvania, had asked, "My brother says I'm a pretty good
football player and I'm thinking of turning professional. Only trouble is,
I'm a girl."

The response she got was promising.

"You may not be able to break the sex barrier and join the Eagles, but
there's a place waiting for you on the Pittsburgh Hurricanes," the editors
replied. "Professional female footballers are the brainchild of theatrical
agent Sid Friedman. [He] Recruited the first team—USA Daredevils—
in Cleveland, O., four years ago as a comedy attraction. Girls didn't think
it was so funny; they wanted to play serious ball. Now, there are four
teams in the all-gal league, including the Hurricanes."

Over the course of a decade, women's football teams sprung up across
the country. Many were no more than local affairs. And while some
teams knew and played one another, others seemingly arose of their own
accord, fulfilling the wishes of their players. Some—spurred by the ambitions, but not the brains, of the agent Friedman—dreamed of a national
women's football league to mirror the NFL itself. For a time, this dream
seemed far from impossible. And eventually, it became a reality with the
formation of the National Women's Football League in the early 1970s.

In the press, the players' looks were always described before their playing abilities. The women had to answer questions about whether playing football meant they supported women's lib. They always had to talk about what their (male) partners thought about their affinity for this contact sport, even though the league existed in a post-Stonewall world and many of the teams served as safe places for lesbian women to be themselves.

The women competed against each other. In some cases they even hated each other. Some teams didn't even know others existed, because they never played each other at all. But what they all had in common was a love for a game society told them they shouldn't (and couldn't) be playing.

Even as they battled each other on the field, players also battled for control of the league and their teams off the field. In some cases, they took on the male owners; but most often, they were subject to the whims, decisions, and financing of the men bankrolling and coaching the teams. The men in women's football controlled the money, and they weren't willing to invest the same resources or long-term capital, or provide the same number of chances that men's teams are given. The women played, and practiced, and hurt their bodies, often for no payment at all.

Still, in at least nineteen cities around the United States, from 1974 to 1988, the women of the NWFL broke the mold for what a football player was supposed to look like. Thousands of people came to watch; perhaps to gawk at first, but then, in the end, to cheer on the players. Though the fanfare wouldn't last, the players got to experience what it felt like to hear the roar of a crowd whenever they scored a touchdown or won a game. And it was exhilarating.

They were Linda Jefferson, the best halfback to ever play the game, who had five straight seasons with the Toledo Troopers where she rushed for over 1,000 yards and averaged 14.4 yards per carry. She would go on to become the first Black woman inducted into the Semi-Pro Football Hall of Fame and one of only four women in the American Football Association Hall of Fame. They were Oklahoma City Dolls quarterback Jan Hines, who led her team to delivering the Troopers their first loss after five undefeated seasons, as well as the Dolls' own undefeated season during which they allowed opponents only eight points all year. They were Rose Low of the Los Angeles Dandelions, a first-generation Chinese American and multisport athlete who legitimized the game during TV appearances alongside Billie Jean King. And they were Trooper Mitchi Collette, who has become a legend in the sport and has kept a women's football team going in Toledo for fifty years.

o———o

In many ways, the 1970s were the perfect time for a women's professional football league to take hold. It was during the pinnacle of second-wave feminism and the women's liberation movement, and women were gaining ground in athletics, as well. The passage of Title IX in 1972 and Billie Jean King's victory in the "Battle of the Sexes" in 1973 set the stage perfectly for the NWFL to debut the following year. But perhaps the world wasn't as ready for the league as the athletes may have hoped.

Though it didn't last, the legacy of the NWFL and its players endures today. More and more, women are becoming an integral part of professional football at all levels, from reffing and commentating to coaching and being NFL owners. There are at least four women's football leagues operating in the United States today, none of which would have existed without the NWFL.

Even while relegated to the sidelines and lacking equal opportunity or access to participate in its evolution, women have persistently managed to find a way to immerse themselves in the sport. Today, statistics show that the number of girls who play eleven-person football is on the rise, while the number of boys is declining.

This is a trend that's only increasing: The Utah Girls Tackle Football League started in 2015 with fifty girls and grew to over four hundred by 2018, doubling in size each season. All-girls tackle teams have also popped up in Indiana and Georgia. Beverly, Massachusetts, has an all-girls flag football team. And in February 2021, Nike announced that it had partnered with the NFL in a multiyear initiative (with five million dollars in funding) dedicated to growing girls' flag football in high school athletics. This rapid expansion can be credited to the increasing visibility of girls who play: *if you see it, you can be it*. And none of it would exist at all without the women of the NWFL paving the way.

Today, because of Title IX and the women who were determined to make an impact in women's sports, there are ten times as many girls participating in high school athletics as there were in 1972. That's an increase of more than 1,000 percent. The NWFL and the women's opportunity to play were both the result of the women's athletic expansion and equality movement, and also made them active participants in it.

"In a very few years from now, professional football could be changed in a big way, regarding women participants. Under Title IX, women must be given equal opportunity in athletics, in public high schools and universities," a woman named Pam Royse wrote in a 1978 Toledo Troopers' game program. "And so it may be, that out of Some-Town, USA, comes a new breed of female football player. Having had the advantages of competing with and against men, she is physically better for that experience."

○———○

During the Super Bowl LIII telecast in February 2019, Antoinette "Toni" Harris—a little-known female community college football player at the time—appeared in a new Toyota commercial. The commercial celebrated Harris, who played free safety on defense, as the first woman in history to be offered a college football scholarship in a full-contact position from a four-year university. By the end of her community college football career at East Los Angeles College, Harris had received six scholarship offers. In February 2020, she appeared in the "NFL 100" commercial spot opening for Super Bowl LIV, alongside a handful of NFL legends and football trailblazers.

It's not hard to look at Harris's recent achievements and trace them back to the NWFL. East Los Angeles College (ELAC) is the same school that Rose Low attended when she first started playing football for the Los Angeles Dandelions, a team that formed in 1973. It's an uncanny connection that threads far deeper than most people realize.

"When I was a student at ELAC in the early seventies, one of our female professors and coaches, Flora Brussa, went to Washington as part of a team to write Title IX. That law made it possible for our women's sports program to begin," Low explained. "When that door opened for us, who would have imagined that a female would play on the men's [football] team fifty years later and then be offered a scholarship to play at a four-year school? Maybe because a few of my schoolmates and I dared to play tackle football back then, a seed was planted for the women who followed to try."

Harris isn't the first woman to ever play football on a men's team at the college level. And she isn't the last. Sarah Fuller, a senior at Vanderbilt University and goalkeeper on the women's 2020 SEC Champion soccer team, became the first woman to play in a football game in a Power Five conference in November 2020 when she successfully executed the kickoff at the start of the second half, cementing her place in the history books. She also became the first woman to score in a Power Five conference when she flawlessly kicked an extra point during a game in December that same year. But without those who came before Fuller and Harris, particularly those women who played in the NWFL, their achievements may not have been possible.

Royse predicted this very scenario: "Our new breed of athlete goes to college somewhere on an athletic scholarship. She is a good athlete, no doubt about it, and after college she decides to make a career in football. Shortly afterward, a men's professional team takes its cue, realizing the publicity advantages of having a woman on the team. They offer her bigger money than a women's team could ever dream of doing."

But Royse cautioned women against taking that step, believing that when "a woman crosses that line in professional football, she takes with her everything the women's teams have fought for and won." Royse saw this crossover coming, where women would become athletic and talented enough to compete on men's football teams, but that wasn't their overall goal. The goal was to develop and grow the NWFL to such an extent that women wouldn't have to compete on men's teams—they'd have a thriving league of their own. "That woman" who joins a team of men "may gain a fabulous salary, but at the expense of her integrity, and that of every woman athlete," Royse reasoned.

When talking about the legacy of the NWFL, we're not just talking about women's football specifically. We're talking about the women who continued to pave the way for women *in* football, just as those who came before them did. When you look at professional football today, women are involved in nearly all facets of the game—media, promotion, coaching, ownership, social media, photography, broadcasting, and analysis.

In September 2020, history was made yet again when two women—Jennifer King for the Washington Football Team and Callie Brownson for the Cleveland Browns—worked on the sidelines as assistant coaches while longtime NFL referee Sarah Thomas was on the field. It was the first time three women stood tall on the gridiron in substantial roles during a regulation NFL game. Thomas also became the first woman to referee the Super Bowl, when she served as a down judge in Super Bowl LV.

The evolution of women in football didn't start with the NWFL and it didn't end when the NWFL folded. But it will always remain a significant point on the vast timeline of women's football history. The women of the NWFL were the first—but they have not been recognized or included in the narrative of achieving the milestone of playing professional football.

○———○

Still, this is a story not of the league itself, nor of the men who funded and ran it. It's not the story of how the NFL might change, or of a future where America has a robust ecosystem of women's football teams across the country. Instead, this is the story of the women who played the game, the glory and pain it brought them, and, ultimately, what it meant to them.

During our research for this extensive project, we realized that telling a story that adequately captured the comprehensive history of the NWFL was impossible, due to the sheer number of women who played. Over six hundred players were involved in the NWFL during its run as a league. We reached out to as many of them as we could find, listened to their experiences on and off the football field, and gave them the attention they deserved, which is long overdue. Some of the stats in this book may be disputed or documented differently in different primary source documents; we have done the best we can to be as accurate as possible, but it's hard to report on a league that lacked the mainstream attention or respect to have its records documented consistently in real time.

The players we were not able to reach or find, or who have passed away, have stories that deserve to be heard, too. While we were not able to highlight every player on every team, this book is for all of them—for every single woman who took the field and made it her own. Our goal is to write these women back into the narrative of football, where they have always been and undoubtedly belong.

o———o

While the groundbreaking story of the NWFL's most successful team—the Troopers, the winningest team in pro football history, men's or women's—is beginning to be told and they are well known in Toledo itself, the rest of the league remains largely unknown. Until now, memorabilia that help tell the league's story—newspaper clippings, hand-drawn football plays, team schedules, weathered game-day programs, old team clothes and uniforms, and many other significant items of that era—have remained hidden away in library archives and in basements and closets in players' homes. Beyond the physical collections, however, are the voices of the players themselves, the stories of their lives on and off the field, and what the NWFL meant to them.

Not all teams were as successful on the field as the Troopers, of course. And that was to be expected from adults with no formal football experience. Toledo's biggest rival was the Detroit Demons. It wasn't an on-field rivalry so much—the Demons didn't stand a chance against the Troopers and never managed to beat them—but there was no love lost between the teams. There were literal brawls on the field, and in one game, the Demons felt the hometown officials were being overly favorable to the Troopers, so they got in their cars during the third quarter and drove back to Detroit.

But that Detroit team is remarkable, too: It began as part of Friedman's outfit as a gimmick team named the Detroit Petticoats. However, once the women got a taste of the game, they wanted to be taken seriously as a football team. They eventually rebranded themselves as the Demons and joined the NWFL. When the team decided to become a serious football operation and many of the original players left, "they left behind a team of not-so-gorgeous women who desperately wanted to play football, and a bunch of patrons who, after seeing one game, never returned," wrote the *Detroit Free Press*. "It seems that once the girls put on the pads and helmets, the pretty, perfumed sight became bloody bad football."

Even still, the players were undeterred. Just one year later, the press rebranded them from a fledgling group of terrible football players to a bunch of edgy women trying to subvert patriarchal ideas of femininity. The *Times* of Shreveport, Louisiana, ran a story describing a mother of four who swigged beer in just her shoulder pads in the locker room after the game, players whose boyfriends wouldn't watch them play for fear the women would be injured, and a player who wanted to make sure people knew they may be playing football but they weren't members of the dreaded women's lib movement.

They may have been threatening the status quo in some ways, but not in any real way, they seemed to be saying. But change happens because everyday people refuse to cave to societal expectations. Yes, social movements are created on picket lines and in organizing meetings, but also in smaller acts involving individuals deciding to live the lives they want to live, naysayers be damned. In that way, the players were unwitting activists, whether they saw themselves that way or not.

These women came from diverse ethnic and racial backgrounds, largely from working-class homes. They were gay and straight; they were factory workers and mothers; they were beauticians and truck drivers. They overcame sexism, injuries, exhaustion, stereotypes, harassment, skeptics, and their own lack of training to become the first women's pro football league in US history. This is the story of the girl gridders who took America by storm: the women of the NWFL.

The league itself was a Hail Mary pass: a long shot, something with a high likelihood of failure. It's the pass you take because why the hell not, because the ball is in your hands and if you don't do it, the chance for success goes from slim to none. The Hail Mary that was the NWFL may not have been a completed pass, but for a while, as it sailed through the air toward its receiver, it looked like it had a shot.

Gloria Jimenez, Toledo Troopers
Photo provided by Gloria Jimenez

PART I

GAME DAY (1976)

IT WAS TOTAL DISBELIEF, TOTAL SHOCK. IT WAS A LONG WAY TO TRAVEL TO LOSE YOUR FIRST GAME IN YOUR ENTIRE CAREER. IT WAS A LONG RIDE HOME...A LOT OF CRYING, A LOT OF HEARTBREAK.

—GLORIA JIMENEZ, TOLEDO TROOPERS

CHAPTER 1

A HEATED CONTEST

It was a sweltering July night in Oklahoma City. At the 8 p.m. kick off it was still 92 degrees; down from a high of 99 earlier in the day. The heat, the local paper explained, was "wilting."

The Oklahoma City Dolls were opening their 1976 season—their first season—by playing the Dallas–Fort Worth Shamrocks. "Man, I'm ready," Doris Stokes, the Dolls' starting right halfback, told the *Daily Oklahoman*. "I'm not scared about it at all, just excited." Stokes was a twenty-one-year-old student at the University of Oklahoma and wore her hair in a big, perfectly round Afro, clocking in at 5'8" and 135 pounds. "I think we can handle Dallas," she continued. "We really think we're going to impress some people." She was ready to "pop somebody good."

"It would not surprise me if we were to have a sellout the first night," Mike Reynolds told the *Daily Oklahoman*. Mike, along with his brother, Hal, were co-owners of the new Oklahoma City team. The Reynolds brothers hired an advertising agent to sell ads for the game programs, and sold reserved season seats for eighteen dollars per person for the seven home games. "It would surprise me if we have less than 4,000," continued Mike. "Taft Stadium will seat 13,500, and it would not surprise me to have 13,500 there the first night."

Mike later changed his estimate to six thousand fans on opening night. In reality, his lowest estimate was correct, and approximately four thousand people forked over the $3.50 to watch the debut of women's professional football in Oklahoma City. And four thousand people, for a new team and venture, was nothing to sneer at. "My friends all like the idea. They all bought tickets to watch us play," tackle, full back, and middle linebacker Frankie Neal said. "They all say, 'I've just got to see this.'"

Some residents of Oklahoma City were already learning what it looked—and felt—like to have women on the field. In order to prepare for game play, the Dolls had been scrimmaging against local high school teams. Charlotte Gordon recalls the boys laughing at the Dolls, until they got out on the field together. "The greatest joy I got was beating the high school players when we would scrimmage them," the two-way player said, reveling in the fact that the women had shut those boys up and showed them they could hold their own. It was a good day when the boys would walk off the field shaking their heads and saying, "Oh, man, they really play." Their skill, Gordon said, was a surprise to everyone, except for the players themselves: "We knew what we wanted to do, and we knew how to go about it."

Built in 1934, Taft was designed in part for high school football games. The seats sat on top of concrete and faced the sun. The fans just about burned up in the heat.

In histories of Taft Stadium, many teams that have played on its field are mentioned: the high school teams that used it; its brief stint as the home of the Oklahoma City Plainsmen in the late 1960s; and for several seasons in the 1980s and 1990s it hosted the Oklahoma City Slickers, a professional soccer team. Not usually mentioned are the Oklahoma City Dolls—another professional sports team that played on the field—erasing the team from the sports history of the city and stadium. Even the stadium's Wikipedia page, often an indicator of which events make it into popular memory, failed to mention the Dolls until recently. (They weren't the only NWFL team that wasn't seen as legitimate enough to be remembered: for example, despite the fact that another NWFL team, the Dallas Bluebonnets, played in Texas Stadium, their name is nowhere to be found on the venue's Wikipedia page or in most reported histories of the venue.) But on July 31, 1976, women's professional football debuted in Oklahoma City.

"I was nervous," end Debbie Sales—known to her teammates as "Tinker"—said after the game. She ran out for the very first play, saying, "Oh my god," over and over in her head. But she "got over it real quick."

Tinker might have been right to worry. After all, the Dallas–Fort Worth Shamrocks were veterans, playing football together as a team since 1974. The Shamrocks had been strong competitors the previous year, losing only to the fabled Toledo Troopers. Many of the Shamrocks players had also played for the Bluebonnets, and continued on after the Bluebonnets folded following the 1974 season and the two teams merged. The Shamrocks were scheduled to play the Dolls for the first two games of the 1976 season, one game in each city. This July night in Taft was the first.

The *Daily Oklahoman* described the matchup as "a cliche"—veteran team versus newcomers—and noted that the DFW team outweighed the Dolls "by about 15 pounds a girl." Prior to the game, the Shamrocks tried to intimidate the Dolls by asking to borrow a belt, which they then sent back by claiming it wasn't big enough to fit around the player who needed it. They were also known to play dirty, the kind of players who would put their fist in an opponent's stomach to push themselves up after a tackle, just to get in an extra jab.

But Hal, the Dolls' head coach, felt confident that the speed of his players would overcome the pure heft of the other team. He said their game plan against the Shamrocks involved not running too much through the middle; this was because the Shamrocks' noseguard, Beverly Sandles, had at least seventy pounds on Dolls center Terri Talley. On offense, the team was looking out for two players in particular: Dallas' fullback, Deborah Canfield, and their two-way player, Sandi Beck, considered the Shamrocks' best athlete. "Our defense," Hal said, "is really going to have to watch out for her in passing situations." And with nearly six Shamrocks players going both ways, Hal hoped the Dolls would be able to wear them down. Hal planned to call plays from the sideline, but gave quarterback Jan Hines the freedom to call an audible anytime she felt it was necessary. "It's nice to have a quarterback who's intelligent enough," Hal said, "and can call the automatic."

The 5'4", 128-pound QB trusted her line for protection from DFW's hefty defense. Under her helmet, Hines sported a mess of brown waves that came down just below her ears and had small eyes that narrowed when she grinned. "If I said I wasn't nervous, I'd be lying," she said before the first game. "But when game time comes, I'll be ready."

Hal believed that "if they do what [the coaches] taught them in practice; if the line blocks well; if the defense doesn't make any big mistakes," then the Dolls would come out victorious. Charlotte Gordon, who had reveled in the Dolls' victories over the city's high school boy teams, said at the time: "I have no doubts—no doubts at all—that we can't beat 'em."

○————○

The game was attended by the family of the Oklahoma City kicker, Mary BlueJacket. Her brother came in all the way from Phoenix. Her mother, worried to death that BlueJacket would get hurt, and being a stout Catholic, brought her angels to the game.

BlueJacket grew up in Colorado, but spent summers visiting her dad's family in the town of Bluejacket, Oklahoma. That her last name reflected that of the town was no coincidence. Beginning as a train station in 1871, the tiny town in the northeastern corner of the state was named for Mary's great-grandfather, Rev. Charles Blue Jacket, a Methodist minister who served as the town's first postmaster in 1882. Reverend Blue Jacket was a descendent of Blue Jacket, chief of the Shawnee nation.

Since then, generations of BlueJackets descended from the Reverend have played football in the town that bears their name. This football dynasty is detailed in a 2014 article from *Tulsa World*, establishing the long history of football in the area and the family who has played it. The article's lead photo features Ginni Satterwhite—the older sister of Mary BlueJacket who played for the Dolls—and Satterwhite's grandchildren and nephew, who played on Bluejacket High School's team. Satterwhite, the article claims, is "the matriarch of Bluejacket football." But there is a glaring omission in that story: Mary. She is a BlueJacket who played professional football and lives in Bluejacket. Yet she wasn't included in a story about her own family, who dominated the sport in their town.

This omission is just one more example of women in football being erased from its history.

The town itself is located in Cherokee Nation. Small and rural, Blue-jacket is less than half a mile across. There were under three hundred people living there in the 1970s, when BlueJacket moved there, though it had over eight hundred during its most economically flush period at the turn of the twentieth century. (A new convenience store opened in 2014, owned by BlueJacket's sister, Satterwhite.) State Highway 25 runs directly through the downtown, where there is a high school and a post office.

Still, the town had an allure for BlueJacket as a young girl. While she loved Colorado, with its mountain air and range of seasons, BlueJacket enjoyed going back to Oklahoma to spend time with the local kids her age. She felt a connection to this place, where her father, who was Shaw-nee, had grown up (her mother was white). She made a vow to herself: when she graduated high school in 1973, she was going to move to Blue-jacket, where she'd made friends on her visits and where her sister had moved first.

But she'd been naive, not realizing that the local kids would be eager to get out of their small town once they graduated. BlueJacket arrived in Bluejacket, but all her friends were gone.

After nine months, BlueJacket got bored and decided to move 185 miles southwest to the city: Oklahoma City. She got a job at a grocery distributor, lifting boxes in the warehouse, making her strong. One day, while her friend was visiting from Denver, BlueJacket spotted something in the newspaper about a new women's football team. She'd grown up throwing the ball around with her brothers, but never dreamed of being able to do that in "real life." So when she read about the team, she didn't fully believe it. There was no way this could be real, she was sure of it. Her disbelief almost caused her to disregard the ad altogether, but her friend convinced her otherwise.

You don't have any friends in town yet, BlueJacket's friend argued. *You should go and meet some people your age,* she pushed. BlueJacket relented. She went to the tryouts, taking the first step toward playing football for the three years she would later describe as "the best of my life."

Months later, on that hot July night in 1976, BlueJacket was on the field. Her family was in the stands, and the Shamrocks, though the more experienced team, were making a poor showing. Indeed, one Dallas–Fort Worth coach admitted his team "really didn't play good ball." The local Oklahoma City paper called the Shamrocks "pitiful." And so, despite the Dolls being novices—and even playing a little sloppily—they were able to capitalize on two Shamrocks errors in the second quarter to pull ahead and hang on for victory.

On the Shamrocks sideline, the players were calm. They were used to the game atmosphere. The Dolls sideline was livelier, full of pacing, jumping, and yelling.

On the field, however, the Dolls had a different philosophy: silence. In the face of the incessant trash talking from their opponents, the Dolls tried not to give the Shamrocks the satisfaction of a response. Dallas–Fort Worth was known to especially revel in the trash talk. "What they really say, you couldn't print," Dolls offensive tackle Melissa Barr told the *Daily Oklahoman*. "It's unbelievable some of the things they say they are going to do to you." The Dolls believed that by ignoring the trash talk they would throw off their competitors, who were trying to get a rise out of them. Refusing to engage in a back-and-forth with opponents also meant they could concentrate on the game in front of them, as opposed to interpersonal conflicts.

"There's no sense in me coming up there and telling her [the other team] when it's coming," said BlueJacket. "She'll know when I hit her."

Even still, the Shamrocks' big mouths brought out BlueJacket's competitive side. During one of the Dolls' games—though she can't recall which one—fullback Cindee Herron remembers BlueJacket coming into the huddle, complaining about all the jabbering coming from the player she was guarding on the line. "I'm gonna break her finger," BlueJacket snapped. After the play, BlueJacket returned to the huddle a little sheepishly. "I think I broke it!" she said.

In the first quarter, when Oklahoma City nearly scored a touchdown, Hines turned to the other Dolls. "They're scared, they're really scared," she said. "Boy I'm sorry we didn't make that one, but we'll get 'em next time."

Two Shamrocks miscues—a bad punt snap and a fumble—happened within fifty-seven seconds of play. These two errors meant the Dolls only had to go twenty-six yards for two touchdowns. The first, a bad snap, was recovered by Dolls linebacker Jean Derry at the Shamrocks one-yard line (Derry played only one season; her career was cut short by bone disease). Then, twenty-year-old Herron, defensive coach Dee Herron's wife, took off from the backfield around the left tackle to score, giving the Dolls a 6–0 lead. Herron had sent Cindee into the game with instructions to "Get in there and knock the shit out of them, hon!"—which she promptly did.

For their second touchdown, the team had to work a little harder. After the Dolls recovered a fumble at the Shamrocks twenty-five-yard line, Hines completed a twenty-four-yard pass to Sales—Hines's only pass of the first half. Once Sales caught the ball, however, the team seemed to forget their game plan to avoid running up the middle and into Shamrocks noseguard Beverly Sandles. On their first three downs, the Dolls ran the ball directly into Sandles, who stopped them in their tracks. On fourth down, however, Hines ran around the right side of the offensive line for the touchdown, followed by BlueJacket's successful two-point PAT. (Discussed in detail later in the book: field goals after a touchdown were worth two points in the NWFL, as opposed to the standard one point).

Even against their more seasoned rivals, the Dolls went into halftime with a 14–0 lead. They struggled during the second half of the game. Still, after the Shamrocks opened the half with a forty-nine-yard touchdown drive, the Dolls managed to hang on. In the end, Oklahoma City won 14–6.

After the game, there were still a handful of Dolls on the sideline who hadn't gotten any playing time during their first game. Coach Herron approached each one and gave her a hug and a kiss on the cheek and said, "I know how hard you worked for this and I'm sorry we didn't get you in. That's just the way it worked out. We'll get you in next time."

Even though it was an adjustment for the players to go from practice to a live game, the women seemed to acclimate pretty quickly. "I felt really good out there," Sales said at the time. "It's a lot different from practice in that you don't know who you'll cream—or get creamed by." The win was a big deal for the team in terms of establishing their confidence. The

Dolls, admitted Shamrocks coach Jackson, "could be in the running for the championship, if they keep playing the way they played tonight." This was a nice bit of foreshadowing.

Even so, the press was unimpressed. "An artistic success it wasn't," proclaimed the *Daily Oklahoman*. "Dallas played pitifully at times and that, coupled with the conservative offenses and dominating defenses, wilting heat, long concession lines, and first-game mistakes, made the fare, well, rather dull." Imagine a men's team being criticized for having "a dominating defense"!

Still, the Dolls had made their mark. And in 1976, the rest of the teams in the league—including the unstoppable Toledo Troopers—would soon come to find out that this team was for real. The balance of power in the NWFL was about to shift.

o———o

Oklahoma City's second game was a rematch with the Shamrocks, this time on DFW's home turf. Only two weeks had passed since their first meeting. Hal told the papers that his team was "ready for them." Their game plan was to pass more, and Hal noted that they'd "saved quite a few" of their plays in order to surprise the Shamrocks.

This was a very different game for the two teams. In the first game, the Dolls struck first. But in the second, it was the Shamrocks who pulled ahead 12–0, with two first-half touchdowns. Even so, OKC didn't stay down for long, hitting back with a touchdown and two-point conversion just before halftime, bringing the score to 12–8. Stokes rushed twenty-five yards to score, and safety Cathie Schweitzer caught the PAT pass.

Halfway through the third quarter, the Dolls sealed the win. Hines completed a forty-five-yard touchdown pass down the left sideline to Sales, doing exactly what coach Hal had wanted his team to do: pass the ball more. "Tinker made a tremendous catch and just outran 'em down the sideline," Hal said. Stokes, Herron, and running back Pebble Myers combined for 239 yards rushing.

What the first two games established was the partnership of quarterback Hines and receiver Sales, who would be a dream team for the Dolls.

Sales became a key, trusted receiver for Hines and, together, they made some of the biggest plays in the biggest games.

BlueJacket credited the team's "self-control"—their refusal to engage with DFWs slinging insults—with helping them pull out the back-to-back wins. "They were out for blood, out to kill," she said. "They were out more to hurt us than to win. They were so mad, [the defensive lineman] would stand there and pound on us instead of going after the ball carrier."

The team gelled really well, which became apparent early on. Gordon described them as having "a lot of team spirit." "I thought a lot of times when women got together they tended to spat and have problems, but not us," she said. "We're a together team, and this is going to prove that myth about women completely wrong. We're going to tear it to pieces."

One example of that kind of camaraderie happened after Stokes scored her touchdown. Stokes was lining up on the end so she could protect BlueJacket while she kicked the extra two points. She was down in her stance when she heard a Dallas player yell out, "Thirty-three! Thirty-three! I will put you on your butt!"

It was then that Stokes realized that *she* was number 33, and that there "was about to be a battle." When the ball was hiked, Stokes braced herself for impact. But she never felt a thing. *What's going on?* Stokes wondered.

One teammate walked up and said, "I heard what she said." She had put that Dallas player down on the ground.

"I wasn't going to let her touch you," she told Stokes. From the beginning, the Dolls saw themselves as a unit and they had each other's backs.

Despite the excitement of their second win, the Dolls suffered a blow during the last play of the first half of the game: Sandy Glasgow, the Dolls' defensive end and defensive captain, was in pursuit of a Shamrock and got clipped, severely injuring her knee. She had surgery, which sidelined her for the season. Glasgow was a twenty-six-year-old cardiovascular assistant with long, straight dark hair that made her look like a Charlie's Angel. It was sad for the fans, who knew Glasgow as the voice behind a radio commercial for the Dolls. But it was sadder for the team, because Glasgow was one of the leaders, always giving pep talks and getting spirits up.

The Dolls were very concerned, and not just about Glasgow herself. They needed all the leaders they could get—because their next opponent was none other than the most successful and most feared team in the NWFL, the Toledo Troopers.

The Dolls were right to worry.

CHAPTER 2

A RIVALRY IS BORN

Linda Jefferson described herself as a "run-of-the-mill Black girl," who was "thinking of becoming a millionaire." Before becoming the star halfback of the Toledo Troopers, Jefferson was born and raised in a working-class neighborhood in Toledo, Ohio. As a child, she honed her speed by running up and down her street, until someone suggested she go out for the track team. Soon, she could run the forty-yard dash in just 4.9 seconds.

Despite calling herself "run-of-the-mill," Jefferson recognized not just her own untapped athletic potential, but that of other girls as well. She lamented the lack of investment in infrastructure and coaching, even in her early days. For example, Jefferson's high school girls' track team was run by the athletes themselves, because the coach didn't care enough to pay attention. And despite running on track teams since the age of eleven, Jefferson didn't learn how to get out of the starting blocks until her senior year of high school. "If a coach could take the time with me to teach me the fundamentals," she said, "I think I could get my one-hundred-yard-dash time down to ten seconds flat." That she was able to accomplish what she did without proper instruction is a testament to her own dedication and innate talent.

Jefferson was a natural athlete. She eventually won several medals in track in Junior Olympic competition, for the long jump and the 440-yard relay. She played basketball for the Toledo All-Stars, a women's team in Ohio (despite being only five feet three inches), played softball whenever she could, and, of course, played football for the Troopers. On top of it all, she worked part-time at UPS—from midnight to 4 a.m.—and took classes at Toledo University.

Jefferson had decided to try out for the Troopers after her friend suggested she join. It was the team's second year in existence, 1972, and the Troopers were still a fledgling independent outfit. In fact, an organized league of teams like the NWFL was still just a dream then. Despite all this, the only reason Jefferson hadn't joined the new team the year before was because she was seventeen and still in high school; as such, her mother wouldn't let her play. Jefferson was the fourth daughter, born when her mother was twenty-one years old. Her mother preached the importance of getting an education; school was the priority.

She started as a split end because she could be protected and avoid being tackled. Eventually, however, Troopers coach Bill Stout moved her to halfback because of her speed. That's where things really took off.

In fact, Jefferson was a major reason the Troopers were undefeated for five straight years (in the three seasons they played before the NWFL started and the two they played as members of the league). But while Jefferson got much of the credit, she herself attributed her success to her teammates. Specifically, Jefferson praised her blockers for opening up holes and holding off the other teams' defenders. "If they give me a hole that's as small as my body I can make it," she said. "If they give me a hole as wide as one foot I can make it."

o———o

By 1976, the year the Dolls joined the NWFL, the Troopers had a lot of momentum. They still hadn't lost a game. Jefferson had made national television appearances and been on the cover of *womenSports*, the magazine cofounded by tennis star Billie Jean King.

With all that attention, coach Bill Stout (the new president of the NWFL at the time) and the Troopers board of directors thought a billboard to promote the team would be a great advertising move. They decided to place it overlooking the Toledo Sports Arena, a venue on Main Street with over five thousand seats that was then home to the International Hockey League's Toledo Goaldiggers. The goal was to target already existing sports fans by alerting them to another local team they may not have been aware of.

There were a lot of selling points the billboard could have advertised: the team's five straight undefeated seasons, or the fact that they had a 28–0 record. Instead, they went with just two words at the top: "Pretty Tough." In the center of the billboard were three smiling faces, Jefferson, the face of the franchise, in the middle, and two white women on either side of her, a brunette to her right and a blonde to her left. At the bottom it simply said, "Toledo Trooper Football."

The billboard spoke to the rock and the hard place that Troopers management found themselves between. They had an incredible product to promote, one that should have been appealing simply for its quality. But they had the challenge of sexism to overcome.

Throughout history, women athletes have been reduced to their looks, and advertisements have focused on making them appear conventionally attractive and feminine and, therefore, nonthreatening. Even today, nearly fifty years since Title IX, women are overwhelmingly represented in advertisements in sexualized ways—if they're featured at all. Despite evidence from a 2014 study in the *Journal of Sports Management* that "consumers prefer portrayals focusing on sportswomen's skill versus their sex appeal," women athletes are still more often than not "presented in sexually provocative poses versus highlighting their athletic competence." Ads featuring women athletes overwhelmingly emphasize their femininity and perceived heterosexuality. And this emphasis, in turn, trivializes women's sports.

That's why, in an article about Jefferson being a "superstar of women's pro football," the writer felt like he needed to assure the public that "she is one of the most attractive, and without a doubt, superbly built superstars in pro football." And while this "superstar" was "fast becoming a commodity" within the competitive world of her profession, nevertheless, the writer assured readers that Jefferson was just as "at home in a dress with neatly coiffed hair as she is in shoulder pads behind a face mask."

Yes, the players were tough, but the billboard also needed to reassure (male) fans that they were also pretty—and predominantly white. The proof was in the image. And other teams were moved to offer similar "proof": for example, the illustration used to advertise the OKC Dolls was of a thin, white, feminine woman in a football jersey, with long, blond hair billowing in the wind.

But the Troopers billboard wasn't just insulting, it was a lie. If you showed up at a Troopers game to see the women on the billboard perform on the gridiron, you'd only be able to watch Jefferson. The other two women weren't actually Troopers—they were paid models. Despite the fact that the team had over twenty women on the roster, none of them, aside from Jefferson, was deemed attractive enough to be used to promote the franchise they were responsible for making successful. For some of the women, it was a slap in the face. "It didn't sit well with us," said Eunice White, who played with the Troopers for seven seasons. "We were a very diverse group of women. They didn't need to go outside of the team to achieve the image they were looking for." Ruth Zuccarell, who played for six seasons, said the players "just didn't understand why they used models. . . . I guess we weren't pretty enough."

Zuccarell was apparently considered appealing enough to appear alongside Jefferson in another ad, one that ran in newspapers and pictured the two women in street clothes rather than their Troopers uniforms, under a tagline that called women's professional football "semi-sweet." You know, because the women might be flattening each other to the ground, but they're still at least a little sweet and, again, nonthreatening.

○———○

Toledo began their 1976 season playing against the Oklahoma City Dolls. The Dolls were fresh off their two victories over the Dallas–Fort Worth Shamrocks, barely a month before.

The Troopers were ready to take on this new team, and reaffirm their dominance over the league. Sure, the Dolls had won their first two games, but they were the new kids in town. Most importantly, the Troopers had never lost a game. (There was one major change to the season's lineup: Lee Hollar, who had played quarterback for the Troopers' first five seasons, had joined the service. She was replaced by Pam Hardy, who at five feet tall and just one hundred pounds, was one of the smallest players in the league.)

To prep for the season, the Troopers had been training with Coach Stout in Toledo's Colony Field, as usual. Colony was more of a prairie than a sports field, but they made it work. To achieve their years of dominance, the Troopers practiced fifteen hours a week, despite the fact that most of them held down full-time jobs during the day. And, as Mitchi Collette said, "Heaven forbid you ever miss a practice."

Sometimes two hundred spectators would watch them practice from lawn chairs. And there were times cars would drive by and men would shout, "Get back in the kitchen!" out the window at them. But the Troopers were undeterred.

Against the Dolls on Saturday, August 21, 1976, the Troopers set out to do what they'd done all twenty-eight times they'd taken the field for the past five seasons: win.

"[That the Troopers were undefeated was] like all we ever heard," said Dolls quarterback Hines. "Everybody knew that they had started the league and everybody knew they'd never been beaten." Not only that, she added, the Dolls were concerned about facing Jefferson. But despite the Troopers' reputation, the Dolls felt confident.

"We'll lose eventually," Jefferson told *womenSports* the previous year, "because as our coach tells us before each game, there's not a team in the world that can't be beat." The Dolls wanted to be the team that finally succeeded where others had not.

Two days prior to the game between the Troopers and the Dolls, the match had been advertised in the local paper: "Okla. City's Newest Professional Sport!" the adverts screamed, next to a black-and-white illustration of that smiling, helmetless football player whose long hair streamed behind her. On game day, the local paper ran a story about Jefferson: "Dolls Meet Linda, Toledo Tonight."

Jefferson had an afternoon of press scheduled for her in Oklahoma City prior to game time, hot off her status as *womenSports* magazine's

"WomanSport of the Year" the previous summer. But unfortunately Jefferson showed up to the airport two minutes late for her flight to OKC, forcing Dolls owner Mike Reynolds to frantically call and get her flight rescheduled. She arrived in the Sooner State three hours later than scheduled, which meant she had to hurry through her media appearances.

Still, Jefferson's promotion worked. Three thousand two hundred fans forked over the $3.50 for a ticket ($1.50 if they were a child), though that still left a lot of empty seats at Taft Stadium. The "majority" of the crowd were there "out of curiosity," Dolls general manager Mike Reynolds told the papers. "A lot" of people who came "aren't even interested in football." But the fanfare around the game created "a big-event atmosphere," according to Hines, full of people who had shown up to watch the Troopers and to see what this new league was all about.

It didn't take long for both Toledo and Oklahoma City to realize that, on some level, they'd each met their match. The teams were incredibly evenly balanced, something players on both sides immediately understood. At the same time, the Dolls probably caught the Troopers a little bit off guard; the Troopers, after all, had considered the new team a sort of warm-up game for their season. It was the beginning of a rivalry between the teams that would last until they stopped playing.

"We had a lot of respect for them," said Oklahoma City's Hines, "but . . . it was important to us to beat them."

The first half was scoreless. The closest either team got to scoring was in the second quarter, when the Troopers managed a first and goal at the ten-yard line. Three plays later, the Troopers made it to the two-yard line. But when quarterback Pam Hardy attempted a bootleg play—in which the quarterback runs with the ball toward the sideline after it's snapped—on fourth down, she was stopped by the Dolls' right linebacker, Cindee Herron. Meanwhile, the Dolls offense never made it past Toledo's twenty-seven-yard line in the first half.

○———○

After a bad snap by the Dolls halfway through the third quarter, the Troopers finally struck: a five-yard rush by Jefferson put the Troopers on the board. Gloria Jimenez kicked the extra-point conversion, and Toledo led 8–0. The Dolls immediately answered with a seven-play, fifty-eight-yard drive that ended with quarterback Hines rushing for twenty yards to score a touchdown. For this, Hines gives "all the credit in the world" to right end Charlotte Gordon: "[She] pulverized her defender. She just pancaked that girl. . . . I could not have scored without that block."

But after Gordon's crucial block, Hines still had to fend for herself. Just as Hines was getting to the goal line, she could see a Trooper coming at her and knew, instinctively, that she would dive at her. So Hines dove first, stretching out with the ball as far as she could in midair. Hines knocked over the pylon on the right side just as the Troopers player hit her legs, spinning Hines around in the air. But it was a touchdown.

When Dolls kicker Mary BlueJacket's extra-two-point attempt was blocked, it appeared the Troopers would pull out another victory. But two minutes later, trailing 8–6, Dolls nose guard Tina Bacy tackled Jefferson for a two-yard loss; then came a six-yard loss for the Troopers. And, with eleven minutes remaining in regulation, a group of Dolls tackled Toledo punter Barbara Church in the end zone for a safety, tying the game at 8–8. The score would remain that way until the end of regulation.

Bacy's defense is what Hines credits with the Dolls' success that day. "She was tall and slender, and she was able to shoot the gap on the deep ends of line," Hines recalled. "And she was an extremely disruptive player. She caused a lot of problems for them when they went off end. She caused fumbles." Bacy also helped hold Jefferson to less than one hundred rushing yards for the first time in Jefferson's career. Bacy played only one season for the team, during which Mike Reynolds said she was their "best defensive player." Her career was ended due to a knee injury that required surgery right before the 1977 season.

Reflecting on it now, Toledo's Collette says that the Troopers innately realized they'd finally found a worthy opponent. "We were a small team as far as our average height was 5'4" and our average weight was 140. We were tiny, but we were mighty," said Collette. "When we went to Oklahoma City, their average height was 5'7.5" and their average weight was [141]. They were good and so were we."

More than that, says Jimenez, is that the Dolls were playing on their home turf, and they had a sideline full of players. The Troopers showed up with far fewer players, meaning that many of their players played both ways or, in Jimenez's case, hardly came off the field at all. "That was the most beat-up I've ever been after a game," she said. "The team was very good."

o———o

Being on a relatively new team, Hines wasn't familiar with the league rules. After regulation ended with a tie score, Hines recalls saying to the referee, "Oh wow, I get to tell my grandkids that we tied." And he said, "No, you don't. You have to play sudden death." That's when Hines said her adrenaline spiked. "The tie end was kind of OK and that was something to brag about and tell people about, that you tied this team—but I just absolutely did not want to lose."

There was a coin toss, which the Dolls won. In the huddle, BlueJacket gave the team a pep talk and an incentive: "Let's just wrap this up," she said. "I'm tired. Let's go for a beer." The motivation worked—the Dolls took the ball and the Troopers never even touched it in overtime. Hines recalls that at the end of every practice, the team would practice "fun trick plays." One of those plays was a hook-and-lateral (colloquially known in football circles as a "hook and ladder"); another was a flea flicker. They had never expected to use any of the plays in a game setting. But both came in handy, and helped the Dolls pull out the victory.

On their second play, the Dolls ran the hook and ladder. Hines flicked a pass to right end Gordon, who then lateraled the ball to halfback Doris Stokes for a thirty-five-yard play, with fifteen extra yards added on because of a face mask penalty. This got the Dolls down to the twenty-yard line. Gordon and Stokes were shocked when their coach called the play in such an important game because, despite the number of times they'd run the play in practice, they'd never managed to complete it. The women were both speedy—Gordon with a slow first step, but then she'd take off—which made it hard for them to get their timing down when executing the play. But, Stokes remembers, "it just flowed so smoothly . . . in the game."

Two plays later, Hines ran a version of a flea flicker play, in which the defensive team is tricked into thinking the offense is going to run the ball when they really intend to pass it. Hines completed a perfect nineteen-yard pass to her tried-and-true left end, Tinker Sales—the only pass reception of the night for the five-foot-five player.

It's a moment Hines will remember forever, one where "everything was in slow motion." She'd made the decision to go to the left because they'd run the ball to the right all night. Hines wanted to bring "the element of surprise" by going the other direction, but was afraid to make the call herself at such a high-stakes moment. Then, as she was going into the huddle, she heard her coach call her name above the roar of the crowd. "I looked over and he's giving me a signal to run it to the other side and I'm thinking, 'Oh, thank god.'"

"I remember rolling out to my left, and I can remember seeing my receiver [Sales], and it was almost like looking down a straw, and I could see only her," said Hines. "And the ball just kind of jumped out of my hands and jumped into hers. And I was never really conscious of throwing it. But I guess I did, 'cause that's what they said in the paper." Thanks to some unconventional play-calling pulled from their bag of tricks, the Dolls won, 14–8.

Hines thought they still had to try to kick the extra two points, and didn't realize the game was over, despite the fans that rushed the field after the touchdown. She wandered around, wondering how they were going to get all the people off the field so BlueJacket could kick the PAT. "And then I realized the game was over," she recalled.

Fifty years later, it is still the proudest moment many of the Dolls players can remember. "We shut Miss Jefferson down!" Gordon said. Cindee Herron was given the game ball that day. "We really felt like we'd done something," she remembered.

For the Troopers, the loss was crushing. Collette describes it as "devastation." They didn't expect to start their season losing for the first time in five seasons to a brand-new team. The way they saw it, they weren't training five days a week in the middle of a prairie—putting their bodies on the line and risking injury for essentially no money—just to lose to a group of women who had just shown up on the scene.

"The look on all my coaches' faces was like, 'Tell me that didn't just happen,'" said Collette. "I remember getting on the bus and going back to the hotel and a lot of the players that had been there before me, they were crying. Because we never knew how it was to lose."

Jimenez, too, remembers the crying. "It was total disbelief, total shock. It was a long way to travel to lose your first game in your entire career," she said. "It was a long ride home . . . a lot of crying, a lot of heartbreak."

There was one thing that the entire Troopers team agreed on: there was no time to grieve this loss. They had a season to continue, and they were determined not to lose again.

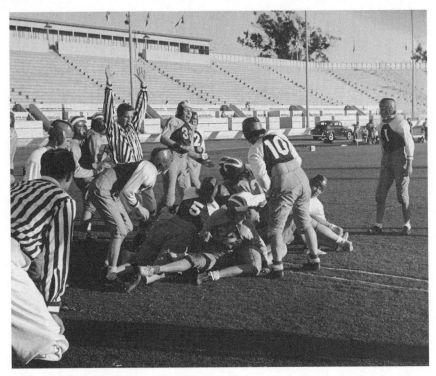

The Marshall Clampett Amazons of Los Angeles score the winning touchdown against the Chet Ralph Hollywood Stars, 1939
Life magazine/Getty Images

PART II

HISTORY (1896–1970)

———

WHEN I READ THE AD IN THE PAPER FOR
PLAYERS, I THOUGHT IT WAS A GAG.

—MARGE WATSON, CLEVELAND DAREDEVILS

CHAPTER 3

THE ORIGINS OF WOMEN'S FOOTBALL

To the Dolls and the Troopers and the Shamrocks—to women like Linda Jefferson and Mary BlueJacket—it must have seemed in the 1970s like they were the first women to set foot on the gridiron. But, the fact is, women began playing football almost as soon as the sport was invented. And that was at least eighty years before the NWFL.

American football rules were created and established sometime in the 1880s. In what is believed to be the first recorded instance of women playing the sport, on November 21, 1896, according to an article published in New York City's *Sun*, a scrimmage was set up as the entertainment portion of the night at Sulzer's Harlem River Park outside its casino before a masked ball for a men's social club. Ten women, most wearing short dresses, lined up into equal sides, five-on-five, and were pinned with Yale or Princeton colors. While the male crowd was expecting something light and gentle, the women had other plans. They came to play, *really* play. And they weren't there to pussyfoot around for the sake of entertaining a bunch of men.

Once the kickoff happened, all bets were off.

"Princeton won the ball, and a girl in a short black skirt and orange-colored stockings started the game by kicking the ball over into the crowd of lookers-on that surrounded the gridiron. The others made a rush and both teams tackled the front line of spectators," described the *Sun*. From there, the game turned into a continuous, scrappy melee and as the men in the crowd looked on, they were so excited by the girls' unexpected aggression they began climbing over each other to get a closer look.

"Police Captain Haughey of the East 126th street station had been watching the game and keeping close to the players" the *Sun* article continued, "with a number of policemen he got in the way of the crowd and drove it back."

In the end, the scrimmage was stopped by the police before it was finished, out of fear for the girls' safety. The spectacle was never meant to be taken seriously; it was merely a gimmick for those who organized it and a source of entertainment for the men who watched it. But the thrill of watching women compete in such an aggressive sport was likely not lost on anyone in the crowd that night or by those who read about it in the newspaper the next day.

"It illustrates how captivating the concept of women's football was to male spectators, even back in 1896," wrote Neal Rozendaal, author of *The Women's Football Encyclopedia*, in 2016. "Other recreational 'powder bowl' events were held across college campuses in the ensuing decades, but these exhibitions were unusual and nonrecurring, and they were universally treated by the press as more farce than competitive football."

○————○

Such "farces" continued in the early twentieth century. It was November 1926, the halftime of an NFL game between the Chicago Cardinals and Frankford Yellow Jackets. And, in one of the most frequently cited "exhibitions" in women's football history, the Frankford Lady Yellow Jackets took the field. Occurring as it did during the break from "real" play, the Lady Yellow Jackets were set to compete against a couple of men in a brief and playful scrimmage for the crowd, much in the same way a court jester was trotted out in front of a king to elicit laughs from the royals.

Despite even this lighthearted intention, few, it seems, were laughing. "Even the Frankford A. A. Ladies' Auxiliary," wrote the *Philadelphia Inquirer*, "in the shape of eleven pretty girls in grid togs, cavorting and performing the Charleston, did not rouse the crowd from the gloom of Chicago leading 7–0." There's no indication that the Lady Jackets did indeed run a few football plays after doing the Charleston and cavorting across the field that afternoon. Even if they had, the *Inquirer* didn't find the football portion of the halftime show engaging enough to include in their postgame write-up. The entire thing wasn't meant to be taken seriously. It was sheer amusement. (Even though the paper deemed the halftime amusement as "a particularly dead one.")

In any event, the male football players of Frankford rebounded in the second half and went on to beat Chicago 33–7. And though the *Philadelphia Inquirer* discussed them briefly—in their extensive recap of the entire championship game from start to finish—there's little information to be found as to what became of the Lady Yellow Jackets and their halftime adventures, and if they ever cavorted again.

Throughout the early twentieth century, male spectators, and those who made money off the women's football "gimmick," continued to treat women's football as a spectacle of amusement. But at the same time, the many women who participated in these exhibitions or charity games really wanted to play, and not just perform as a sideshow for hoots, hollers, and laughs. They wanted more respect.

Like for so many women athletes throughout history, and even today, respect and opportunities were hard to come by, especially in football. But when the opportunity did arise, those women who actually stepped onto the field took full advantage, even if it didn't last long.

That's exactly what happened with the Cavour (South Dakota) High School girls football team in the fall of 1926. Often overlooked in women's football history circles (perhaps because the team did not participate on an amateur or professional level), the Cavour High School team certainly deserves remembering. They weren't just a halftime novelty. They played full games from start to finish, tackle and all. And they garnered community support and plenty of national media attention along the way.

Without enough boys to fill the roster for the Cavour football team, a group of girls decided to form one instead. They called themselves the "Alphas and Betas" and squared off against each other in pregame matches before other area high school and college games.

"Their existence was short-lived and eventually squashed by prevailing authorities," Chantel Jennings wrote in The Athletic, "but for a few weeks in central South Dakota in 1926, a group of female football players put a town on the map as a community rallied behind its favorite football team. That team just happened to be composed of girls."

The Cavour team stopped scrimmaging after numerous complaints from other schools and colleges arose. Women desisting from play after community outrage is a pattern that repeats itself continuously throughout women's football history.

The overall consensus was that the girls shouldn't play interscholastic football, for the same nonsensical reasons that plagued aspiring female athletes in the nineteenth and twentieth centuries: it was too risky for their health. Thanks in part to scientific literature written by men— such as Dr. Edward Clarke's Sex in Education; or, A Fair Chance for Girls published in 1873—there circulated many unsubstantiated claims and assumptions that declared it extremely dangerous and physically hazardous for women to overexert themselves, especially during menstruation. Women were seen as too dainty and too demure for athletics, and their delicate female organs were to be protected at all costs. Health, beauty, education, and reproductive ability were far more important. Therefore, physical activity was to be light and recreational. As a result, almost the whole of society believed that women who engaged in too much physical activity would be at risk for hysteria, fatigue, sterilization, and even cancer.

Not much had changed by the 1930s. Still, there are numerous reports of a handful of women's football teams popping up throughout the decade in different parts of the country, barnstorming their way into the hearts of fans. From Toledo, Ohio, all the way to Los Angeles, California, women were suiting up in shoulder pads, helmets, and cleats, gleefully ignoring the detractors and warnings about their "health."

Two teams in Ohio butted heads quite regularly in 1930 and 1931 and attracted a lot of national attention. Two men named Herman Metzger and Dick Lazette coached the teams, and the players wore uniforms that were previously used by the town kids' league team and bought cleats on credit from an athletic supply company. The first game was a success. Fan turnout was high and the teams actually made money. But the negative feedback soon began to outweigh the positive.

"We played exhibition games wherever we could," Metzger told the *Toledo Blade* over four decades later. "We ran resistance from people who thought the idea of girls playing football was objectionable. . . . The more national publicity we got, the more negative mail we got. Dick finally got a letter from Mrs. Herbert Hoover maintaining that we were exploiting womanhood and the thing kind of cooled off and died after that."

The fact that Lou Henry Hoover, the First Lady of the United States, decidedly weighed in on the matter is surprising, considering her esteemed reputation of being a staunch supporter of women's rights and opportunities in education and athletics. In 1923, Mrs. Hoover joined the National Amateur Athletic Federation (women's division) and worked hard to improve the participation of women in sports. She often preached about the value and importance of physical activity for women, and how it helped develop strength and character. The women's division was made up of hundreds of members that included Girl Scouts of America leaders, physical education teachers, and teachers from women's schools and colleges across the country.

If Hoover did, in fact, pen a letter criticizing Metzger and Lazette's football teams as "exploiting womanhood," it's ironic because her organization's motto was "A sport for every girl, and every girl in sport."

By "sport" she must not have meant football.

○——○

In October 1939, history was made as the first full-contact women's football game to be played in Los Angeles took place at Gilmore Stadium. The Chet Relph Hollywood Stars faced off against the Marshall Clampett Amazons of Los Angeles in front of two thousand five hundred spectators. NFL rules governed the game, which consisted of twelve-minute quarters. The *Los Angeles Times* was on hand to cover the game in full detail, and *Life* magazine would feature a two-page photo spread of the players in the November 22 issue.

During a time-out, the *Life* photographer snapped a playful photo of the girls pouring jugs of water over each other's heads in an attempt to cool off from the heat. In another photo, Amazon halfback Babe Culler is smiling widely with a large, white plaster Band-Aid strip clinging to her bloodied cheek. Of course, interspersed between photos of game action is also one of Mary Zivalic, a 205-pound center, hiking the ball between her legs at the camera with the caption saying she likes to play football because "it helps keep her thin." (This tongue-in-cheek imagery in the media is yet another constant in women's football history.)

The players wore regulation uniforms along with their own tennis shoes and played with an undersized football. They also wore circular, spongelike rubber pads over their breasts for protection (there's also a picture of this in the *Life* magazine spread). Lois Roberts, who played in her bare feet and could punt the ball fifty yards, and Shirley Payne, a quick and slithery halfback and two-way player, were the stars of the game for the Amazons. Payne's forty-five-yard interception return helped seal the victory for the Amazons, 12–6.

Initially, the overall reception of the contest at Gilmore Stadium was positive, with newspapers around the country picking up the story and marveling at the athleticism of these would-be housewives and fair maidens. *Life* magazine was especially complimentary, and pleasantly surprised by the aggression and the quality of play on the field.

"It was no powder-puff battle. The girls were rough and tough. They kicked each other in the stomach, dirtied each other's faces, tackled and blocked savagely, knocked four girls unconscious," the magazine reported. "And, strangely enough, they played good football, seldom fumbling or running away from their interference."

But, as with previous women's football matches, the compliments only went so far. The article also went on to describe the reactions of "doctors" who had heard about the game and were "horrified" at the thought of it.

"Football, they said, is a dangerous sport for girls. A woman's body is not heavily muscled, cannot withstand knocks," read the article. "A blow, either on the breast or in the abdominal region, may result in cancer or internal injury. A woman's nervous system is also too delicate for such rough play. It would be better, they thought, for the girls to stick to swimming, tennis and softball."

Dick Hyland, a renowned sports columnist for the *Los Angeles Times* and a former Olympic athlete, wasn't a doctor, but he was also appalled at the idea of women playing football. He dedicated an entire column to mocking the event, one week before the game was even played.

"What, WHAT, is the world coming to? The loving, clinging vine now are 'smashing types and good hard blockers!'" Hyland wrote in a condescending tone. "I don't know what all this feminine activity is supposed to prove in the world of sports. In fact, I'm wondering if the report doesn't belong in the entertainment pages or over with the crime news."

There was no follow-up column after the game took place. Perhaps Hyland felt there was no need to actually attend and watch for himself. He had made it clear that the game wasn't important enough for him to cover or take seriously. It didn't matter how well the athletes played or that, despite the fact that they emerged from the fray with a few bumps and bruises, they were still able to make it home in time to put dinner on the table, as they would have been expected to do by society's rules. Or that both teams continued playing, traveling to different cities to take part in more exhibition games—the Amazons and Hollywood Stars even went abroad to showcase their football skills in Guadalajara and Mexico City. For Hyland and the like—and, it seems, the *Los Angeles Times*—there was no place for women in football.

o———o

Others who were a little more open-minded decided a rule change was in order to make the game safer for women. Not long after the first Los Angeles game, a new brand of girls' football was introduced. Stephen Epler, a former Nebraska schoolmaster, had introduced six-man football for boys in 1934 so the sport could be played safely and for fun at town playgrounds and schools. In 1939, he decided to revise the rules to create a similar game for girls with no tackling, a smaller field, and a lot more passing. It was essentially the beginning of what is now known as powder-puff football, a seemingly less aggressive form of football played by women at the high school and college level.

Epler's form of girls' football quickly caught on. After-school programs and high schools all over the country adopted and employed it. But not everyone bought in. Tom Brislin, a writer for the International News Service, reported in December 1939 that the Pennsylvania Department of Instruction and the Pennsylvania Interscholastic Athletic Association, which controlled nearly nine hundred member high schools in the state, disapproved of the "establishment of female football" in Pennsylvania high schools—even when played under Epler's new rules—and essentially banned girls' football from the state.

When the *Bradford Evening Star* ran a portion of Brislin's article, the editorial staff put it in place of its regular sports column, "Speaking Of: Sports by Sikes." At the end of the article, they added their own pithy little commentary:

"The writer along with many others are against women participating in the football sport. It is too rough of a game and despite the precautionary measures advocated serious injury will be unavoidable. The members of the fair sex better try baseball or basketball to keep their curves instead of the gridiron sport." (Ironic, since girls have been historically and systemically excluded from baseball, too.)

But women didn't stop playing tackle football—doctors, Dick Hylands, new rules, and high school athletic associations of the world be damned. In 1939, down in Atmore, Alabama, seventeen-year-old Luverne Wise became a kicker for the Escambia County High School football team. Wise decided to join the team because she and her friends were tired of the "football is man's game" rhetoric. Coach Andy Edington offered her a tryout, not expecting Wise to actually take him up on the offer. After practicing with the team and showing off her Carli Lloyd–like kicking skills, she made varsity. Wise played again in 1940 during her senior year and did more than just kick extra points and field goals. She also threw a few PAT passes and earned an All-State honorable mention as a quarterback. Wise's goal after graduation was to coach a girls' football team.

In Montrose, Colorado, a group of eager women got together to hold their own tackle football game in the mud. No serious injuries were reported but a few jerseys "got red-streaked from some mildly bloody noses." And in 1941, a women's professional football league attempted to launch in Illinois. The league was said to consist of eight teams, including the New York Bombers, Chicago Bombers, and Chicago Rockets. The two Chicago teams clashed in an exhibition game midsummer at Spencer-Coals field under regulation football rules. The goal was to play a schedule of games throughout the fall season. But this league never made it that far. What little media build-up and excitement preceded that first exhibition game and the launch of the league fizzled out.

In some cases, extenuating circumstances allowed women a chance to play. While most young men were still overseas during World War II, schools and colleges across the nation were suspending football seasons and campus activities, including Eastern State Teachers College in Madison, South Dakota. But in the fall of 1945, Eastern State decided to hold its homecoming weekend to help celebrate the end of the war. And what homecoming would be complete without a football game?

With only three men enrolled for the fall semester, the women of Eastern State dared to wonder if they should step in, much like women did in baseball, with the formation of the All-American Girls Professional Baseball League (AAGPBL). They decided, *Why not*? Roger Holtzmann of *South Dakota Magazine* wrote of the event, "uniforms presented a minor problem, and not for the reasons that might come to mind first. After five years in storage, apparently without mothballs, the college's jerseys were rife with holes and most of the pads were literally coming apart at the seams."

Thankfully, they were able to round up some spare uniforms for everyone to play. Though the game went on as planned and the homecoming was a success, the girls of Eastern State who played that day never took the field again. Despite how much fun they had and a high turnout of friends, family, and alumni, they never expected anything to come from the event. It exists merely as a fond memory, one they can happily share with their great-grandkids—that time *they* got a chance to play football.

○———○

Looking back at the history and timeline of women's football, there's a predominant cycle here. Yes, there was always an audience for women's football, and there were plenty of women who wanted to play. But opportunities to play were few and far between. When women did get a chance to participate in an exhibition game or try to start up a league, it was more of a novelty than a legitimate opportunity.

The initial media and fan support of these exhibition games and startup leagues were attributed by Rozendaal, in *The Women's Football Encyclopedia*, to the unavoidable curiosity that surrounded women playing a men's sport, particularly a sport that was deemed too rough and complicated for them. Games were often written about and described like a circus act—one that would pop up from time to time in a city or town nearby and that was it.

"They gained some media coverage over the unusual premise but then quickly disappeared again after one game, provided that the 'game' took place at all," he wrote. "The media was fascinated by the idea of women's football as an attention-grabbing oddity, but it rarely provided any reports of the games themselves or treated the sport seriously."

The potential was always there, and had been there since the beginning of football—since that first women's scrum held at Sulzer's Harlem River Park in 1896. But no one knew quite how to harness it and turn it into something viable: something that would attract fans on a regular basis, give women who wanted to play football a real opportunity, and eventually make enough money to sustain itself. No one had the creativity or wherewithal to market and promote women's football in the right way, and no one had the motivation to transform it from a gimmick into a serious business venture.

No one, that is, except for a steely-minded, ostentatious theatrical promoter from Cleveland, Ohio.

Enter, Sid Friedman.

CHAPTER 4

THE "P. T. BARNUM" OF WOMEN'S FOOTBALL

"**B**efore you read the next few paragraphs, you'd better make sure you're sitting down," read Terry Casey's sports column in the *Tribune* of Coshocton, Ohio, in 1967. "While it seems somewhat strange and unusual, a CLEVE-LANDER is planning on organizing an ALL-GIRLS football team to barnstorm against professional men's teams. You might say this stretches 'equal rights' a bit too far, but SID FRIEDMAN of Cleveland is serious, or at least so he says."

After making his initial announcement to the press, Sid Friedman's phone rang off the hook with calls and questions, just like he had anticipated. And he was all too happy to oblige. "It's a dangerous sport," Friedman is quoted saying in an interview with the United Press. "But there are enough women who weigh 300 pounds, 250 pounds, who could do it. There might be one exceptional woman in the country who could do it better than a pro star."

Sid Friedman was cut from the same cloth as P. T. Barnum. Though he never ventured into the circus business, Friedman—a stout middle-aged man with sagging cheeks and a giddy used-car-salesman vibe—was a self-proclaimed public relations expert extraordinaire, who dabbled in everything from beauty pageants and talent shows to sports management. In the 1960s, the Cleveland, Ohio, resident ran the All Star Theatrical Agency and had previously managed the wrestling referee career of MLB player Jimmy Piersall and claimed to have managed NFL Hall of Famer Bobby Mitchell.

But it was his unique approach that set him apart from other promoters. Friedman once held a competitive event for the go-go dancing world record; he held another for the longest a harmonica trio could play without stopping. He wasn't above promoting any kind of event, if he knew it could make money. And the more outlandish and wackier the idea was, the better.

"He loved to promote with the press and get attention for doing wild and unusual things," said Rozendaal, who researched Friedman for his *Women's Football Encyclopedia*. "The one thing I found on him that I always find fascinating is he was sort of an official for a number of beauty pageants. And he came up with an idea of a Miss Outer Space pageant. It was, in essence, a beauty pageant where the winner would be promised a first shot to live on the moon, should we ever make it there in the 1960s."

America did make it to the moon, though Miss Outer Space never got to live on the moon. But his most outlandish idea of all was starting a women's football troupe. In both cases, Friedman was banking on existing fascination and curiosity. The space race was already captivating the world, and women had been playing football for themselves and before crowds, intermittently, for decades. Still, even in the 1960s, women's football was seen as no less ludicrous than it had been in 1896, or 1926, or 1931, or 1944.

But where others had failed, Friedman believed he could succeed, and turn women's football into the "greatest show on earth."

As such, Friedman has a complicated legacy. On the one hand, the only way for Friedman's scheme to succeed was if he found and supported a group of women talented and athletic enough to make his vision a reality. On the other hand, Friedman's motivation from the onset was, simply, to make money.

Friedman's rise is an example of an all-too-familiar story. He acted completely in self-interest, and he even expressed regressive and sometimes misogynist ideas about women athletes. Yet, still, he unwittingly made strides for women's sports. Without intending to be, Friedman became an important figure in the history of women's football and provided opportunities where none had previously existed.

o————o

Friedman sought to model his athletic troupe of women much in the same vein as the Harlem Globetrotters—lots of flashy moves, crowd-pleasing antics, exciting competition, and plenty of entertainment. His football team would compete hard, put on a good show, and leave the audience wowed, wanting more. This was the game plan and Friedman wanted to stick to it, but his stubbornness would come back to haunt him later on when he brought more women's football teams into the fold and one in particular—the Toledo Troopers—became so good, he took it upon himself to suggest they throw a couple of games to keep the fans invested. It did not go over well.

Still, at the beginning, Friedman's goal was to start a single women's football team and have them compete against men for show. He had seen and heard enough about women's football throughout the previous decades to know it was an untapped attraction. Moreover, Friedman had his fingers on the pulse of not only the sports industry, but the entertainment industry as well. He seemed to understand both landscapes implicitly. It only made sense that he found a way to fuse the two together.

All Friedman needed was some start-up capital. A smooth talker, Friedman found that convincing Cleveland-based investors to bite on his idea wasn't too hard. In the summer of 1967, Friedman devised a plan and by August, he made his grand announcement in the papers.

He declared that he was starting a women's football team that would compete against amateur and semipro men's teams. And they'd do so around the country, in a must-see barnstorming tour for the ages. Friedman's all-girls team would wear men's uniforms and equipment, and play by standard football rules.

In order to achieve the financial success he was after, Friedman planned to recruit the best women's football players he could find. As he had anticipated, the free advertising he received from newspaper articles featuring his announcement helped him get the word out about tryouts for his all-women football troupe. He was looking for thirty-five to forty girls to join his squad. By September, Friedman announced that he had already signed eighteen girls and had found the perfect name for the team: the USA Daredevils (they would eventually evolve into the Cleveland Daredevils).

Marcella Sanborn was one of the first women to try out for Friedman's troupe. In between raising her sixteen-year-old daughter, Claudia, and the hours she put in as a supply supervisor at the Ohio Bell Company, the thirty-nine-year-old tried out after seeing the announcement in the paper. Sanborn, who became a standout quarterback on offense as well as a safety on defense, impressed onlookers far and wide over the course of six exhibition games, even hard-nosed sportswriters. She was selected by the infamous Bud Collins of the *Boston Globe*, as noted in the Introduction, as the 1967 Athlete of the Year over NFL players like Johnny Unitas and Joe Namath, and praised as a "60 minute woman."

Sanborn wasn't alone, of course. Others tried out and made the team, too. Friedman had little trouble filling the roster. His next step was to fill the head coaching position with a legitimate and recognizable football name. It just so happened that Marion Motley—an NFL star and former Cleveland Brown—was looking to get into coaching. A decade earlier, when he first retired from pro football in 1955, Motley had hoped to secure a coaching position with the Browns or with another NFL team. But his former team, and subsequently, the rest of the league, Motley surmised, discriminated against him because he was Black. Consequently, he wasn't able to obtain a single coaching job. Motley was forced to find work elsewhere, working as a salesman, as a construction worker, and at the post office.

After years of inquiring about coaching positions and being rejected time and time again, a coaching opportunity finally opened up—only it wasn't in the NFL. It was with Friedman's startup Daredevils. The *Cincinnati Enquirer* announced his hiring with the condescending headline, "Who's Gonna Guard Girdles?" as if to imply no one in their right mind would coach a women's football team. Motley didn't see the difference. For him, it was an opportunity to coach a team and one he welcomed.

With Motley on board, Friedman got the extra clout he needed to really sell his women's football troupe to the public. As one of the best players in the NFL and an Ohio native himself, Motley's name carried a lot of weight. When Friedman made the official announcement about Motley's hire, newspapers from Texas to Minnesota jumped on the story. And, as he had done so fervently before, Friedman made the most of the free publicity.

"This isn't going to be any joke. We plan on having toplight coaching. We don't want any fly-by-night operation. It's going to be strictly major league," Friedman told the *Scranton Times Tribune*. "After watching some of the action, I was amazed at what ferociousness they have on the gridiron. These girls said they'll play any men, as long as they get paid. Most of the women are married and some have children. They're just big, strong and tough girls."

Motley ran the team as if he were coaching any other professional football team. Practices were tough and he put the women through their paces. The goal was to practice for six weeks straight and get the team ready to play its first exhibition game by November.

"This is a barnstorming venture," Friedman explained to the *Dayton Journal Herald* in mid-September. "We're not going to try to run up big scores—just show off the girls' running, passing and kicking abilities. But I don't think we're going to lose a game."

As for who the Daredevils' opponents would be, Friedman boasted that he had "offers galore" from men's teams as close as Michigan and as far as Salt Lake City, Utah. But for the 1967 season, the Daredevils only played six games. Their overall record was 1–4–1—with all of the losses coming against men's teams and their one win and tie coming against another all-girls start-up team from Detroit, called the All-Stars (though this record is disputed, and listed as 3–1 in some sources). Overall, fan turnout was decent. But the Daredevils' biggest draw was when they played against an all-male squad in Erie, Pennsylvania, and nearly won the game.

o————o

One can imagine Friedman, with the leaves crunching under his worn, polished shoes and his tie flapping in the fall breeze, ambling his way across the damp grass where his football team was stretching in preparation for their 1967 game in Erie. He might have smiled slyly and adjusted his suit jacket as he looked them up and down. He believed that his team, the Daredevils, were not only going to make him a lot of money but also garner him plenty of national notoriety to boot. This wasn't an average football team full of average players, after all.

"How's everyone feeling tonight, ladies?" Friedman may have asked, his gruff voice filling the space between them.

The semicircle of women before him, including Sanborn, would have hooted and hollered, some raising their helmets high into the air with one hand. They would have been eager to get on the field and get the game started. They had played in a few exhibition games against men's teams so far and though they'd lost every single one, the action on the field was enough to satisfy any rabid football fan's curiosity. No one expected the women to win, of course. That wasn't the point. Watching women of extraordinary size and athletic skill showcase their talents up and down the gridiron was the draw. That's what sold the tickets.

As people filed in one after the other, Friedman's penchant for showmanship would have begun to take over. "Might be the biggest audience we've had yet," he might have said, nodding over his shoulder at the crowd. "Let's give them a good show, ladies. That's what they paid for. Who knows, maybe this is the night we beat the men into the ground."

The women in full uniform and pads wouldn't have cared too much about showmanship. They weren't in it for that or the measly stipend Friedman paid them per game. They were in it because they loved football and wanted to play. Friedman offered them that chance, so they took it. And they played their hearts out every single game, whether against men or women.

The Daredevils didn't win on that afternoon in Erie, Pennsylvania. But they certainly came close. In front of a crowd of four thousand, Sanborn told the *Boston Globe*, they only lost by two points, 31–29 (though the Oil City *Derrick* newspaper reported the final score as 31–27). The "show" was just as good as Friedman had anticipated it would be.

○——○

In the first season of its existence, Friedman's gamble on his women's football troupe paid off. But, being as ambitious as he was, Friedman wanted to take the venture another step further. The Daredevils games against the women's team in Detroit gave him a taste of what could be an even bigger attraction than the one he had originally envisioned. He wanted to expand, to bring women's football into the national spotlight, not just in the Rust Belt area of the country, but maybe even the world. He realized he could do more than just put together a traveling women's football troupe that played against men for the mere spectacle of it—he could start other women's teams to compete against each other, and maybe even an entire women's football league just like the NFL. No one had ever attempted such a thing before. Naturally, Friedman wanted to be the first. And he would call it the Women's Professional Football League.

Friedman's first order of business was to change the name of his USA Daredevils to the Cleveland Daredevils. Next, he would start other all-girls teams in nearby cities like Erie, Buffalo, Philadelphia, and Detroit. Proximity was key, as it would limit travel costs. And from a publicity standpoint, his Daredevils were already known around those areas. His plan was to keep the barnstorming idea in place, with his Daredevils continuing to play against men, while introducing other girls' teams into the mix for a bit of interleague play. But before all the logistics were in place, Friedman started first and foremost, as he always did, with the press. He announced his new idea for expansion and dropped some former NFL player names as possible coaches for good measure. United Press International (UPI) took care of the rest.

The following news brief was circulated nationally:

Women in three National Football League cities will leave the steam iron for the gridiron next year and give the men a little competition. Theatrical agent and promoter, Sid Friedman, who formed the Cleveland Daredevils, an all-girl football team, this year, plans to expand his venture to Pittsburgh, Detroit and also into Erie, PA. Friedman said the league will start practice next June and play a 26 game schedule in addition to barnstorming the country. He said he had an offer to provide halftime games for both the Detroit Lions and the New York Giants.

Friedman had big aspirations for expanding his women's football venture into a league. But convincing others to buy into his new vision wasn't as easy as he had anticipated. Despite the momentum and hype the Daredevils created, drumming up financial support, participation, and media attention for additional teams was a tough go. By September 1968, Friedman managed to field only one new team: the Pittsburgh All-Stars. Like the Daredevils, the All-Stars roster consisted of women sixteen to thirty-two years old who, by day, were schoolteachers, stay-at-home moms, aspiring athletes, students, secretaries, and more. The team would later be coached by a retired NFL player: Charley Scales, former running back for the Pittsburgh Steelers.

"You can't help a 'double-take' when you see pretty Martha Eaton adjust her football gear. She's a willowy blonde (5'11", 145 pounds) with high cheekbones and, by day, a secretary in the personnel department of Eazor Express," wrote Judy Ludlum of the *Pittsburgh Post-Gazette* in an article titled "Purse-Toting Footballers Draw Stares." "Recently married, she and her husband Jack are avid tennis players. (He ranks first in men's doubles in the Western Pa. Lawn Tennis Association.) Also an enthusiastic skier, she spent the last two winters in Vail, Colo. Martha, who is 28, used to play 'touch' football with her two brothers often and now feels she is ready to tackle 'rougher stuff'."

In late fall of 1968, the Cleveland Daredevils and the Pittsburgh All-Stars played against each other only a few times. The All-Stars won the first meeting between the two teams, 22–12, in what was most likely a practice scrimmage. The "big debut" happened on November 29 in Pittsburgh at Bethel Park High's stadium. Both teams scored a touchdown and a two-point conversion, and the game ultimately resulted in an 8–8 tie. A reported crowd of sixteen hundred "enthusiastic" spectators were on hand to watch the contest unfold.

Due to a three-and-a-half-hour bus ride, the Daredevils were a bit late in their arrival and the start of the game was delayed. But the women did not disappoint once they hit the field. It was apparent to everyone in the stands and on the sidelines that they were serious about football, and they came to play for claps—not for laughs. The spectators were pleased with the physicality and skill of the players, and the game was successful enough to encourage Friedman to keep forging ahead with the development of his women's professional football league in spite of a lack of teams.

o———o

By the end of 1968, Friedman was more determined than ever to expand women's football into other cities. But his luck didn't change much in 1969. He was still having a hard time getting teams up and running in his target cities. Friedman—being the creative, out-of-the-box promoter that he was—decided to test the international market, instead.

Toronto, Ontario, wasn't too far from Cleveland or Pittsburgh; and if push came to shove, the teams could always meet at a neutral location somewhere in the middle. With the help of former Canadian professional football player Fred Robinson, Friedman started the Canadian Belles. Robinson, who also had a brief stint in the NFL with the Cleveland Browns, signed on to coach and recruit players. Like Friedman, Robinson wasn't afraid to talk up the team and the future of women's football in order to create some hype—even if he embellished the facts here and there.

"There have been teams in Cleveland and Pittsburgh for several years and they draw an average of 5,000 fans for games," Robinson boldly said in a *Windsor Star* article in May 1969. It didn't matter whether or not Robinson believed what he was saying about the fan turnout or how many years the Cleveland and Pittsburgh teams had been in existence, at least not to Friedman. Robinson's words not only gave Friedman's startup league free publicity, but also enticed more players to try out, and planted a seed of intrigue for prospective fans. And that was far more important.

Still, these two men shaped the entire public narrative for the supposedly women-centered enterprise. Robinson continued to do interviews and recruit players for the new Toronto team, while Friedman turned his attention to promoting the league in Canadian newspapers. He advertised the Belles, along with the Cleveland Daredevils and Pittsburgh Hurricanes (no longer the "All-Stars"), as participating teams for the 1969 season (while also throwing in the Detroit Petticoats even though they were not yet an official franchise). Friedman described the league as a barnstorming venture that would play in both Canada and the United

States in regularly scheduled charity and exhibition games. The goal was to start training camp in July, start full practices in August, and start the official season in September. With four teams in the mix, Friedman could pit the two teams with the best records against each other in a championship-like game at the end of the season. The advertising and promotional possibilities alone must have made him salivate.

It was all coming together, finally. Or so Friedman thought. For some reason—maybe the lack of a solid investor, an inability to find a coach, or not enough players to fill a roster and field a team—the Detroit Petticoats never got off the ground by the time football season arrived. But Friedman kept pushing forward. It seemed as if nothing was going to deter him.

"My goal is to have the first all-women's professional football league," Friedman told the press in November 1969. "When the team in Detroit is finally organized, we'll be ready. We've played several exhibitions already this season and drew 7,000 fans up in Toronto and another 6,000 in Pittsburgh. All we need is some national exposure and we can double, even triple those figures."

According to Friedman, the 1969 season was going well—even without a fourth team. He boasted that his teams were drawing large-enough crowds that he was able to provide each of his players a steady salary, book them top-notch hotels, and pay for their meals and expenses on road trips. Friedman also mentioned that he had brokered a deal with the NFL to showcase his teams during halftime on national broadcasts, but the plans fell through because "the bands just didn't want us stealing their show."

For Friedman, walking the fine line between fact and fiction had become something of an art form. He did it well. And like any good showman and promoter would do, he talked positively about his teams and painted a bright picture. For that reason, it's hard to know whether or not the crowd sizes at the women's football games were as big as he described or if the possible halftime show deals with the NFL he mentioned were legit, especially when reporters took him at his word.

These inconsistent and untrustworthy news stories would foreshadow the coverage the NWFL would receive just a few years later, making it hard to tease out truth from wishful thinking. The reporting was often sarcastic and demeaning, due to sportswriters being overwhelming male, and Friedman was often the focus—not the players themselves.

o———o

Ever since the summer of 1967, Sid Friedman had been propping up women's football in the press to heights it couldn't quite match in reality. He talked of barnstorming across the country. He talked of a multicity league, with teams from coast to coast. He talked of filling the stands from end to end, having games on national television, sharing the national spotlight with the NFL, and having an official, thriving women's football league of his own. But these things never fully came to fruition, beyond his grand promises. They were nothing more than lofty aspirations of a man who, by now, wanted women's football to catch fire more than anything else in the world, because of everything he had put into it so far. It's as if he believed the more he talked about what could be, the more likely it was to come true.

As the 1969 football season came to a close, Friedman continued to remain "optimistic" about women's football catching on in the near future. Such optimism must have derived, in part, from the fifty thousand dollars of his own money and two years of his life he had already invested in the project. And he also had gotten to know the players and believed in their talents and ability. While he had yet to establish an official and legitimate women's professional football league, other than in name alone, thus far, he had accomplished one major feat that his predecessors had not. Naysayers aside, Friedman managed to turn the concept of women's football from a "gimmick" into a "real possibility."

In doing so, Friedman's league gave hope to women athletes of all ages. Like that one young woman from Lewisburg, Pennsylvania, who had contacted the *Philadelphia Inquirer* "Action Line" and confessed she wanted to play professional football.

But for good and for ill, women's football was growing *beyond* Friedman's vision, and his control. In 1971, two other all-women football teams organized independently of Friedman—the Detroit Fillies and the Pittsburgh Powderkegs (also coached by Scales). They had their own ownership, coaches, and players, and played a handful of games against each other. After finding some success in recruiting players and attracting fan support, both teams discussed the possibility of inviting other teams into their mix.

And that's when the power dynamic of women's football began to shift. Friedman was no longer the only one in town organizing and promoting women's football games. There was new competition on the block, in the form of the players themselves. Some players for the Detroit Fillies also played for a team called the Midwest Cowgirls. Both teams had the same owner and coach: Dave Pierce, a twenty-eight-year-old public relations consultant, like Friedman. Still, Friedman continued to run and operate his own group of teams, with the belief that Pierce and others would fail where he had succeeded.

By spring 1971, Friedman was still at it. There was little development on the expansion front. But that didn't stop Friedman from talking about his women's professional football league in the same grandiose, sweeping way he had for the previous four years.

In *Family Weekly*, a national newspaper magazine supplement that was popular at the time, Friedman's picture appeared alongside the likes of Dick Martin from *Laugh-In*, Los Angeles Lakers legend Wilt Chamberlain, Jack Webb from *Dragnet*, the US treasurer of the United States, Dorothy Andrews Kabis, and a handful of other "famous people" in a popular weekly question and answer series called, "Ask Them Yourself."

The question Friedman received was: *Is it true that you are planning an all-girl pro football league to start in April of 1971?*

Friedman answered as only he could, with a little embellishment and a lot of flair:

"My girls teams will participate in two leagues—East Coast and West Coast—in the fall. My East Coast teams will be in Buffalo, Cleveland, Toronto and Pittsburgh, and my West Coast teams will be in Vancouver, Seattle, Washington, Portland, Los Angeles and San Francisco. The winner of the East Coast will play West Coast in December in the Super Bowl. We start practice in April."

At the time of Friedman's statement (made in March), the Cleveland Daredevils, the Canadian (Toronto) Belles, and the Pittsburgh

Hurricanes were the only functioning teams in existence under his thumb, and the Hurricanes weren't yet playing games. By the time fall rolled around, Friedman had managed to add only two more teams to the fold: the Buffalo (NY) All-Stars and the Toledo Troopers. There was no West Coast Division. The teams played each other sporadically, but the Troopers and the Daredevils played the most and often against each other, with the Troopers winning every game. Losing got under Friedman's skin, since the Daredevils were his original team and he had put so much effort into propping them up in the press. But he had bigger things on his mind than the scoreboard.

Yes, women's football was growing, but not to the scale that Friedman had desperately wanted. As the single creator and czar—a title bestowed upon him by numerous journalists—of his women's football venture, and the teams within it, Friedman could oversee and expend only so much of his time and money. And with two more teams under his umbrella, Friedman's overhead costs rose considerably—stadium rentals, programs, coaching salaries, player salaries, transportation, and hotel fees all began to add up.

If Friedman really wanted to expand all the way to the West Coast, he would need to invite others into his operation to invest and share costs. But that would also mean he'd have to relinquish sole control. And that's not something Friedman was too keen on doing. This was his brainchild that he had nursed from nothing into something and introduced to the world at a time when no one else was talking about women's football, and he wasn't ready to compromise on it. In the end, that kind of limited thinking only hindered Friedman from doing what he had always wanted—to turn his women's football endeavor into a legitimate league and a national phenomenon.

o———o

Women's football, ultimately, would rise and thrive not because of, but in spite of, Friedman. And the successes of these teams were, of course, due to the sacrifices of their players. This shined through, occasionally, when reporters at the time talked not to the male owners and coaches, but to the players themselves—though it was the exception rather than the rule.

In an extensive feature for the *Chicago Tribune* back in November 1969, when the Daredevils were first gaining recognition, Renee Sebo wrote about the team. She attended practices and spent time at Friedman's office, where he continued to conduct business and run promotions for other events and beauty pageants while simultaneously managing the team. Whatever preconceived notions Sebo had going into the story were quelled once she spoke to the players and watched them play. She quickly realized it wasn't some gimmick after all.

"But now as they run and throw and catch, you can see they're not afraid and they're good," she wrote of the Daredevils. As for her opinion of Friedman, Sebo was keenly aware of his background and penchant for embellishing. Still, she concluded her article with a certain amount of positivity.

"Friedman has grand ideas for the Daredevils and women's football, like TV commercials, play at halftime during the pro games and tours of military bases. And he's optimistically thinking of the day when a girl will get paid as much as $1000 a game. An average crowd at a Daredevils' game now numbers 5,000—mostly curiosity seekers," she wrote. "Cleveland people respond to the Daredevils with, at best, 'a novelty,' and, at worst, 'never heard of them.' 'When I read the ad in the paper for players,' says Marge Watson, an eager tackle, 'I thought it was a gag.' Now, puffing hard in the warm, bright sun, she knows better.'"

Dallas Bluebonnets vs LA Dandelions
Photo provided by Joyce Johnson, LA Dandelions

PART III

THE BIRTH OF THE NWFL (1971–1974)

I'VE HAD A COUPLE OF MINOR CONCUSSIONS, A LOT OF SCRATCHES AND BRUISES. I'VE HAD MY BELL RUNG GOOD, AND I'M NOT ASHAMED TO TELL YOU I'VE CRIED.

—BARBARA O'BRIEN, DALLAS BLUEBONNETS

CHAPTER 5

THE TROOPERS' REIGN BEGINS

"I did not pose for that," Gail Dearie, now eighty, said of the iconic photo. "We were having a scrimmage at practice. I had just stood up after the huddle. I was thinking about my route for a play. And a [European] photographer snapped that picture. Apparently, she liked what she got. She thought it was worth trying to send it to *Life* magazine. The picture really took off. Now, we say 'it went viral.' A lot of things happened as a result of that picture."

In June 1972, *Life* published a photo spread with a short article about a new women's football team—the New York Fillies. (The Fillies, however, appeared *without* the support or blessing of Sid Friedman. They were not under his umbrella of teams, and were owned by someone else.) *Life's* writeup of the Fillies was only the second such feature about women's football in the magazine's history.

Twenty-nine-year-old Dearie from Red Bank, New Jersey, was one of the players featured in the photos, and one photo in particular stood out from the rest. Dearie is clad in a grass-and-dirt-stained white jersey with the number 84 on the front, her long blond hair falling out of her large gold helmet and down onto her shoulders, and her high cheekbones and full lips distinguishable underneath the thick gray face mask. The full-page photo contrasted beauty and brawn, and it attracted national attention.

In spring of that year, before Dearie became the most recognizable Fillie on the roster thanks to the *Life* magazine photos, she was working in New York as a go-see model in commercial print media when her husband showed her a wanted ad in a national paper looking for women to join a new professional football team. Dearie was intrigued and decided to see what it was all about. Her main reason for going, she said, was to "put away a slap-in-the-face kind of attitude that some people have about athletic ability and women—not being able to use it fully because it didn't seem feminine."

She wasn't the only one. Nancy Berardino, a seventeen-year-old from Far Rockaway, had also seen the advertisement. Her twenty-four-year-old sister, Lynda, wanted to try out for the team as well. Dearie, the Berardino sisters, and Dearie's friend Carol Brown were among the hundred or so women who showed up to the Fillies callout.

"Some of them had never played football before. Some didn't know very much about the technicalities of the game," Brown told *womenSports* magazine in 1974. "But every woman there wanted to be a professional football player." The women who showed up for the tryout did so with the hope of proving wrong anyone who didn't believe they could play football, and also because they loved sports and wanted to take advantage of the opportunity to play.

Dearie stood tall above the crowd, not just for her athleticism but also because of her beauty. In truth, Dearie was the perfect person to dispel the myth that a woman couldn't be both a good athlete and feminine at the same time. While she turned heads wherever she went in the city, it often frustrated her that her looks were the main thing some people chose to focus on. Like all women, there was much more to Dearie than her outward appearance. She was a mother of two, a wife, a devout Christian, a model, and a part-time college student. She was also an athlete.

When Dearie finally got the opportunity to step on the football field on the day of football tryouts, she turned heads for a different reason—her height at five feet eight inches, athletic ability, and strength made her the perfect wide receiver or tight end. "It was legitimate," Dearie said, recalling the tryout. "They weren't making fun of women, if you know what I mean."

o———o

Dearie and Brown made the team, along with forty other women from the surrounding New York City area, ranging in age from sixteen to forty years old. They were promised twenty-five dollars per game, fully funded by Fillies owner James Eagan: a cocky New York City attorney.

Eagan started the New York Fillies because he believed it was a solid monetary investment, and was hoping to make some extra cash on the side. It was certainly not because he wanted to help elevate women's football. For him it was a business venture, nothing more. He didn't care about the women's dreams or aspirations on the gridiron. To Eagan, the women were simply a means to an end.

"They drew 6,000 at three dollars a head in Erie," the young and slick Eagan told the *Philadelphia Daily News* before the Fillies debut game. "Can you imagine that kind of crowd in Erie, Pa.?"

Eagan knew very little about football and the game itself, and spent time at practices familiarizing himself with the rules. He brought in Bill Bryant, a former semipro football player, to be the head coach of the Fillies and he hired additional assistant coaches to handle all the technical stuff, like training the team and getting them ready to play their first game in front of what Eagan anticipated to be a huge crowd.

Bryant did his best to teach the Fillies plays on the offensive and defensive side of the ball. "I'm trying to teach these girls the fundamentals," he told the *Daily News*. "You have to start at the beginning and some learn quicker than others. These girls are a lot more serious than you think. They're playing to win." But when Eagan, who was quick to shave expenses, decided not to purchase medical insurance for his players, all four coaches quit the team in "protest and disgust" the night before their first game.

The fact that the women were willing to play without insurance coverage indicates how badly they wanted to be out there, how deeply they understood what a rare opportunity they had. It also shows how little concern Eagan had for the well-being of his players.

The Fillies officially clashed with the Midwest Cowgirls (owned and operated by Dave Pierce and, like the Fillies, not associated with Friedman) on Saturday, May 13, 1972, at Randall's Island Downing Stadium in New York City. The Fillies were outmatched in both skill and physicality, and the Cowgirls crushed them 28–0.

The defeat on Randall's Island was a wake-up call for Eagan. Till then, he somehow hadn't realized he needed a competitive team in order to attract fans and bring in the kind of revenue he desired. His lack of football acumen not only showed when he spoke to reporters after the game, but was also evident in the on-field product. Being a New York City team, the Fillies attracted the press in droves to cover their debut game. But the poor field conditions and low quality of play were all reporters needed to confirm their initial skepticism. They went all in on their criticism.

"Yellow flags fluttered like leaves in the final throes of autumn," mused one article from the Associated Press. "With inadequate lighting at the 22,000-seat Downing Stadium on remote Randall's Island, no official scoreboard, and a wiseacre announcing the plays from atop a sidelines table since there was no access to the official press box, it was a little tough to keep atop the action."

Despite his team's drubbing and the fact that the Fillies put up more injuries—ten in total—than points on the scoreboard during the game, Eagan remained steadfast that the team would get better and be more competitive as time went on. But that didn't happen. After three more games and three more losses (one to the mighty Toledo Troopers, 34–0), the lack of fan support, and a financial loss of twenty thousand dollars, Eagan decided to disband the team.

Carol Brown took it upon herself to search for a new financial backer for the Fillies and interviewed a handful of high-powered businessmen. But nothing ever materialized. Even so, the players continued to practice in Central Park and play games sporadically from 1972 to 1975, after renaming themselves the New York Herricanes.

The struggles in New York City had not gone unobserved. From his Cleveland perch, Sid Friedman watched the downfall of the New York Fillies and was most likely pleased. If the Fillies had really taken off along with the competition between the independent teams popping up around him, then less attention would be paid, both in the physical and monetary sense, to his own nascent women's football enterprise.

But Eagan had been a flawed owner from the start. Friedman had more knowledge about the game and had time and experience on his side. And despite his setbacks in getting a national league off the ground, Friedman had the Toledo Troopers, who were quickly becoming the main attraction.

When the Troopers joined Friedman's Rust Belt group of teams in 1971, he saw it as a sign that his venture was growing—exactly the way he'd planned it. But what he hadn't counted on was a group of women who knew their worth, and a male coach who was willing to be their biggest advocate.

o———o

Bill Stout was not the first man to be surprised at the skill and commitment of women on the gridiron. To fully understand the Troopers' origin and how the team excelled under Stout, it's important to note the rich history of football in Ohio and why it is the most logical place for women's football to have taken root.

The local games in the 1930s; the Cleveland beginnings of Sid Friedman's sideshow; the NWFL fielding long-standing teams in Toledo, Columbus, and Cleveland; even the teams that persist today: for a century, Ohio has been a mecca for women's football. That is no coincidence, because the roots of the game of football itself are baked into the state's history. Ohio isn't just a *women's* football mecca; it's a football mecca in general, and a love for the game and a culture that revolved around and revered the sport already existed there. The seeds were planted for women's football to flourish in the Buckeye State. They just needed someone to tend to them.

Baseball may be America's pastime, but football is Ohio's. On Friday nights in the early twentieth century, the mill towns would shut down for football games. As early as 1922, Ohio State University built a sixty-six-thousand-seat stadium, a shrine of sorts, which was at the time the largest poured-concrete structure in the world. Before there was the NFL, there was the Ohio League, a loose alliance of independent, semipro teams—not all that different from the women's football teams under Friedman—from cities including Toledo, Cleveland, and Youngstown. The Pro Football Hall of Fame is located in Canton, Ohio, the same place the NFL was born. In Ohio, parents put their boys in the sport from the time they are in elementary school.

Ohio's game day football—as described by Danille Christensen Lindquist in the academic paper "'Locating' the Nation: Football Game Day and American Dreams in Central Ohio"—is "a multifaceted event grounded in both historical contexts and live performances." This event, says Lindquist, creates a sense of both identity and cultural belonging in those who participate.

This lionization of football exists in Texas, too, another state that fielded several long-standing teams in the NWFL. Many people are familiar with a more modern portrayal of that culture in shows like *Friday Night Lights* or movies like *Varsity Blues*, but there is a long history of football being embedded into the culture of Texas. "Football is Texas, a culture grounded and affirmed in all the necessary ingredients of rules, traditions, folklore and legend," John Henry writes in the *Fort Worth Star-Telegram*, "all of it passed down from a fraternity of coaches and players and towns whose people have basked in the prestige from the game."

Throughout the entire United States, too, football is almost like a religion. Some people go to church on Sundays to say their Hail Marys; others sit around the television and turn on the football game, hoping to see a Hail Mary of a different sort. Americans worship their teams like they do their gods, and everything else ceases to matter while the game is on. Game day is a holiday, a holy day.

For girls growing up in this culture, forced to always be the spectator—in Ohio and Texas, yes, but also anywhere in America—it was only natural that there would be an overwhelming feeling of missing out. While there may have been other sports that were becoming more accessible to girls in the seventies, like rec league basketball or softball, those sports were consolation prizes. As much as the girls loved playing them, in Ohio at least, football was *the* sport: lionized by their friends and family, and always off-limits to the girls. If they were lucky, they could scrimmage with their brothers or the neighborhood boys, but that was as close to tasting organized football as they ever thought they could get. The reality of putting on pads and helmets and jogging out onto a real football field, with fans in the stands cheering them on, was one that existed only in their wildest daydreams. Even though girls were gaining ground in other sports leading up to and after the passage of Title IX, they were still shut out of football. And, in Ohio, this meant shutting girls out of the sport that mattered most.

But that didn't make football matter any less. Just how much football mattered—to these girls, in this state—was evident in the Troopers' first tryout.

o———o

More than eighty women showed up to try out for the Troopers in 1970. But Stout only wanted twenty-two: the best athletes, the most committed players, who would put in the work he knew would be required to turn a bunch of rookies into champions. His players practiced five nights per week in Colony Field, a weed-covered patch of grass hidden between US 23 and a rundown section of Toledo.

There were plenty of teams whose coaches believed they were more than a gimmick and viewed them as real athletes. Bill Stout, however, would be the first to go to bat for his players and help them create and envision a league that took them as seriously as they took themselves. He would also continue the tradition of women's football in the Rust Belt city of Toledo, located near the Michigan border and on the shore of Lake Erie.

Stout was a former All-City noseguard for DeVilbiss High School in Toledo whose pro football dreams had crumbled. Before he began coaching the Troopers, he was a struggling factory worker with a gambling problem. He felt like he was out of options, so he turned to coaching women's football—which he didn't take seriously until he saw the dedication and determination of his charges. He was a white man in his late twenties who carried his weight in his belly and wore mutton chops down his cheeks. He almost exclusively wore that very 1970s brand of athletic shorts and a polo shirt, a whistle draped around his neck.

Stout enlisted Carl Hamilton to coach the Troopers defense. Hamilton, a stocky Black man who wore a dour expression in photos but had a knack for getting the best out of his players, had played football at Bowling Green University. A high school teammate of Stout's named Jim Wright, a white man with a full head of brown hair parted to the side, a crooked smile, and a dimple in his right cheek, came on board as assistant coach. The team played most of their home games at Waite High School, a large brick building near downtown. Another woman who would go on to blaze trails for the women who came after her also has a Waite connection—Toledo native Gloria Steinem attended in the late 1940s.

In the Troopers' first season in 1971, there weren't many options when it came to opponents in Friedman's collection of teams. They played only three games that year, one against the Buffalo All-Stars and two against the Cleveland Daredevils. They won all three by large margins. Almost immediately, Stout internalized the narrative that this was a team of winners, that they were champions, and he began to parrot it until his players believed it, too. It didn't matter that they'd hardly had any competition: his team was the best, and by asserting it he would make it true. Even so, privately, he harbored some doubts as to how successful his team could be. "The brand of football wasn't that good when we started," he later told the *Toledo Blade*. "I never thought people would pay a second time to see us play."

o———o

The 1972 season established the Troopers' core identity: it was the year Linda Jefferson, the greatest halfback in the league, joined their team, giving the offense a jolt. The player—called a "bionic femme," in an article comparing her to O. J. Simpson of the NFL's Buffalo Bills—rushed for 1,179 yards in her first season with the Troopers. She averaged an astonishing 41 yards per touchdown run. Meanwhile, the team's defense, known as the Green Machine, really took shape under defensive coach Hamilton. Now, they were stopping opposing teams in their tracks. "The defensive animal squad is Carl's pride," read a poem from their yearbook, which also indicated there'd be repercussions for any points the defense allowed: "Let them score—it means leg lifts and you wish you'd have died."

Midway through the season the Troopers also acquired Gloria Jimenez, a Mexican American hairdresser who joined the team at the urging of her friend. The two were "young and rambunctious and didn't have enough to do," so they decided to go out for a football team. Jimenez had virtually no experience with organized sports at the time. What she did have, however, was five brothers and a lot of enthusiasm. "My dad always used to say, 'I've got five sons and my daughter plays football.' . . . I had more trophies than all my brothers put together."

Over the course of her time as a Trooper, Jimenez would be a true gadget player, a jill-of-all-trades who could slide in wherever she was needed. She played defensive end, defensive tackle, middle linebacker, offensive tackle, a little bit of fullback, and she was also the kicker. Jimenez played both ways, she played special teams, she did it all. She essentially never came off the field during a game.

When they went 8–0 in their second season in 1972, the Troopers' team yearbook declared them "NUMBER ONE" and "the best <u>damn</u> team in the league." And they were, by a long shot. In games against the Cleveland Daredevils, the Detroit Demons, the Buffalo All-Stars, and the New York Fillies, the Troopers scored 298 points, while their opponents scored just 32. Five of their games were shutouts. Bill Stout got what he wanted; he really was coaching a team of champions.

At least, that was how they rounded out their first two seasons. But their first game of the new 1973 season would be against a new team, the Dallas Bluebonnets (some historical records put this game in the Troopers' 1972 season, citing that season's record as 9–0). When the Troopers got down to Dallas and exited their bus, they walked into a real stadium. It felt as if women's football might just be on an upswing. Goodbye, high school football field, hello home of the Dallas Cowboys.

CHAPTER 6

DALLAS ENTERS THE FOLD

The Dallas Bluebonnets had a rough welcome into the world of women's football. Of all the teams they might have competed against, the Bluebonnets played their first game against the undefeated Troopers.

Not only that, this first match, against the top team in existence, would take place in Texas Stadium, the new home of the Dallas Cowboys. The oval-shaped stadium is best known for the large rectangular hole in its roof—the result of a design plan that was never fully executed and was supposed to involve a retractable roof. Over the years, football superstars like Hall of Fame players Troy Aikman, Emmitt Smith, and Deion Sanders played there.

To the Bluebonnets players, taking the same field as the Cowboys made them feel like they were on top of the world. They were playing in the same venue they watched their idols play in on TV, quite literally living out their dreams. It seemed like a sign that they were finally going to make it, that women were finally going to get the opportunity to play football at the level they deserved. It felt like the world of sports was finally opening up for them. They had no idea they were about to get their butts kicked.

The venue held over 65,000 people. Even so, just 2,842 people paid the three dollars to watch the Bluebonnets and Troopers face off. While getting almost 3,000 fans at a first game is nothing to diminish, that number of people wouldn't have filled even 1 percent of the seats in the stadium. Both things were true: they were playing for a nearly empty stadium, but also attracting thousands of fans to their game.

Despite the swanky digs—especially compared to the fields most of the other teams played on—most of the Bluebonnets had to dress for practices and games at home. The locker room in Texas Stadium lacked curtains or doors on the showers, granting the women little privacy. And since there was no equipment made specifically for women's bodies, they had to improvise when it came to protecting their chests: they took kneepads and sewed them to the front of their shoulder pads, creating cushion for their breasts.

The Bluebonnets' first game, on February 18, 1973, had been advertised in the local papers. "Now, even pro football 'liberated,'" proclaimed the *Odessa American*. To explain the existence of a women's football team, the *Dallas Morning News* offered "a tip of the headgear to Women's Lib" (while also making sure to note that most of the players were not "strung out on Women's Lib"; they just want to play football, you see). The papers took care to mention the marital status of the players, assuming all were heterosexual: "most are single or divorced" but "four are married and one . . . has five children." Not mentioned is whether the authors of the stories possessed gaydar.

Even for the Troopers, a confident and experienced team with two undefeated seasons under their belt, walking into Texas Stadium was intimidating. There was the sheer size of the place—the Troopers were used to playing smaller-scale venues, like a high school football field or, in some cases, a corn field—but there was also the fact that the Bluebonnets were standing there, nearly forty players deep, in their brand new uniforms: cyan-blue jerseys paired with United Nations–blue pants. The Troopers, on the other hand, had fewer players and were in their practice jerseys; Friedman reportedly hadn't let them wear their beautiful game jerseys, kelly green with three stripes at the shoulders: a white stripe sandwiched between two goldenrod stripes.

So the Troopers were a little out of their element, being in the big, shiny stadium and playing on Texas Turf, an artificial surface they weren't used to playing on. On the first play of the game, quarterback Lee Hollar tossed the ball to Jefferson and it bounced off her leg. Jefferson picked up the ball and ran it back ninety-two yards for a touchdown. After that, their nerves were settled. It was just a football game, and they knew how to play football.

"We thought we were all that and a bag of chips," said D. A. Starkey, who at 5'2" and 145 pounds played both ways for the Bluebonnets. "Come to find out, after I saw us play, we were like junior high."

Despite two Troopers being carried off the field on stretchers—casualties of adjusting to the artificial surface—the Troopers trounced the Bluebonnets, winning the game 37–12. Jefferson rushed for 209 yards on ten carries, scoring five touchdowns: the 92-yarder, along with 42, 13, and 15-yarders. Her fifth touchdown came on a 53-step screen pass. It was the kind of stat line that would propel any NFL running back to the football spotlight, earning him numerous accolades and awestruck statements in the sports section of newspapers across the country. But while there were game summaries written, Jefferson herself received little fanfare or nationwide attention.

On the Bluebonnets end, quarterback Barbara O'Brien scored their first touchdown on a one-yard keeper. And linebacker Willie Johnson broke her finger during the game, but stayed and played the entire thing.

A warm welcome into women's football, from Toledo to Dallas.

○————○

The Bluebonnets began less than a year earlier when, one night, a group of women were doing what they did most nights: hanging out in one of their favorite lesbian bars in Dallas, Texas.

At the time, there were several women's bars that dotted the blocks comprising Oak Lawn, known as Dallas's gayborhood. It was 1972 and the blocks that would eventually gentrify and be considered a trendy place to live were still gritty and seedy. The bar where the Bluebonnets were born was without pretenses: the bulk of the joint was taken up by the bar itself, the rest by a small dance floor and some pool tables. Groups of women chatted, pairs of women flirted, and everyone had one eye on the door. Should the police show up and raid the place, the women would be ready to keep their hands and eyes to themselves at a moment's notice.

Among the fold was D. A. Starkey, a hard-drinking, loud-talking butch woman—a self-described "dyke"—who was always looking for some kind of fun. Or trouble. That night, one of Starkey's friends brought in something she'd found in the *Dallas Times Herald*, an ad that caught her eye: it was two lines in the personal section, looking for women to try out for a professional football team.

Starkey wasn't the kind of person who read the paper, so this was the first she'd heard about any football team. And it didn't matter to Starkey that she'd never played football before. She had plenty of softball experience, so she knew she could catch the ball, and she was excited at the prospect of getting to smash into people. If there was one thing Starkey liked, it was being aggressive and shoving people around; if there was another, it was playing sports. Football would be the perfect melding of those interests.

That night, the lot of them decided they would go try out.

o———o

The women who played in the NWFL bucked convention in ways that went beyond simply taking the football field. While it is not true for all of them, of course, many of the women who played in the league were gay.

It's a common assumption that women who play sports are lesbians. And this assumption is often meant as an insult, so as to demean these athletes for breaking out of the conventional roles and expectations of women. Yet while this isn't always the case, it is true that many queer women often do play sports. And historically, as Susan K. Cahn writes in her 1994 book *Coming on Strong*, sports teams have often been places where lesbian women could find community and acceptance in an otherwise hostile world.

The other place that many gay women found a community was in women's bars. If not for bars, "our history would have been decidedly different," Dallas gay historian Phil Johnson told *Triangle* magazine in 1997. "The bars are our roots and our foundation. It was from them that everything else sprang." Johnson pointed out that gay bars existed before any other queer organizations—like churches, choruses, sports teams, or publications. For many of the Bluebonnets, the worlds of bars and athletics fit together seamlessly.

As a league, the NWFL (which launched in 1974) existed in an America just a few years removed from the Black Cat Tavern uprising of 1967 and Stonewall Inn uprising of 1969. Those events happened in Los Angeles and New York City, respectively, both large, more liberal cities than others in the country. And most of the NWFL teams were located in smaller towns, or in less liberal areas of the country. Even still, the resistance was trickling inward from the coasts. Many of the Bluebonnets players hung out in women's bars together, or knew each other from the softball leagues organized out of those spaces. And so, the NWFL began at a time of major change for gay Americans.

In fact, the same year the Bluebonnets were formed, Dallas held its first gay pride march. June 24, 1972, was a blazing Texas summer day, and a crowd of about two hundred people marched through downtown Dallas carrying signs that said, "I'm one, too" or "Gay is as American as Apple Pie." The *Fort Worth Star-Telegram* described the more than three thousand onlookers as "calm but a bit startled," and coverage leaned in hard to stereotypes: the paper described participants as "men in jeweled sandals, hot pants and halter tops" and "women adorned in Levis and t-shirts." Marchers pointed out to the press that they were still victims of harassment and homophobic violence, that they could be fired for being gay. "That's why we're marching today . . . ," one marcher told the *Telegram*, "to let people know we have the same rights as a heterosexual."

But not everyone in the Dallas queer bars was following the queer liberation movement, or was even aware of the shifting political tides. Dallas "wasn't like Stonewall," Bluebonnets quarterback Barbara O'Brien says today. For her part, Starkey was too busy getting drunk and picking up women to pay attention to politics. She left those details to other people in the community; thinking too much about being up against the world would spoil her fun, and that was all Starkey wanted in life. She was constantly chasing the next adrenaline rush, whether it was on the field or in the bars.

For lesbians in the NWFL, they knew that being who they were was a risk. There were places you could be safely out and places where you couldn't. One of those places where you were (mostly) safe to be gay was in a lesbian bar. Dallas had a particularly robust lesbian bar scene. While some cities struggled to keep even one women's bar open, at one point in the 1970s, Dallas had as many as five.

It is perhaps no surprise, then, that so many of the women who hung out in the gay women's bar scene at that time were drawn to the Bluebonnets. Many of the women were athletic and played on various sports teams, like softball and soccer, that were organized through the bars. They saw football as an extension of that. But more than that, these women were experts at creating community spaces when the world was a hostile place for people like them. In that way, the teams and the bars served much the same purpose.

These bars were such big supporters of the league, and the players were such an integral part of Dallas's lesbian community, that local women's bars bought ad space in their game-day programs. In a 1977 Dallas–Fort Worth Shamrocks program, The Maidenhead, "a women's cocktail lounge," advertised its "Steak Out" nights on Wednesdays and Sundays at 8 p.m. Another bar called Sassy's, also known as Too Sassy's, advertised itself in the program as "celebrating a new era for women." And there was an ad for Jugs, which opened in 1975 and was owned by Joe Elliott, a legend in the Dallas lesbian scene. When Jugs closed its doors in the 1990s, it was the longest-running women's bar in Dallas. They offered twenty-five-cent beer on Tuesday nights.

The bars, however, were not always as welcoming to Black women as they were to white ones. Even within a marginalized community like the gay community, Black folks were often discriminated against. Some venues would require multiple forms of identification from Black patrons, while not asking the same of white ones, as a way of excluding them.

The fact that they were gay was both important and unimportant to the queer women on the Bluebonnets. They were there first and foremost to play football. That so many of their friends were there, too, and their sheer number—in addition to the way sports teams can often feel like families—combined to make the Bluebonnets a place where any woman, gay or straight, could be herself. However, "we weren't that open," O'Brien, the Bluebonnets quarterback, confessed. The gay players knew who the other gay women on the team were, "but we weren't advertising our sexuality."

The Bluebonnets were not unique in having a large number of gay women on their roster. Sometimes, when teams traveled to games, the home team would bring the visitors out to their favorite local gay spot. Oklahoma City Dolls kicker Mary BlueJacket estimates that her team was about 50 percent gay women, and after the games, the lesbian women would go out to the women's bars while the straight women went home or elsewhere. On the road, however, the women would party together in their motel rooms as a team.

Romances, hookups, and interpersonal drama sometimes made their way into the locker room as a result. There was at least one hookup between Los Angeles Dandelions players. Two members of the Dolls were a couple. And Rose Motil, the quarterback of the Columbus Pacesetters for three games in 1974 (until she tore her ACL), lived with her partner, Pacesetters fullback Mary Morrison, in an apartment on Ohio State University's campus near German Village. Motil graduated high school in 1971 and came out the following year, and frequented popular Columbus women's bars in the seventies, including Summit Station and Mel's.

One player for the Columbus Pacesetters in the 1980s, Vickie Pardue, remembers the team's trainer "wrapping her ankle too good," after which the two slept together. "And we all know how that turned out," the player smirked on a Facebook post. Then Deb Fry started playing, and her girlfriend Suzanne became the team's money girl. After Fry and Suzanne split up, Suzanne and Pardue dated for the next seven and a half years.

On the Bluebonnets, Starkey and CoCo Manson dated for a few years (and, in true lesbian fashion, remain friends to this day). Starkey says that when the two would have a fight, sometimes they put their pads and helmets on and went into the yard to get their aggression out. "We would go after each other," Starkey said, and then say, "okay, that's over."

Starkey came out to her parents when she was just fourteen years old. "My dad said, 'Well, sister, that's a hard life. Good luck,' and it was never spoken about again." It was never an internal struggle for her, the way it is for some people. Starkey has always been exactly who she is, which, in her words, is "just a dyke." Her butch presentation made that fact hard to hide, and she says that any taunts or names she was called in public never bothered her. "That's what we were!" she said. "It didn't hurt my feelings."

"Men would just call us dykes, and, you know, 'Come here, let me show you what a real man is,' and stuff like that," O'Brien remembered. "I thought it was pretty disgusting. Right? But consider the source."

Toni Gibson recalls that some of their worst harassment came after they'd done pep rallies with the Dallas Cowboys. The Cowboys players, she said, "understood our struggle" and "couldn't have been more nice to us." But they'd show up to practice and there would be a group of harassers—mostly men—waiting for them. "If you played football, everybody called you a 'queer' automatically. And the other word was 'dyke.'" It was dangerous at times, Gibson said. "At that time, you could have done anything you wanted to a gay person and everybody would have turned their head."

One night after a game, Gibson, Starkey, Manson, and a few other players went to eat at a Denny's they frequented. A man approached their table, threw a wooden nickel on it, and said, "This is what y'all are worth. You bunch of dykes."

Gibson says that when they went out as a group, their safety felt more precarious because the group of women who were read as lesbians were conspicuous; there were more of them, which made them more noticeable. In Leslie Feinberg's novel *Stone Butch Blues*, there is a phrase for this phenomenon: the "geometric theory: two people like us in public are more than double the trouble." As Cat Moses explains in the 1999 paper "Queering Class: Leslie Feinberg's 'Stone Butch Blues,'" "One butch . . . on the street is likely to be perceived as a freak and subjected to harassment; two or more together are a freak show, a traffic-stopping phenomenon, an invitation to violence."

In the early 1970s, police raids were still happening in gay bars, and owners, staff, and patrons of the establishments were routinely arrested just for being inside. For decades, women had to be wearing at least three items of "women's clothing" in order to avoid being arrested. But even that didn't guarantee safety; police could create reasons to take someone into custody. "For a long time, you just didn't wanna be caught in the gay bar," said O'Brien, "'cause the Dallas police would be raiding it."

During the decades in which police often targeted gay bars, raids predominantly impacted the most marginalized queers: Black and Latinx, transgender, and working class. "Upper-class cross-dressing women," writes Moses, "have always been more tolerated than working-class butch women." Moreover, Joan Nestle, a femme lesbian who frequented pre-Stonewall women's bars, points out in her collection of essays that upper-class butches like Vita Sackville-West and Radclyffe Hall have been idealized as trendsetters and fashion icons. Yet this idealizing, Moses adds, occurred even while "working-class butches have long been objects of hate, scorn, and ridicule." Butches and drag queens were also most harshly targeted in vice raids on gay and lesbian blue-collar bars, because they were "the most visible gender transgressors." That is, upper-class queers were more likely to gather in someone's private home than they were to go to a bar where they might be arrested.

Perhaps this is why—according to Paula Bosse, who runs the local history website Flashback: Dallas—it's incredibly difficult to find positive media stories about Dallas's gay community prior to the 1970s. "There are plenty of negative items that appeared in the local newspapers, most of which invariably focused on reports of vice raids or were generally one-sided psychology-based discussions of 'aberrant behavior,'" she writes on the blog Central Track, "but there is almost no mention at all of gay culture." It wasn't until the gay community in Dallas began organizing in earnest following Stonewall, and taking their complaints to the courts, that the raids subsided. By that time, Starkey remembers getting caught making out with a girl in her car, but the police telling them to just go home.

For someone like Bluebonnets player Betty Young, Dallas's lesbian bars were where she discovered that she was not "a freak" and that there were other people like her. She grew up in a Christian family in Pennsylvania before moving to Texas. Young knew from a very young age that she liked girls. She thought of herself as "a strange little creature" because of her love of "boy things." She dealt with conflicting messages: that she "should have been a boy" but that she "couldn't have boy things."

It always felt natural to her, though, to gravitate toward the things the boys were doing: wearing jeans and button-down shirts, playing sports, flirting with girls.

Young recalls feeling "terrorized" about being found out, which she was on more than one occasion. As a teenager, girls would tell her she would be "the perfect boyfriend"—if only she were a boy. They would kiss her, as practice for kissing their boyfriends. They'd never heard about being gay; a girl heard that someone in Denmark had had "a sex change" and said to Young, "We'll go do that so we can get married!" They didn't know anything about what it entailed or what the surgery would mean, they were just looking for a way to be together.

In high school, Young's mother found a note that a girl on the cheerleading team had written to her daughter and was "almost hysterical." That's when Young understood: this needs to be hidden. When Young moved from Pennsylvania to Texas, she kept in touch with a girl back home. Young says that when the girl's parents found out, they put her in a psychiatric hospital. After Young moved to Dallas, she began hooking up with the daughter of the missionary family Young's family was staying with. Her parents found a note from her to Young; the girl's mother confronted Young and called her "the devil."

"It was kind of like a witch hunt thing," she recalled, her voice shaking as she described that time in her life. "I didn't know there were any other beings like me until I was eighteen years old so this was a lone journey of [feeling like] a freak of nature."

When Young found out that other gay people existed, and she learned what the word "homosexual" meant, it was a relief. She knew instantly that's what she was. The first time Young walked through the doors of a gay bar and looked around, it was "an epiphany," she said, one that "lifted [her] to the heavens." Shortly after that is when she found out about the Bluebonnets, through the new friends she'd made at the women's bars, which she describes as "another lift-off."

Dallas's lesbian bar scene became Young's home. She didn't really drink and her family never went to bars because of their faith, "but that was the only place we had," Young said. Tuesday was bring-your-own steak night and the bar would provide the potatoes and salad. "Going to the bars was not to go to bars," said Young. "It was our community. It was like home for us."

Today, there are very few gay bars left in Dallas, as they've mostly closed, following a nationwide trend of queer bars closing as it becomes safer and more acceptable to be gay in public. But a few still exist, including the Round-Up Saloon and Dance Hall, where Young and her wife like to go out dancing. They often run into former Bluebonnets teammates, like Norma Featherston. "I started running into all my old teammates" at some of the women's nights, Featherston said. "Now we're older and we're . . . going dancing rather than playing football."

With bars being such a central focus of lesbian nightlife, hard drinking came along with it. Starkey came from a family of alcoholics and she struggled with it, too. She describes herself as "a blackout drunk" who "doesn't remember shit" from the years she spent drinking and using drugs. She went to prison twice for DWIs. Finally, in her midthirties, she got sober.

Bluebonnet Lory Masters, too, got sober in 1983. "There were a lot of us that were alcoholics back then," she told the *Dallas Voice*. "The bars were the only place we had to go to be ourselves, and when you were in the bar, you drank. You know, people tell a lot of stories about me, and maybe the stories are true, and maybe they aren't. But I can't say they aren't because I was so drunk back then, I don't remember."

The LGBTQ+ community tends to have higher rates of substance misuse than their straight counterparts. It was that fact, combined with Masters's personal experience, that motivated her in 1989 to push for the Oak Lawn Counseling Center—which later became Oak Lawn Community Services—to create the Oasis drug and alcohol treatment program, which was tailored to Dallas's LGBTQ+ community.

o———o

The number of gay women on NWFL teams did more than just provide community for the queer players. Their presence also opened the minds of their straight teammates. Nearly every player openly acknowledged that there were lesbians on their teams; and they followed that up with insisting that it "didn't matter" and that they were "a family."

Especially considering that the teams often existed in smaller towns or more rural locations, where it was less accepted to be gay, straight women on the teams had often never met an openly gay person before joining the NWFL. Hines, the quarterback of the Dolls, says her experience in the league forever shaped her social politics. Growing up in the church and being straight herself, she didn't know anything about gayness until a friend of hers on the team came out to her.

"It took me a few days to work through it mentally," she said. "And I'm thinking to myself, 'I've known this person for a number of years, and never had an issue. Why should things change now that I have knowledge of something that I didn't before? Why should that change my relationship?"

Dolls player Pebble Myers, who was a college student at the time and a self-described "country girl," remembers the gay players asking her if she was gay or had any interest in women. When Myers said no, "that was the end of it." She says the players would congregate by their cars after practices and share stories from their lives. "We talked about our boyfriends," she says, "and they talked about their girlfriends."

It is interesting to think about this league in contrast with another women's professional league, the All-American Girls Professional Baseball League (AAGPBL). Existing during World War II, from 1943 to 1954, it predated the NWFL by three decades. The AAGPBL also had many queer women playing in it; looking at how their straight teammates, and the men who managed the league, reacted to the idea of homosexuality offers a good understanding of how much progress had been made on the issue in the twenty years between the leagues. Unlike the NWFL, which allowed the women to wear the same equipment as male athletes and generally did not police their appearance, the AAGPBL required the women to play baseball in skirts—at the expense of their safety—and attend charm school. Women could be kicked out of the league for having a haircut deemed "too butch," because the owners of the league did not want the women to be perceived as lesbians.

Similar to the NWFL players, many of the women in the AAGPBL came from small, rural towns and had never met a gay person before joining the league. But for the straight women who discovered some of their teammates were having relationships with each other, their reaction was not always one of normalization. Some were horrified, while others thought it was a joke. The fact that the straight NWFL players responded so differently, with an open mind and open heart, testifies to the larger social shifts that had occurred in the time period between leagues.

The women of the NWFL also disprove one dominant narrative: the idea that queer people in red states or "flyover country" always leave for coastal cities. In fact, the NWFL women stayed in their hometowns or home states, and found community among others who had stayed, too. Most of them are still there today; they did not board a bus with a one-way ticket to New York City or San Francisco.

They resisted and persisted, whether in a sport they were told they shouldn't play or by loving people they were told they couldn't love. They may talk about times when they felt unsafe being openly gay. But these cities and towns are also the only place they've ever been queer; they don't know what it would be like anywhere else, nor do they want to.

o———o

Another part of the Dallas Bluebonnets' origin story begins with two brothers. That two-line ad looking for women to play football—the one that galvanized that lesbian bar, where Starkey first heard of the team—had been placed by brothers Joe and Stan Mathews.

They weren't looking to start their own team, necessarily, but that's exactly what they ended up doing. Joe was having coffee with a friend when the topic of women's football came up. A seed had been planted and Joe began testing the waters. He mentioned the idea of a women's team to various people and "they didn't laugh," he said. "The more I thought about it the more I believed a women's team could be formed."

Nearly forty women answered the ad. Tryouts were held at Samuell-Grand/Tenison Park in Northeast Dallas. Samuell-Grand abuts Tenison Memorial, together forming a massive park in the upper Owenwood neighborhood encapsulating nearly 186 acres of land. The women arrived and hung out around the parking lot, trying to size up the operation. Then the coaches asked them to run and do different drills to get a sense of their skill and potential. The ones who seemed promising were asked to come back, though Barbara O'Brien remembers everyone who wanted to play making the team.

O'Brien was nineteen years old and showed up to tryouts after hearing about them from a friend she played softball with. She arrived with an arm she honed playing QB in pickup games with the boys on her street. She could throw a perfect spiral, making her the obvious choice for quarterback. O'Brien was a five-feet-nine-inch-tall young woman with auburn hair who had grown up in a white, middle-class home in Garland, Texas, and was working for AT&T. She learned to play sports because her mother loved sports, and passed that love down to her daughter.

Joe, who had been a buyer for Sears in Dallas at the catalog order house for twenty-seven years, tapped a robust collection of experienced men to coach the team. Head coach Rich Benat had played four years of collegiate football at Bridgeport, Connecticut. When Benat, an assistant football coach at the University of Bridgeport, was contacted by Joe with the offer to coach a pro team, Benat said he would "jump at the chance." He moved to Dallas and got a job as a life insurance salesman. It was only after he had agreed that Joe told him it was a women's team. "I watched one practice," he told the *Dallas Times Herald*, "and the girls were so enthusiastic, I knew they could play. It was just a matter of teaching them the right techniques."

Joining Benat on the coaching staff were offensive coordinator Eddie Jackson, a former baseball and football star at Wiley College who was known as the team motivator; defensive line coach Mike Anderson; Bob Daily on offensive backfield; and Stan coaching the quarterback and receivers. Joe served as the team's general manager.

Benat lasted only a few months as the coach of the Bluebonnets, however. While coaches and players on many of the teams often boasted that watching them play would be just like watching men, or that they were coached no differently than they would have been if they were men, there was a line and Benat crossed it. He was rough on the players; to them, it didn't feel like his treatment was being done for their benefit; instead, they felt it was because he thought them incapable, or the equivalent of a high school team. He talked down to the women, treating them as if they didn't know what they were doing and were incapable of learning. And he didn't seem to understand that any ignorance came from the players' lack of exposure to formal football coaching.

With Benat out, Anderson, a former semipro player who was about the same age as the players, took over the head coaching role. That's when the team really blossomed. He respected the women and developed off-field relationships with many of them, even employing a few of the players at his lawn-care business. With a coach who helped them tap into their potential and cared enough to be patient with their learning curve, the Bluebonnets quickly learned the mechanics of the game.

o————o

"We were starting from what little boys started at, I'm sure, in junior high or something," O'Brien said. "We just had to learn every aspect of the game." They went through the basics, like how to get into a proper stance, how to tackle, and how to do a stunt when on the line. They learned pass patterns and running plays. They learned how not to get hurt while tackling someone else and how to fall. They did strength-building exercises, particularly for their necks.

Most of the women were in their twenties, but some were younger than that. Carol "CoCo" Manson and Toni Gibson were both seventeen. Gibson's family didn't approve of her playing "a man's sport." Her grandparents were ministers and her grandmother was appalled that Gibson would go out for a sport like football. This grandmother believed women shouldn't be doing a lot of things, including wearing pants, so football was definitely a no-no. Luckily for Gibson, she didn't need to ask her parents to sign a waiver to let her play, since by this time she'd already been married—which emancipated her—and divorced. Gibson joined the line.

Some women showed up hoping to find a girlfriend. Lory Huitt (who later changed her last name to Masters) agreed to go to tryouts to support her friend. Once she got there, she looked around and "saw all those cuties," she told the *Dallas Voice*, and said, "Where do I sign up?" A blonde with a mix between a Farrah Fawcett blowout and a Brigitte Bardot bouffant, Masters was famous for playing in white, elbow-length evening gloves, which she wore because she hated getting dirt under her fingernails when she got down on point. She played tackle, though she didn't do a whole lot of actual tackling.

The Bluebonnets practiced for four hours each Saturday and three hours each Sunday to prepare for their season, which the *Dallas Morning News* said meant they were "pretty serious about this whole football thing."

Early on, the Dallas Cowboys supported the Bluebonnets. It was a big deal to have the support of their NFL team, and at one point, they even had a pep rally together at Forester Field. Players like Harvey Martin and Roger Staubach stood onstage with the women, legitimizing a team that may have otherwise been considered a joke. The fact that they played in the same stadium sometimes made the Bluebonnets feel like the Cowboys' "little sister team," though it doesn't seem that the team provided any other funding or support for the Bluebonnets.

The Cowboys players didn't make the millions of dollars NFL players make today. Still, with the formal recognition of the Players' Association in 1968 came the first collective bargaining agreement and guaranteed salaries: a $9,000 season minimum for rookies and $10,000 for veterans, while the average salary in the league at that time was around $25,000.

Meanwhile, the Bluebonnets crossed their fingers they'd get the twenty-five dollars per game they'd been promised. Though they didn't play for the money—how could they, there wasn't any—the discrepancies in pay and funding were huge. And these discrepancies raise the same questions asked today: What does it mean for a men's professional team to support the local women's team? Does it require more than lip service, a couple of public appearances together, and a photo op in the *Dallas Morning News* of former Cowboy Pettis Norman buying a ticket to a Bluebonnets game?

Of course, at the time, the Bluebonnets took what they could get.

∘———∘

The Bluebonnets were also known for their size: the players on their line were big. Biggest of all was Bobbie Grant, who, at 5'11" and 265 pounds, was an intimidating presence on the field. While the press had a field day insulting her size, her opponents were more worried about how they were going to get through her. For her part, Trooper halfback Linda Jefferson said she found the trick: run around her. "She's very slow, but you get her in a line and no two women can move her," Joe Mathews said. "We don't have to worry; nobody is going through where Bobbie is."

Grant played center, defensive end, and defensive tackle. Her team-mates called her Super Sugar, a nickname she liked. As a kid, she would watch football on TV with her brother, analyzing games and dreaming about being like NFL players Deacon Jones and Bob Lilly. She worked full-time at the Dallas YWCA and kept herself in playing shape, she told *Ebony* magazine, by eating "ordinary soul food," avoiding candy, drinking four glasses of milk, and working out twice a day at the YWCA. In addi-tion to being a big on-field presence, Grant was big off the field, too. She loved to be recognized for being a member of the Bluebonnets and, in her spare time, sang in her own band, Super Sugar Soul Revival.

Players like Grant found a place where their bodies and size were valued. No matter what the press said about them, the bodies that were mocked as being unattractive or unfeminine off the field were intimi-dating and desired on it. The NWFL challenged traditional ideas about weight and body image for women: value was not always in being lithe and thin, for example, because you couldn't then be a good linebacker. No one cared how feminine you were while executing a tackle, so the gender of butch and more masculine women was not policed the way it was on the streets.

Of course, there were sometimes exceptions. There was the time Joe Mathews asked the Bluebonnets players to have a more acceptable presen-tation off the field. Starkey remembers him coming into the locker room and telling the women, "I want y'all to wear a dress on the plane." The women responded by laughing him out of the locker room. They roundly rejected the idea, being clear that it wasn't going to happen. "I think most of us at that time were like, 'you can't make me.' You know?" said Starkey. She cites the fact that many of the players were gay and were already re-jecting many of the gender norms imposed on them, so they felt comfort-able pushing back against Mathews. This was another stark contrast from the AAGPBL of the 1940s and 1950s, where the women felt they had no choice but to play baseball in skirts if they wanted to play at all.

Generally, however, the focus was instead on what a body could do, and when it comes to football, size can be a very good thing. There was a Troopers player who desperately wanted to be a cheerleader; but at her size, no squad would take her. On the football field, however, her body was an asset. "Being on the football field was all about empowerment," said Pacesetters player Linda Stamps. "We had several linewomen who were six-feet tall and a couple hundred pounds. They'd get trained and, in about six weeks, they'd be walking taller and fully into themselves. They owned their bodies. That's the kind of thing football did for women."

Pacesetters trainer Julie Sherwood remembers the football field as "the first place that I ever was where your weight wasn't something to be ashamed of." At the time, much like today, fatphobic society perpetuated the idea that the lower the number on the scale, the more attractive a woman was and therefore the more value she had. But while off the field, larger women were discriminated against, Sherwood said that on the gridiron "people took you seriously." She credits her playing days as giving her the confidence to feel like she didn't have to lie about her weight when she renewed her driver's license.

These were just some of the many things that male football players never had to deal with, on or off the field. In contrast to the Bluebonnets, all the Dallas Cowboys had to do was go out and play.

o———o

The Dallas women had a reputation for playing dirty. Nearly fifty years later, they're happy to admit that reputation was earned.

Some of the players chalk it up to being taught to play football by men who were treating them no differently than they would treat male athletes. "Acting like ladies" wasn't going to fly in a pile on the field. At the time, there were far fewer rules around what kinds of tackles and holds were illegal. Today, a player isn't allowed to dive for another player's knees to try to injure them, but at the time, anything went.

What the Bluebonnets players may have lacked in football skills they tried to make up for by taking their opponents out. During an on-field scrum, when none of the dirty tricks could confidently be pinned on any particular player, they would pinch, bite, stick their fingers through the ear holes of helmets—anything to take another player out of the game.

Starkey, in particular, lived for the intensity. And she didn't care whether or not she was fighting fair. There were rumors that she kept a tally on her helmet of players she'd taken out, but Starkey says that wasn't true. "Getting into the excitement of it was just exhilarating, and I was kind of a bully," she said. The fact that she was "kind of aggressive" meant that the football field gave her a place to take that aggression out—often at the expense of other teams.

Sometimes, however, her teammates got the brunt of her attitude. She remembers one game when quarterback O'Brien accused her of not doing a good enough job blocking the other team's defense. Instead of trying to get more blocks, Starkey decided not to block at all on the next two plays, so O'Brien would know what it felt like when Starkey *really* wasn't getting any stops. After that, Starkey says, O'Brien "shut that shit up." The Bluebonnets coaches weren't spared Starkey's big mouth, either. "I would rebuke authority. . . . If there's a leader, I'm butting heads with 'em," she said. "I was kinda the renegade on the team, 'cause I always wanted to fight."

After games at Texas Stadium, there would be tables set up for meet and greets with the other team. This was less of a friendly "getting to know you" event and more of an opportunity for players to find the person who had taken them out or done them dirty and get out their frustration about it. "There'd be people walking around, asking, 'Where's Gibson, 32?' and you knew they weren't doing it to be nice to you," Gibson remembered.

Needless to say, the Bluebonnets were a rough and tough outfit from start to finish. This was even the case when another Mathews brother decided to start a women's football franchise of his own in California. This new team, the Dandelions, would soon find out just how dirty Dallas could be on the field.

CHAPTER 7

DANDELIONS BLOOM

It was a classic early-spring day in Los Angeles in April 1973: the sun hanging high in the sky and not a cloud in sight. Rose Low and a few of her friends at East Los Angeles College (ELAC) headed down the Pacific Coast to Santa Monica Beach, looking for a break from the everyday rigors of school. Low, a petite and seemingly shy nineteen-year-old college sophomore, with long crow-black hair that dipped down past her waist, had heard an announcement about a new women's professional football team that was forming in the LA area. As an athlete, and someone who grew up wanting to try any sport she could, Low was especially curious. On the way to Santa Monica, she knew they'd be driving right by Hollywood High School, where tryouts were being held. She told her friends about it. Since they were heading in that direction, they decided to stop to see what the tryout was all about.

They never made it to the beach.

When they first arrived, Low and her friends mixed in with the rest of the women on the field, including twenty-one-year-old college student Joyce Johnson; twenty-seven-year-old Gail Werbin, an aspiring film-maker who held a master's degree in cinematography from USC; eighteen-year-old physical therapy major Janet Grassly; thirty-year-old mother and PBX operator Barbara Patton; and many others. The youngest potential players sitting in the bleachers that day were eighteen, and the oldest was thirty-two.

o———o

That day, Robert "Bob" Mathews, forty-two, stood in front of Low and the other women in a tan sport coat and a striped tie. Soft-spoken with a full head of dark hair and long sideburns, Mathews had worked his way up from an electrician to a supervisor for an electrical contractor, and was an aspiring businessman. He certainly looked the part, as a white man in professional attire.

The women listened as Mathews explained the purpose of the tryout: he was forming a new women's professional football team, which would compete against other all-women's teams. Players would be paid a salary of twenty-five dollars per game, provided they attended practice before the games, and all travel expenses would be covered in full. Uniforms and equipment would also be provided. All the players had to do was buy their own cleats.

Mathews's presentation was thorough and convincing. It was obvious he wasn't just some guy off the street who woke up one day and decided to start a women's football franchise. He knew about women's football teams in other parts of the country, including the Detroit Demons—rebranded from the original 1972 Midwest Cowgirls/Detroit Fillies—and the Toledo Troopers, of course. And his brothers, Joe and Stan, already owned a team in Dallas called the Bluebonnets. Mathews once told the *Sportswoman* that he had been interested in giving women a chance to play football since 1965, and now was the time to do it because he thought society was finally ready to accept it. With his brothers already in the mix, Mathews was ready to take the plunge and spearhead a "pioneer venture" that would launch women's football in California.

In order to drum up the funds, Mathews managed to find a group of investors willing to back him and help bankroll fifty thousand dollars to start a women's football franchise. This initial investment consisted of an unofficial price tag of eleven thousand dollars, as well as funds for the team's equipment, uniforms, travel expenses, and player salaries. The investors included Cecil Proulx, a contract negotiator for the US Air Force;

Ed Addinton, a sales manager for a car dealership; Pat Hogan, a finance company office manager, and his wife, Joyce; Howard Olds, a local grocer and businessman; and Jerry Patterson, the director of athletics at Hollywood High and also an assistant coach for the team. Together, the investors formed California Women's Professional Athletics, Inc. And they named the team the LA "Dandelions" after Mathews's wife suggested, "They're pretty spring flowers that you just can't kill."

After Mathews spoke, it was Patterson, wearing sunglasses and a bright orange spring jacket, who addressed the group next. Patterson gave a pep talk about expectations, and wanting to help develop the Dandelions into "something [they'd] enjoy and be proud of."

Other coaches on the initial Dandelions staff included former All-American George Boerner and Walt Butler. Bob Edwards, an illustrator and art teacher who once tried out for the NFL's LA Rams, was appointed head coach; this arguably made him the first Black head coach in pro football history.

At first, Edwards believed the potential Dandelions players were too feminine. "You want good women players, go to El Toro (the Marine base), the Police Academy or a track meet," he told the *Los Angeles Times* at the time. "Of course, I might be judging them too harshly." Edwards's preconceived notion about the women standing in front of him was based on the typical feminine stereotype—demur, fragile, unathletic—one that he would have never applied to a group of aspiring adult male football players. Little did he know, he was about to be proven wrong.

Patterson led everyone onto the field to warm up and throw the ball around. Low was surprised by how organized everything was. There were skill tests for throwing and catching, other football-related drills, and the coaches on hand were fully engaged as they went along. She had never been asked to throw a football before, let alone hold one in her hands.

It was almost surreal.

◦——◦

Before Title IX passed in 1972, women were only allowed to participate in limited athletic activities. Football was definitely not one of them. "We couldn't do what the boys did," Low recalled. "Even run a mile around the track—the boys ran and the girls had to walk. We were like, 'What's wrong with us?'"

But the limits placed on women athletes didn't deter Low and other women from wanting to play sports. It only made them want to play more. Low's athletic curiosity had peaked back in high school, but by the time she graduated in 1971, she hadn't had a single opportunity to play organized sports for her school.

Then, Title IX happened and her entire sports world—and many other women's sports worlds—magically opened up. "All of a sudden, there were a few more sports that we could play," Low said. "We jumped in."

While in college, Low participated in almost anything that was offered: field hockey, badminton, archery, and a handful of other sports that she hadn't been allowed to play in high school. With Title IX in play, different colleges were now able to organize all-women's teams, which could compete against each other.

Low was overjoyed. For the first time in her life, she was able to take part in competitive sports, and it sparked something in her that hasn't waned since. It was part of the reason she wanted to become a physical education teacher. But not everyone was as thrilled. Low was first-generation Chinese American and the second-oldest child with three brothers; her parents had certain expectations of how her life should go, and it didn't involve sports or athletics. It definitely didn't involve football.

Low's mother had high aspirations for her daughter. She wanted Low to be a nurse or a pharmacist. Getting a job as a physical education teacher wasn't even on her mother's radar. "My parents immigrated from China. Being immigrants, they worked so hard to get us through school. We were so poor back in the day," Low said. "My parents worked multiple jobs. And they wanted to make sure we had a good future. When I told my mother I wanted to pursue physical education, she said women just didn't do that."

Still, Low couldn't resist the pull. She studied physical education in college, participated in athletics, and, without her parents knowing, was now trying out for—*God forbid*—a football team. Low had always been athletic since she was little and had a "good arm." She played pitcher in softball and as she tossed the pigskin back and forth to other would-be gridders that day on the field, she could feel the eyes of Edwards and Patterson watching her. They never said a word to her about playing quarterback, however, and had her try out for free safety instead. Low didn't care what position she played; she was content to be out there, trying a sport she hadn't ever gotten to play before. She knew there was a lot she had to learn about football, from simple things like how to block and what the coaches meant when they said, "First and ten," to more complex aspects like defensive schemes and offensive plays. Learning was part of the process, and Low was more than happy to welcome the instruction. Others were, too.

Coach Edwards, who revealed that he hadn't expected much at the start of the tryout, was encouraged with what he had seen so far. "My first motivation, when I first heard about it, was I thought it would be a nice opportunity to come down and meet a few ladies and get a few phone numbers," he joked. "Now I have about 35 phone numbers, and about 35 have mine. And it's not like I thought it would be."

Edwards saw potential and, at the very least, something to work with. Except for the women who had just shown up for fun and weren't taking tryouts seriously, and those who couldn't commit to the practice schedule, Edwards felt the coaches had all the pieces they needed for a complete football team. Still, they'd need to toughen the players up and get them in game shape. Patterson agreed, and also felt "a quick, fast team would be ideal."

The coaches were prepared to put in the necessary time before the Dandelions' first game. This was just a few months away: Mathews had arranged for the Dandelions to play his brothers' team—the Dallas Bluebonnets—on Sunday, July 22, 1973, at Long Beach Veterans Memorial Stadium. That schedule meant the players who made the team and were fully committed to attend practices had exactly twelve weeks to get properly conditioned, get to know each other, learn their offensive and defensive positions, study the plays, and get ready for their league debut.

It was a whirlwind for Low, who had gone to the tryout on a whim. But on the day they were given their uniforms, it became real. Each player was issued a helmet, a pair of shoulder pads, a jersey, football pants, and additional pads for those who needed extra padding to protect their breasts.

Low had asked for a larger helmet herself, because she wasn't willing to cut her long hair and had heard horror stories from the coaches that players on other teams would try to grab onto it to tackle her. She decided to twist her hair up into a bun on top of her head and slide her helmet over it to keep it in place instead. It worked. With her hair problem solved, Low was eager to get started. And there were thirty other women from the tryout who, like her, were ready to give the Dandelions their all.

o———o

Overall, the Dandelions roster was racially diverse, as were many of NWFL teams. In reflecting back on their time playing together, many of the women—regardless of their race—recall this diversity with fondness, and often refer to their teams as being "like family."

For many of the white players, it was the first time they had really spent any significant time in close proximity to women of color. Even still, players reported very few experiences with racism or tensions arising from racial differences. After a game in Albuquerque, where Dallas and Los Angeles had traveled to play each other at an in-between location, Bluebonnets members recall attempting to go to a bar that would not let the Black women in; the entire team decided to leave rather than separate or tolerate the blatant discrimination of women whom they considered to be "sisters."

Oklahoma City Dolls players Charlotte Gordon and Doris Stokes, both Black, remember some insensitive comments being made. They chalked them up to the white women having such little exposure to Black people prior to joining the team. Neither said that the comments made them feel unwelcome or impacted their feelings of safety or solidarity on the team.

The fact that so many of the white players had not spent much time around women of color before joining the NWFL, on the Dolls and most of the other teams, speaks to the segregation in urban planning and development, and the legacy of redlining that has upheld systemic racism by geographically separating people along racial and ethnic lines.

And yet, of the women tracked down from the league today, those who have stayed in touch with each other often break down along racial lines.

For example, the Bluebonnets who are still friends today are mostly white, gay women; when a Black player was contacted, frequently the players she was still in touch with were also Black. This breakdown speaks to a level of interracial connection and solidarity that didn't necessarily translate long-term away from the football field.

The on-field and sideline solidarity that did exist between women of different races, however, was likely helped by two things. One was a shared class background. With so many of the women coming from working-class backgrounds, there were similarities that may have lessened some of the racial and cultural differences that manifested. The other was the fact that, though they may have all come from different places, and each had her own story, they had something in common: they were all women who were subverting societal norms, doing something they were told women shouldn't do, at a time when expectations for women were even more limited than they are today. Regardless of race or sexual orientation, there was a shared experience in being up against the world, together.

In addition to Low, the Dandelions roster had twenty-two-year-old Vickie Garcia—a stocky Latina with a strong arm, a booming voice, and a comedic flair—who was a clear-cut frontrunner at quarterback. Aside from watching football on television, Garcia had little experience with organized football. She'd never been in the huddle or called plays before. And she quickly realized that watching it and actually doing it in real time were worlds apart. "The hardest thing is learning all of the plays and calling them at the right time," she told the *Los Angeles Times*. "The quarterback gets hit a lot but if you can't take hitting, you've got no business in football."

Joyce Johnson, who had to drive all the way from school to Long Beach for practices, braving the twenty highway miles of dense LA traffic, had plenty of agility and the speed required for halfback on offense. With her tomboyish demeanor, athletic build, and brown seventies-esque coiffed hair parted in the middle, Johnson fit the bill of a women's football player to a T. But it was her football acumen that made her stand out the most. "My boyfriend was the captain of the football team in high school," Johnson explained. "I was the spotter at football games. I'd sit next to the announcer in the booth and tell him who tackled who, and what number jersey it was. I was an avid watcher. I just liked the game a lot. You name it, I knew it when it came to football. I was a real scholar of the game, so to speak."

Susan Hoxie was an unemployed twenty-three-year-old living at home with her parents when her mother showed her an ad in the *Los Angeles Times* about the Dandelions' tryout. "She said, why don't you go ahead and do this?" the Oregon State University graduate recalled. Her mother was ill with terminal cancer at the time and wanted Hoxie to go out and do something fun instead of sitting home and taking care of her every day. At first, Hoxie was skeptical. But she had seen the *Life* magazine photo spread featuring Gail Dearie and the New York Fillies from 1972, and knew women's professional football was happening elsewhere in the country. With no job and a supportive mother who was excited for her to play football, Hoxie figured, *Why not?*

Hoxie was pleased to learn that the Dandelions were a legit outfit. After running a few passing routes during the tryout, she knew she was good enough to make the team. Coach Edwards pegged Hoxie for wide receiver, and the five-feet-six, pixie-haired brunette was thrilled. While she wasn't the fastest on the field, she had "great hands" and loved catching the ball. That was the easy part. Learning routes and verbiage came with practice, but like every other woman on the team, Hoxie was eager to learn. "They were surprised how coachable we were," she said of the coaching staff. "They found us more willing to learn than men. We didn't come in thinking we knew everything. And they were surprised at how good we were based on the fact that none of us had played organized football."

As soft-spoken as Hoxie was, and as physically small as she may have appeared, when she got out on the football field she looked forward to hitting people—hard. "Especially when I've had a bad day," she said in an NBC documentary about the Dandelions. "It gives me a chance to take out my frustrations and get a little aggressive."

At thirty years old, Barbara Patton was a working mother with two children. When the Dandelions began practicing, Patton would often bring her son, Marvcus, her daughter, Debbie, and her nephew with her to practice to save on childcare. She was a winsome and charismatic woman with an infectious smile, and had an uncanny ability to brighten up anyone's day. But when she donned a helmet and pads, she became a spirited linebacker who loved to tackle and smash her opponents to the ground. "I can play a good hardy game," Patton once mused, "go home and eat dinner, and then go out dancing."

Rounding out the roster was tight end/receiver Lori Blankenship, halfback Ginger Ford, center Kathy Greenwood, linebacker Pam Brown, and cornerback Charlotte Raff. All were in their early twenties.

Every single Dandelion who made the cut and appeared on the final roster was excited to finally get a chance to play a sport many of them had never thought possible, let alone on the professional level. They practiced three nights per week, wherever they could find a spot, and often at local high schools. Players who had full-time jobs had to go straight to practice after working a full day, others had to commute from another town or county, and stay-at-home mothers had to figure out childcare. By the time they arrived at the football field, they had little time to socialize and get to know each other on a deeper level—something Low regrets.

They were so focused on the task at hand. Every minute of practice was spent working on drills, plays, and conditioning. It made for long and taxing days, both emotionally and physically. Practices were hard. Edwards didn't take it easy on the players simply because they were women. He treated them the same way he would have treated a men's team: respectful, encouraging, and tough. "We liked that," Johnson said. "We liked that [the coaches] treated us just like a men's football team. They played semipro ball. So they treated us the exact same way. But it was hard. They were not easy practices at all."

After running through drills and plays, Edwards would make the team run laps while wearing all of their equipment. "That was hell," Ann Strohecker Beebe said in an interview with Channel Nine Sports in Los Angeles in 1995. Beebe was the team's punter (she could punt the ball forty-five yards) and also played tackle and tight end. She was twenty-six at the time and, like Hoxie, was unemployed. Growing up as a Stanford football fan, Beebe thought she'd give women's professional football a try, knowing full well it wouldn't be a full-time, paying job. She commuted to Long Beach from San Fernando Valley, forty miles each way. But to her, it was worth it. "I'm really glad I did it," Beebe recalled. "Because it was taking a real reach to just go out and see something because of an ad I saw in the *Los Angeles Times*. I went out there and there were a whole bunch of people I didn't know, it was a reach for me."

For those three months from mid-April to mid-July 1973, the newly formed Dandelions worked diligently on becoming a team, and a competitive one, at that. They practiced so much that, by the time July rolled around and their first game against the Dallas Bluebonnets was on the horizon, they were desperate to play a different team instead of constantly scrimmaging against each other. "We didn't know how tough the other teams were going to be," Beebe said, "but we loved that we were finally going to get to play a real game."

Everyone was excited for the chance to get in the game—everyone except for Low. Low was unable to sign a contract for the 1973 season, because she was actively involved in college sports at ELAC. "I kept asking everybody, if I signed with the Dandelions, which is a 'professional' team, what would that do to my amateur status? Would that hurt the status?" Low recalled. "They had the rules for the men but for myself it was like—I can't jeopardize my college team. So I kept going to the practices. I was a member of the team, but I chose not to play in 1973. It was disappointing because no one knew if the team or women's football was going to take off or not, and I desperately wanted to be a part of it."

Since Title IX was still new, Low wasn't able to get a straight answer on what was acceptable under the rule as far as being able to play a professional sport as a female college athlete—not even her coach at ELAC knew what to tell her. At the time, Low was playing five other sports in college and didn't want to disqualify herself from being able to participate. So she reluctantly removed herself from the official Dandelions playing roster, but made a concerted effort to remain active on the team as much as she could. And she was there on the sidelines for that first game against Dallas, even though she couldn't play.

○———○

On game day, poised to contend with the Dallas Bluebonnets, the Dandelions felt a mixture of nervousness and excitement. As the minutes ticked toward the two o'clock kickoff, they huddled together on the sideline of the football field at Long Beach Veterans Memorial Stadium. They had practiced, absorbed, and devoured as much football information as they possibly could in the months leading up to the game. There was nothing more for Edwards and the rest of the coaching staff to do but lead their team of football newbies out onto the grass, give them the football, and hope they had soaked in enough information to make a game of it. It was also a chance to see if enough fans would turn out to see the Dandelions in action. Yes, they practiced hard. But could they replicate the same energy and aggressiveness in front of a real, live crowd? Could they live up to the hype?

Los Angeles already had a stellar reputation as a big-time professional sports town. The Rams, the Dandelions' NFL counterpart, were just beginning their seven-year run as NFC West Champions (1973–1979), the majority of which were under head coach Chuck Knox, and defensive end Jack Youngblood was the draw. The Lakers were basketball royalty, having been to the NBA Finals seven times since the team relocated to California from Minnesota in 1960, and in 1972, won their first (of many) NBA Championship. And the Dodgers had already brought three World Series titles to the City of Angels.

The Dandelions had a lot to live up to, especially if they wanted to be taken seriously as a professional team. They were competing for fans in a big city atmosphere, where pro sports ruled the town and athletes were as popular as Hollywood actors.

"I have absolutely no idea what's going to happen (today)," Johnson said before the game to a local sports reporter. "I really don't know who's going to win. All I hope is that we can prove to people that this is not a joke."

Hoxie's ill mother, who had first shown her the Dandelions announcement in the paper and encouraged her to try out for the team, passed away a few weeks before the first game. For Hoxie, it was bittersweet. "We both knew she wasn't going to make it," Hoxie recalled. "She was hoping to make it long enough to see me play my first game. She had

had cancer for so long, it was a relief when she passed away because she wasn't suffering anymore." Hoxie couldn't suit up for the first game. She had injured her thumb in practice and the workers' compensation doctor wouldn't let her play because it wouldn't be covered. Like Low, Hoxie was relegated to the sideline. All they could do was watch.

As the bleachers filled up with fans, the Dandelions got ready for kick-off. Even though it was also their first season as a women's professional football team, the Bluebonnets had played regulation games before. They had already competed against two other seasoned and experienced teams: the talented Toledo Troopers and the roughcast Detroit Demons. The grass on the football field that day wasn't the only thing that was green—when the ball sailed through the air and the game began, the Dandelions' inexperience showed.

The Bluebonnets quickly struck first as their speedy halfback, Shellie Wall—who could reportedly run the forty-yard dash in 4.9 seconds—took the ball on an end-around for a forty-two-yard galloping touchdown (she added an additional fifty-seven yards on four carries in the fourth quarter). But the Dandelions weren't fazed. They eventually calmed their nerves, and ran Edwards's pro-style offense with reckless abandon. Down one score, they drove the ball down the field on a seven-play, forty-five-yard drive when Garcia hit receiver Pat Smith with a ten-yard pass for a touchdown.

Injuries on the Dallas sideline and penalty flags on the field were abundant, ironically causing the Bluebonnets to label the Dandelions "dirty"—usually it was the Dallas team on the receiving end of that descriptor. They accused Los Angeles of grabbing face masks, tripping, holding, clipping, and even kicking. After Bluebonnets player CoCo Manson had to be helped off the field, Dandelions tackle Linda Danner was kicked out of the game. Whatever *legal* penalties the Dandelions accrued during the course of the game, their lack of official game play was most likely to blame.

The game went back and forth, with the Dandelions taking the lead in the fourth quarter, 12–8. But Wall—the best player of the game by far that day—sealed the 16–12 win for the Bluebonnets with a seventeen-yard touchdown run. The loss didn't damper the Dandelions' excitement of having just played their first game. "Our friends and family came to that game and some of them had on jerseys with my name on it," Johnson said. "It was a pretty big crowd and the game was covered by the local media. That sticks out in my mind the most, how cool it was."

Unlike the show of love and support Johnson and other players received from their friends and family, Beebe's family refused to come see her play. "I was living in LA and my family was still living in Palo Alto. I wanted them to fly down for our first game but they were having none of it," Beebe explained. "They did not approve. There was no way they were going to come down and watch me play. They didn't like me doing it and they probably thought I was going to get hurt. They never got to see me play."

o———o

Despite losing to the Bluebonnets 16–12, the Dandelions received positive reviews from the media and fans. "They're probably the best professional women's football team ever assembled in Los Angeles," wrote a reporter for the *Los Angeles Times*. "The fact that they're first is immaterial."

In front of an estimated crowd of six hundred fans, standout players on the Dandelions included wide receiver Lori Blankenship—Johnson's childhood best friend—and halfback Ginger Ford. Garcia finished the game with two touchdown passes. Considering it was their first game ever as a team, Coach Edwards was pleased with the Dandelions' effort overall.

Mathews was equally pleased with what he saw on the football field, but not what he saw in the bleachers. With around six hundred tickets sold at $3.50 per person, the revenue wasn't even enough for him to break even. He had been hoping for a crowd of four thousand or more to cover expenses and make a little extra on the side. Perhaps the Dandelions' next game against the Detroit Demons would yield better results in the stands as well as on the scoreboard.

"Rugged combat with action that won't quit," read a small advertisement in the *Independent* ahead of the night game between the Dandelions and the Demons on Saturday, August 18, at Long Beach Veterans Memorial Stadium. Mathews was trying his best to portray his team, and women's football, as a can't-miss event. But it wasn't the "rugged combat" that stood out in the Dandelions' second game of the 1973 season; it was their decisive 25–0 win on 213 yards, crushing a Detroit team that was known for being tough and scrappy, if not very good.

Despite a slow start from both teams, the Dandelions took control of the second quarter and never looked back. Blankenship was once again the go-to receiver, while halfback Ernestine Warren occupied the bulk of the backfield role. The Dandelions defense—including Barbara Patton—kept the Demons from being able to move the ball down the field. The game was essentially over halfway through the fourth quarter.

The rout of the Demons was filmed, and re-aired on local television a week later. Even though Susan Hoxie's mother never got to see her play professional football, her father flew up for the game against the Demons. "He spent the rest of his life bragging about me," she beamed.

The Dandelions played only three games in 1973, and finished with a 2–1 record, with both wins coming against the Detroit Demons (they also played a game that year in Albuquerque, New Mexico, against the Bluebonnets, which the Dandelions won). There was a previous game scheduled against the Toledo Troopers on September 1, but it never took place. A brief announcement placed that same day in the *Independent Press-Telegram* gave no explanation other than to say the game had been canceled. Travel issues were most likely the prevailing concern for the Troopers, who would have to fly all the way from Ohio to Los Angeles. Whatever the reason for the cancelation, the Dandelions never got their chance to play against the best team in women's football.

Throughout those first three games, the Dandelions averaged 180 passing yards and 250 yards rushing—impressive numbers by any football analyst's standards. But they averaged only 2,000 fans per game, and Mathews admittedly lost $12,000 on his investment. Still, he wasn't deterred. He was happy about his team's talent and level of play, and focused his energy on generating more fan support and publicity in order to fill the stands.

Joyce Hogan, part owner of the Dandelions along with her husband, handled the bulk of the team promotional duties. After the Dandelions, first game against the Bluebonnets, Hogan felt they had "proved to the doubting Thomases" of the world that women "given the opportunity, the equipment and the coaching, could play not only respectable football, but exciting football." In a Sid Friedman–esque way, Hogan was happy to talk up the football team and share her thoughts with local newspapers as a way to keep the Dandelions and women's football a trending topic of conversation. In his column for the *Los Angeles Herald-Examiner*, sportswriter Melvin Durslag noted Hogan said she had a lot of requests coming in from women around the country who wanted to play professional football. And "if women's tennis and women's golf can make it, why not women's football?"

But Mathews wasn't about to go the same route that Friedman went and rely on hype alone. He knew he needed more than just Hogan's words to convince people and attract more fans. What he needed was some organization and consistency between the independent professional women's football teams that were currently playing. He needed the Dandelions to play more regularly scheduled games, against different teams around the country, so that the fandom could grow and expand, not only in California but across the United States. He needed to establish a cohesive women's football league where every independent team could fall under one umbrella, like the NFL.

That's when Mathews's idea of forming an "official" National Women's Football League was born. And unlike during Friedman's previous attempts, there were now enough teams playing, in different cities across the country, for Mathews to make it happen.

CHAPTER 8

THE NWFL KICKS OFF

On September 15, 1974, Bob Mathews sat at a conference table at the Airport Avenue Ramada Inn near Inglewood in Los Angeles with his hands folded neatly in front of him. He began speaking animatedly, eager to usher in a compelling new era in women's professional football. So commenced the first session of the National Women's Football League (NWFL) executive committee.

While it's not known how many people were invited or who actually attended, the purpose of the meeting was twofold: adopt a "Master League Agreement" and bylaws, and elect and appoint official league officers. Naturally, Mathews was elected president of the NWFL. Bill Stout, the head coach of the Toledo Troopers, was selected as vice president, Eastern Division; Joe Mathews, Bob's brother and owner of the Dallas Bluebonnets, was also selected vice president, Southern Division. Charles Jule, an insurance broker and president of the newly formed California Mustangs, was elected vice president, Western Division. Joyce Hogan, who had already taken on the role as the director of public relations for the Dandelions and was well known in women's sports circles, was appointed executive director of the NWFL.

Nowhere to be found was Sid Friedman; women's football was moving on without him. The "women's football gimmick" he had originally
started was now a full-fledged movement, with other figureheads coming
into the fold. While Friedman didn't willingly hand Mathews and the
other owners the baton, they took it anyway and ran.

"Under the guidance of Mrs. Hogan, the (NWFL) promises to continue the forward growth of football for women and to bring to the
sports-minded the opportunity to see exciting football, played by athletes with dedication to the sport unmatched, anywhere," the committee
announced in a press release about the formation of the league. NWFL
official rules consisted of twelve-minute quarters, a smaller football, and
a fifteen-yard penalty for tackling by pulling hair. And in a reversal from
NFL rules, after a touchdown, a kick was worth two points and a run or
pass play was worth one.

Oklahoma City Dolls kicker Mary BlueJacket suspects that the reason
PATs were worth more in the NWFL is that most of the women had never
kicked a football before, nor did they really have the coaching to teach
them proper technique. Accuracy of conversion kicks was hard to come by.
This was true even on the dominant Toledo Troopers, where kicker Gloria Jimenez described herself as "a horrible kicker." In the years the Dolls
would be dominant, 1977 and 1978, BlueJacket believes her ability to rack
up points by consistently kicking the ball through the uprights gave her
team an advantage. Kicking was harder for the players in this league, and
perhaps the scoring reflected that. The rules were applied to make the game
a better fit for the women who played, and they worked well.

In September 1974, for the first time in women's football history, there
was a formal and legitimate league consisting of seven teams: the Los
Angeles Dandelions, Toledo Troopers, Detroit Demons, Dallas Bluebonnets, Columbus (Ohio) Pacesetters, Fort Worth (Texas) Shamrocks
(started by Joe Mathews as an expansion of the brothers' Dallas team),
and the California Mustangs. The committee was open to expanding to
other teams in other cities with each new season, and planned on playing a regular schedule of games that fall. A schedule of seven games was
promptly released, with the promise that in 1975, the NWFL would play
approximately forty games. It was an ambitious declaration.

The announcement of the formation of the NWFL and its plans going forward made national news. "The National Women's Football League, the first such female league of its kind, was established during the weekend with seven teams which will begin play later this month," stated a blurb in the *Spokane Chronicle*, from the UPI wire service. Two weeks later, the *New York Times* ran a story, too. The word was getting out, but, even so, the league and the players still weren't always respected by reporters.

A game on October 26, 1974, between the Pacesetters and the nonleague Dayton (Ohio) Fillies was covered by the *Cincinnati Enquirer*. "It's no sewing circle," the headline declared, and the sexist insults continued from there. "Anything professional was strictly coincidental," sports reporter Jack Murray wrote, "as America knows big-time pro football. [The women's teams] are more social clubs with pads and cleats." The photo that ran with the story was captioned "pacesetting comes later." It's a theme that continued to replay itself throughout the duration of the league.

Regardless of the media's framing, in the fall of 1974, Mathews was feeling good. He had taken a step in the women's football journey, one that Friedman never could quite make: he had created and organized the NWFL as an official pro sports league that was recognized as such on the national stage.

And that very step of Mathews's would essentially put an end to Friedman's seven-year reign as the "mastermind" and "ringleader" of women's professional football. While Friedman continued to organize games in and around the Rust Belt area of the country (Cleveland, Ohio; Buffalo, New York; and Erie, Pennsylvania), his own plans for a legitimate women's professional football league never fully got up and running. It remained mostly a barnstorming venture that largely featured Friedman's Cleveland Daredevils and the nearby Dayton Fillies. And, despite holding what Friedman billed as the first women's professional football championship game in history in spring 1974, national newspapers and even local media had barely any interest in covering it.

The new NWFL also made way for teams formerly under Friedman's thumb—like the Detroit Demons and the Toledo Troopers—to fully break free and branch out once and for all. Speaking to the *Detroit Free Press*, some of the Demons players revealed that the previous "owners wanted to promote professional women's football as a freak show, roller-derby style." There's some confusion as to which owner the Demons were referring to specifically: there was David Pierce, the owner of the 1971 Detroit Fillies, but also Friedman, who claimed to have started the original team as the Detroit Petticoats in 1967.

Toledo Troopers coach Bill Stout confirmed some of the Demons' claims to the *Detroit Free Press*. He said Friedman "once asked us to throw a game. Another time, he sent out *Hustler* magazine, which wanted the girls to pose in the nude."

When questioned by the same newspaper about his unconventional promotional style, Friedman replied, "I'm in show biz. I wanted a show team. The basic idea was to get a Harlem Globetrotters setup. That's where the revenue in commercials was."

Women's football never brought Friedman the financial success he was after. But he did achieve something else, which likely wasn't even on his radar: he played a significant role in advancing the sport and giving women opportunities to play. Friedman's legacy when it comes to the game is complicated. He was an opportunist and his motives were purely selfish. And yet, he is also the main reason Mathews was able to create the NWFL at all.

It's hard to know whether Friedman was proud that he played such a significant role in the evolution of women's football. But, more importantly, the women who took the field because of Friedman got to be proud of themselves.

Still, the teams were ready to move on. They were ready to be more than a sideshow; they were ready to be the main event.

○——○

Despite Mathews's and the other owners' successes in getting the NWFL off the ground and making the league official in 1974, not much had improved for the players—financially, mentally, or physically. And the Dallas Bluebonnets, who were barely holding their team together after the 1973 season, were falling apart.

D. A. Starkey decided not to return to the Bluebonnets after only two seasons. The request from Joe Mathews that the players wear dresses upset her. And the team was having to take buses to away games they would have flown to in the past, leading Starkey to suspect that the team was hurting for cash. "It got to where it wasn't fun for me anymore," Starkey said. "And if it ain't fun, I don't wanna do it." So she went back to doing what she loved most: drinking, playing softball, and picking up women.

That was also around the time the Bluebonnets lost their young safety, Toni Gibson. During a game against the Troopers, she blew out her knee, essentially ending her football career. Knee and other injuries were a major problem not only for the Bluebonnets but for other teams around the league. In two and a half years, Dallas coach Mike Anderson told the *New York Times*, there had been "eight knee operations and dozens of sprained ankles and wrists." Another team reported six knee injuries requiring surgery in their first season alone. "I've had two knee replacements, I just had my shoulder replaced . . . [and] I've had all kinds of shots in my back," said Starkey. "They beat the shit out of us."

Barbara O'Brien, too, decided not to finish out the 1974 season. She had grown frustrated with the amount of practice the team did for very little payoff—due to the lack of organization and great physical distance between all the teams, they didn't play games all that regularly. Not only that, she'd had three concussions and wanted to get out before she did long-term damage to herself. "Sometimes I cry," O'Brien told the *New York Times* in 1974. "I've had a couple of minor concussions, a lot of scratches and bruises. I've had my bell rung good, and I'm not ashamed to tell you I've cried."

Chronic traumatic encephalopathy (CTE) is a long-term health risk for anyone who plays football, though it wouldn't have been on the women's radars in the 1970s. CTE is caused by sustaining repeated brain injuries, like concussions, but also just by continual trauma to the head. While none of the players interviewed for this book have reported experiencing neurological issues as a result of their playing days, it's likely that the game took a physical toll on their brains as well as their bodies.

The research on women and brain injury as a result of playing tackle football is still in its infancy, but what is known points to full-contact sports impacting women's brains differently than men's. Several studies have found that in sports with comparable rules for both girls and boys, the rates of concussion are actually higher in women. A 2012 statement from the American Medical Society for Sports Medicine highlighted research showing that female athletes sustain more concussions than their male counterparts, report more severe symptoms, and have a longer duration of recovery than men.

However, biases may be impacting some of that research. For example, even the language used to describe the injuries in women has been different in some studies (for instance, one study says men "report" concussion symptoms, while women "complain" of them). Moreover, some of the conclusions drawn by researchers fell into gendered stereotypes (such as attributing the higher reporting of concussion symptoms by women to women being more likely to talk about their problems. This isn't necessarily accurate. And it doesn't take into account the fact that they may actually be less likely to report pain or injury, since they're so often seen as too weak to play "men's" sports like football). Until more research is done, we have to take these preliminary studies with a grain of salt.

"When it comes to female athletes' participation—regardless of age—we're lacking in truly understanding their experience around head injury," Dr. Donna Duffy, program director for the Program for the Advancement of Girls and Women in Sport and Physical Activity and codirector of the Female BRAIN Project, a research team at the University of North Carolina Greensboro, told the *New York Times* in 2018. "We're on the cusp of this; there's a growing body of literature suggesting that biological sex hormones may be impacted or disrupted when a head injury is sustained." Like the fact that research has shown that if a woman sustains a brain injury during the first two weeks of her menstrual cycle, there tends to be a longer recovery time as opposed to during the second two weeks.

There is little research being done on this issue now and there was none at all happening when the women took the field in the 1970s. The Troopers' Collette says she's never been concerned about CTE because she was "always taught that our helmets were to protect our head." But evidence points to the fact that helmets actually increase, not decrease, brain injury risk. This is because players are more likely to use their heads to hit someone if they're wearing a helmet, heightening the likelihood that they will suffer trauma to their brains.

Many of the women shared stories of "having their bell rung." Starkey remembers trips to the hospital following a game where the players would have injuries evaluated, including concussion screenings. Many times, the players never even made it to the hospital to get checked out.

To this day, Gibson has a crooked finger from getting it stuck in the ear hole on someone's helmet while she was practicing tackles, twisting her finger all the way around. She was sure she'd need to go to the hospital, since the top of her finger—from her big knuckle up—was backward. Instead, one of her coaches grabbed her finger and turned it around while she was standing in the middle of the practice field. They sprayed it with a lidocaine numbing spray to kill the pain and told her to get back out on the field. "That's really how they treated us," Gibson remembers. "Like men!"

Injuries and concussions be damned, plenty of women were willing to put their bodies on the line to keep playing football.

CHAPTER 9

FALSE START

One day in 1972, Sunday Jones—pronounced like the Sabbath, she always said—drove by Toledo's Ottawa Park, named for the Ottawa River that runs through it. There, she saw a group of women practicing football.

Jones was tall and lanky, at 6'1" and 150 pounds, with dark skin and a small gap between her two front teeth—a gap that was often visible because Jones was always smiling. She'd never played football, but was a standout on the basketball court. She was itching for an opportunity to try her hand on the gridiron, and she knew Troopers coach Bill Stout from Toledo's recreation department, where she played basketball for a rec league, averaging twenty-six points per game. Like Stout, she graduated from DeVilbiss High School, but there weren't opportunities for girls to play football yet, which she always thought was "a shame." Whenever she saw an opportunity to play sports, she took it.

Jones was more than just an athlete, though. She was also a singer. She aspired to become famous, to see her name in lights. She had missed the launch of the Troopers because she'd been on the road a lot, singing in nightclubs and touring with the rock and soul group the Ohio Players.

But her career wasn't going where she wanted it to, so she came home to Toledo and began working as a hairdresser by day. By night, she

121

would become one of the best receivers in women's football. It seemed only fitting, then, that she would join Linda Jefferson—the sport's best halfback—and the Troopers, the best team in the sport.

○———○

In 1973, the Troopers win streak was still intact. But there weren't many teams for them to play, because they were beginning to clash with Sid Friedman. And he was retaliating against what he viewed as a disobedient child.

The Troopers proved to be one of the more talented women's football teams Friedman had ever seen play—even better than his own Daredevils. Indeed, the Troopers played Friedman's Daredevils two times in 1971, and won each game handily, by an average margin of thirty points. While the team was originally assembled independently, the Troopers participated in Friedman's Rust Belt league of teams and also competed against other independent teams in and around the eastern part of the country. They went undefeated in 1972 with a record of 8–0 (cited as 9–0 in some records because it includes a 1973 game against the Bluebonnets).

Knowing Friedman, he probably saw dollar signs attached to the talented players on the Troopers who were proving, even more than his other teams already had, that women really could play football, and play it well. But he also knew that fans of the sport wanted to see meaningful competition.

Friedman reportedly asked Coach Stout to have his team throw a game or two, because their continued domination wasn't good for him, the growth of his enterprise, or his Cleveland Daredevils' reputation. Friedman may have felt he was doing the right thing for the sport: to keep the drama and suspense alive in every game for the benefit of the crowd (and his wallet).

But the Troopers didn't see it that way. They balked at this idea, and understandably so. "We didn't want to be clowns," said Trooper Nancy "Eric" Erickson. "We wanted to be football players."

The final straw for the Troopers, however, would be when Friedman failed to provide one of the two things he had previously guaranteed the players and teams in his midst: medical insurance. The Troopers ultimately decided to part ways with Friedman, keeping the equipment provided to them as compensation for the unpaid insurance costs. This infuriated Friedman, who was not used to being challenged by the teams of women he organized. They were usually just grateful for the opportunity to play. But the Troopers demanded more.

In retaliation for leaving him behind and going independent, Friedman refused to allow the Troopers to play against any of his teams, which included the nearby Buffalo All-Stars, Cleveland Daredevils, Dayton Fillies, and Pittsburgh Hurricanes. This limited who the Troopers might compete with to the other fledging independent teams around the country—in Dallas and Detroit.

Consequently, the Troopers played only four games that 1973 season, two against the Detroit Demons and two against the Dallas Bluebonnets. Three were shutouts; they scored forty-three and forty-one points in their two games against Detroit and twenty in the shutout against Dallas. Jefferson rushed for 1,780 yards in her first two seasons, a blur in her gold, green, and white uniform. The games were like child's play to the well-oiled machine that was the Toledo Troopers.

Sunday Jones was making her mark on the field, too. In her first two seasons with the team, she had 275 yards receiving, averaging 21.1 yards per reception. She also led the team in pass interceptions in 1973, with six in just four games. The team also acquired Mitchi Collette during that tumultuous third season, a nineteen-year-old UPS worker and coworker of Jefferson's. Collette began her career as a tight end and defensive end before eventually settling at right guard.

In spite of Friedman, the Troopers were now becoming a real organization, in addition to a dominating football team. They had a board of directors, an attorney, and a public relations person to handle media requests. In going independent from Friedman, Bill Stout recognized he would need an organized entity to keep his team afloat. He enlisted Frank Wallace and Harry Eschedor Jr. in creating a holding company called SKW Enterprises, Inc. It was chartered and dedicated explicitly to "the propagation of women's football." The board of directors included Eschedor, who was the chairman, along with Wallace, who was the secretary and treasurer, Bill's brother Mike Stout, and Bill Stout. Bill was a major stockholder in the company, and players signed yearly contracts and were listed as employees.

There was also a vibrant booster club that raised money to support the team. Membership in the Toledo Troopers Booster Club came with reduced ticket prices to home games, bus trip rates for road games, access to meetings with guest speakers, attendance at the annual end-of-year awards banquet, and newsletters with team updates. They sold raffle tickets, ad space in their game programs, and allowed groups to sell blocks of game tickets at reduced rates. Things were moving in the right direction for the entire Troopers organization. Jefferson appeared on national television that year, 1973, alongside Coach Stout on *The Phil Donahue Show*. And Stout brought his younger brother Mike in to coach the team's offense. Mike was an elementary school teacher with a haircut that would later be known as the Dorothy Hamill, and he helped turn the Troopers offense into an even greater force than it already was.

With so much happening in the Troopers' favor, Friedman must have been seething. Here was women's football finally getting the spotlight he'd always wanted—but the team that was receiving it was the one that wanted nothing to do with him.

Still, despite their steps forward when it came to legitimizing their outfit, the Troopers were hobbled by Friedman shutting them out. It's hard to be the best team in the world if you don't have any opponents, after all. But the Troopers persisted, led by Stout's faith in his team and a belief that women's football deserved better than what Sid Friedman could give it. "Not many teams could have survived the many disappointments we had this past year," Stout told his players that November, "and still be on top at the end of the season."

In the end, Friedman's loss of the Troopers wound up being the NWFL's biggest gain. When the league officially organized in September 1974, Stout was part of the executive board and was elected vice president, Eastern Division. His Troopers now had a fresh start, against a new group of teams and competition. Best of all, the arrival of the Troopers gave the NWFL instant credibility.

o———o

Whatever the history between the team and its owners, the Detroit Demons were feeling refreshed and optimistic in 1974 with the formation of the NWFL. They had a new coach, new jerseys (practice jerseys handed down from their NFL counterpart, the Detroit Lions, who adopted the team for a season or two, allowing the players to attend practices but not providing any concrete financial or marketing support), a new vibe, and a new schedule of games as part of a brand-new league. They were also independent of male ownership after rejecting Friedman's vision for them: the team was owned by six players, and they employed five male coaches who said they were "proud" to work for the women.

And the best women's football team in the history of the sport—the Troopers—were part of it all as well. Having both the Troopers and the Demons in his NWFL, Bob Mathews hoped, would not only put the league on the map, but would also help it grow extensively between the 1974 and 1975 seasons.

Rose Low was hoping for the same. So were many of her returning Dandelion teammates. They wanted to keep playing football, and they wanted to see where it could go. For Low, the 1974 season was her chance to finally get on the field for a game. She had finished up her two-year stint at ELAC and was now enrolled at Cal State Long Beach University. Even though she was on the rowing team at Cal State, the university stipulated that student athletes could participate in a professional sport as long as it wasn't the same sport they were playing in college. Low was elated: "I was rowing and playing football at the same time."

Joyce Johnson, who had started out as a halfback in the Dandelions, first season, broke her leg in the off-season. "We'd still get together and play two-hand touch," Johnson recalled. "This one gal who was on the defense kind of blindsided me and broke my leg." After recovering from her injury, Johnson lost some of the speed that had made her a solid halfback, and Coach Edwards moved her to linebacker instead. She took to the new position right away. "I loved playing defense. It was so much better than the one being crushed constantly. I'm really kind of aggressive. I loved knocking people down and doing all of that."

Coach Edwards, who hadn't been exactly sure how much he should throw at his players when it came to the playbook, taught the Dandelions only a limited number of plays their first season. His goal was to have them perfect those initial plays before they moved on to more complex schemes on offense and defense. But for the Dandelions' second season, he tossed that antiquated thinking aside, realizing he had underestimated his players.

"Instead of the simple pro set that we used last year, I'm putting in a multiple offense—which can operate out of a variety of formations—this year, which is more complicated, and they haven't had trouble adapting," he told *womenSports* magazine in 1974. "In fact, I think the coaches on the other teams kind of undercoached the girls, thinking they won't grasp the sophistication of plays." The result was a thick playbook that consisted of several pages of diagrammed plays, and the Dandelions practiced them all with fervor, determined to execute to the best of their ability during their next official game.

Before the NWFL officially formed in September, the Dandelions played against a new kid on the women's football block in early August. Mathews figured one of the best ways to save money was to play regular games against a local team rather than incur travel expenses by flying or taking a bus to Dallas or Toledo multiple times in a season. He convinced insurance broker Jule—who was also appointed a vice president of the NWFL when the league was formed—to launch the California Mustangs franchise along with the backing of forty-one-year-old Lorain Kelly. Kelly reportedly gave up her job with the wire service to help start the team. "We have a five-year plan and a ten-year plan," Jule told a local magazine. "We figure it will take five years before we make any money and ten years before this becomes a real first-class sport with full public acceptance."

This perspective seems to be the only realistic outlook for an owner in regard to what the trajectory for new sports teams are like, when it comes to making them successful. Professional sports leagues require decades to become financially successful. "Leagues in the first few years just don't make money," said David Berri, a professor at Southern Utah University who studies the economics of sports and is coauthor of *The Economics of the Super Bowl*. "And you shouldn't expect them to make money." This was something none of the NWFL team owners seemed to understand.

Both Jule and Mathews hoped to create a California rivalry between their two teams to help drive local fan interest in the Golden State. But the Mustangs' first game was a lopsided 20–0 loss to the Dandelions, who showed why they were the veterans on the field. In front of fourteen hundred fans at Santa Ana Stadium in Santa Ana, California, Ginger Ford ran all over the Mustang defense and scored two touchdowns—one on a sixty-yard scamper and the other on a forty-yard run. Kathy Greenwood caught a forty-five-yard Vickie Garcia bomb for the final score of the day. It was a complete and utter romp.

○———○

When the new NWFL 1974 fall game schedule was released in September, the Dandelions weren't set to play the Mustangs again until late October. Their next game was against the Dallas Bluebonnets on September 29 at Santa Monica City College stadium. A new NBC News monthly docuseries called *Weekend* covered the game; the segment aired in November and featured game footage, including touchdown runs by both Hoxie and Ford, player interviews, and snippets of the Dandelions celebrating the hard-fought win in the locker room after the game while guzzling beers.

During the game, Low—who was the second-string quarterback—went in for Garcia on the Dandelions' second drive. When Edwards signaled to her to get in the game, Low twisted up her long, dark hair and tucked it on top of her head before sliding on her helmet. "My parents are very much against (football)," she confessed while being interviewed before the game. "Because, I guess they're a little old fashioned. They're afraid I'm going to get hurt or something." Low's parents still had no idea that she was playing professional football for the Dandelions, and she didn't quite know how she was going to explain it to them if they found out.

But she pushed the thought to the back of her mind and led the Dandelions down the field for their first touchdown of the game on a handoff to Ginger Ford. Garcia never went back in after that, and Low remained the Dandelions quarterback for the rest of the game.

"You know how competitive women are," Low said, when asked about taking over the QB position from Garcia. "I'm sure she wasn't real happy about it but Vickie was funny. She had her own ways and she talked back to the coaches and stuff. I didn't talk back to them, you know. I was, whatever the coaches said, I'll do. But Vickie had a good arm." Whatever Edwards saw in Low—whether it was the spark she gave to the offense or that she didn't talk back or question his play calls—he liked. "It's hard on me because feminine emotions, they're a little more emotional and show it more," he said, "and as a guy, maybe I'm a chauvinist and I don't want to, you know, make them cry or cuss me out or whatever."

Dallas scored twice on their next two drives and it looked like the Dandelions were going to lose yet another game to the team they considered to be their biggest rival. "Dallas was a tough team," Low recalled. "And they were big." Hoxie noted that their quarterback, O'Brien, was a "tough hitter," and Johnson agreed with them both. "Dallas was the toughest team we played," she said. "Especially O'Brien—this tall, gorgeous person playing quarterback. She got all the notoriety on that team."

As one of the tallest and most athletic players on the Bluebonnets, O'Brien was a standout. But she alone couldn't stop the Dandelions from scoring back-to-back touchdowns—one on a Hoxie run and the other on a Juanita Byars interception that was returned for a score. Late in the game, both Ginger Ford and Hoxie ran for additional touchdowns and sealed what was a blowout game for the Dandelions, 38–13.

As the postgame celebration got underway, Dandelion safety Gwen Moore dumped an open beer over a teammate's head. Cans of Budweiser were popping open left and right. Johnson even took an ample swig from a whiskey bottle. Laughter, cheers, and singing rang throughout the locker room. It was a big win for the Dandelions, but not everyone was celebrating as if they had just won the Super Bowl.

"Wait a minute, shut up!" Edwards shouted, getting back to business. "I want you at practice Tuesday, five o'clock—just sweats." The Dandelions nodded briefly in response and kept the celebration going, unaware it would be the last game the Dandelions would play in the 1974 season.

For their part, the Mustangs folded not long after they began, unable to implement even one year of their aforementioned ten-year plan. This foiled Mathews's plan to increase revenue for the Dandelions by competing regularly against a local team. It wasn't the only letdown of the season. A combination of travel, financial, and scheduling issues continued to plague the league.

For many players on the Dandelions, the lack of game play in 1974 was a huge disappointment. They were devoted to practicing, some commuting from fifty miles away for each practice, and the twenty-five-dollar stipend (eighteen dollars after taxes) they received per game barely covered a tank of gas. "It's not that we are so concerned about the pay," Johnson told the *Long Beach Independent Telegram*. "We were looking forward to traveling, meeting people and playing. Putting all that time into practicing for just two games is frustrating."

Mathews understood the players' frustration, though he never spoke to them directly about it. He, too, wanted the Dandelions to play more games. How else were they supposed to make money and help grow the NWFL? It wasn't for a lack of trying.

But travel issues often sprung up, and it was difficult to raise sufficient funds. When the Dandelions played a local team like the Mustangs, it cost six thousand dollars for stadium costs, medical/ambulance workers, referees, and other incidentals. When they later hosted games at East Los Angeles College against out-of-town teams, they paid for all of the visiting team's expenses, and the cost would double. Averaging one hundred fifty to fifteen hundred fans per game wasn't going to cut it. They needed to consistently average three thousand to six thousand fans to survive. Mathews had now lost enough money that he was struggling to pay the players their twenty-five-dollars-per-game stipend. But financial issues weren't his only concern. The lack of organization and communication within the league and between the participating teams would also prove to be a consistent issue throughout the next few years of its existence.

Yet, the Dandelions soldiered on. Many, if not all, of the women on the team were just content to be able to play a sport they loved. And they knew Mathews was putting up a lot of his own money to make it happen. "We played football because we loved it, and this gave us a chance to play," Hoxie confessed. "A lot of us, including me, were just doing it for the fun of it and for the thrill of being allowed to do something we weren't allowed to do when we were little girls." Johnson was also impressed with Mathews's willingness to pay for the Dandelions uniforms and equipment. "We had brand-new everything. We had good helmets, pads, everything. Anything we wanted," she said. "I can remember at the time even thinking to myself, this is kind of amazing that this guy is willing to put this money out. I'm looking up at the stands and there's nobody there. And he's paying us a stipend, and you know, the programs and everything that comes along with it—it was amazing."

Low didn't interact with Mathews on a regular basis. But she, too, praised him for investing his own time and money into the team and the league. "I know he lost money," she said. "We didn't make very much. I think I made more money doing promotions and the commercials and the TV and all that stuff than I did playing." The television appearances started happening with regularity in 1974. And Low was one of the players who was often asked to represent the team. She was articulate and endearing, and cared very much about the Dandelions as a legit football organization. "We had so much press and opportunity, being out here in Los Angeles," Low said. "I kept getting asked by management to do promotions and stuff. I did the *Joker's Wild* game show and the *Merv Griffin Show* with Billie Jean King and other athletes. That was pretty cool. I was going, what am I doing with these girls?"

Low appeared on the *Merv Griffin Show* on October 10, 1974. The theme was "women in sports," and the guest list included King as well as golfer Jane Blalock, swimmer Donna de Varona, and track star Wyomia Tyus. After the show finished taping, Low and the other guests exited the venue and a large crowd had assembled to greet them. "That is the very first time that several people asked for my autograph," Low said. "That threw me off, and for a moment I didn't know what to do. For the other ladies, it was no problem. They were used to it."

The NWFL billed itself as a professional league, but the players had a hard time placing themselves alongside other professional athletes of King's stature. The league had just been introduced and most of the country didn't even know it existed. Low and her Dandelion teammates were just happy to be there. They didn't have the depth of experience that other women professional athletes had, on or off the field. And they certainly weren't household names. Whenever Low appeared on television programs or was interviewed by local California news reporters, she felt awkward and out of place—though she never let it show. While she enjoyed the attention, it always felt surreal to her. Like every other player in the league, she just wanted to play football.

Still riding high from being on Merv Griffin with a handful of other incredible women athletes, Low was excited to see the episode on television. She hadn't considered the fact that her parents might actually watch it until her brother brought over a color television to their parents' house. He plugged it in and told them all they had "a program to watch." Low began to panic. "I thought, how am I going to explain this? It was hard keeping it from them. But that's how they found out I played football."

Low's parents weren't at all angry or upset like she had anticipated they would be. Instead, they were thrilled. "Afterwards, you know, I had my mom and dad telling their friends, 'my daughter plays football!' It was a relief."

With her secret finally out and the weight lifted from her shoulders, Low had a renewed sense of purpose and commitment to the Dandelions. "I loved the camaraderie," she said. "And being around other people who were interested in the sport. I don't even know how many times we got paid, but after we stopped getting paid we just kept showing up."

For Low and the rest of the players, it was never about the money. "Nobody was getting rich off of it," Beebe said. "And if it's no money and we keep playing, well we just kept playing." Johnson added, "It was really just a lot of camaraderie, making friends and playing a sport you love. That was really the extent of it. It was for no other reason."

Cover of game program between the Houston Herricanes and Oklahoma
City Dolls
Photo provided by Billie Cooper, Houston Herricanes

PART IV

THE HEYDAY OF THE NWFL (1975–1978)

WE JUST WANTED TO PLAY FOOTBALL. IT'S NOT
ANY MORE OR ANY LESS THAN THAT.

—GWEN FLAGER, HOUSTON HERRICANES

CHAPTER 10

TROOPERS FACE
THEIR DEMONS

It seemed as if the steady hum that had been lingering around the NWFL since its inception had finally grown into a reverberating buzz. It was effectively reaching people who still had no idea that a women's professional football league even existed. The league not only sparked interest and created new fans, it also attracted aspiring players and potential new owners. One of those owners was a fifty-eight-year-old former football coach and salesman living in San Diego named John Mulkey Jr.

Mulkey Jr. had always been "nuts" for the game of football. "I was around five or six and I was watching a game in Balboa Park," he told the *Chula Vista Star-News* in May 1975. "Someone came along and stuck a ball in my hands and I've loved the game ever since. I'm always thinking about it, talking about it. I eat, drink and sleep it." After playing in his youth, Mulkey Jr. told the paper, he worked at Villanova University before coaching a championship team at Mater Dei High School in Los Angeles. He then took a coaching job at Marian High School in Chula Vista. "I dropped out of coaching after the '73 season and went into selling," he said. "But I got out of that and went back to coaching because I missed it so much."

While watching a rerun of a game of the Dandelions against the De-mons, Mulkey Jr. felt inspired to get back into football. "I had $7.50 in my pocket and some money in the bank," he said. "I made a lot of calls to determine whether or not I could come up with enough money to pur-chase an NWFL franchise for a San Diego team." Along with receiving "generous investments" from friends, Mulkey Jr. started a campaign to raise funds. He was backed by "mostly women" to get the campaign off and running, and contacted the NWFL office for approval. "Some people think it's a joke, but women's football is big time," he said. "And after watching films of other women's teams playing, I decided I'd really like to give it a go."

After Mulkey Jr. raised ten thousand dollars to purchase and fund a new franchise in spring 1975, the San Diego Lobos were officially born. Mulkey Jr. hired Larry Smith, a man he had known since he was sixteen years old, as the assistant coach, and filled out the rest of his staff. Then it was time to build his thirty-woman roster.

Doreen Gutzmer, a forty-year-old housewife and mother of five, showed up at the first Lobos tryout ready to prove she wasn't past her prime. While Mulkey Jr. was hoping to fill his roster with eighteen- to twenty-year-olds (he had petitioned the league to drop the age restriction to sixteen, but it was an insurance requirement that players be at least eighteen years old), the seventy-some players that showed up at tryouts were all over the map age-wise. From Gutzmer to twenty-seven-year-old Linda Maier to twenty-three-year-old Mary Kay Harding: these talented women quickly made Mulkey Jr. realize he may have been focusing too much on age. Gutzmer turned out to be better than most of the girls who were half her age and made the team. Within several months—by Octo-ber 1975—Mulkey Jr. had been suspended as head coach, and replaced by Jim Cherry.

By August, the Lobos were ready for their first official NWFL game against the Dandelions. And, in nearby LA, Mathews was all too happy to welcome the Lobos into the NWFL fold, excited that another local California team had sprung up again. Local competition was better for his team financially, and he needed all the breaks he could get if he wanted to keep the Dandelions going. "Since the teams currently participating are scattered so far around the country, we try and organize a round-robin competition for local teams," he explained to *Élan*, the East Los Angeles College magazine in 1975. "After we generate enough interest we would then hope to begin some sort of a national title game."

Mathews's plan had always been to expand and grow the NWFL as time went on. But the financial means and fan support lagged far behind his expectations. It appeared that not everyone was on board for women's football as much as he and his fellow team owners were. Society as a whole had a lot of catching up to do with the idea of women showcasing their physical and athletic ability in such a masculine-coded way. But how long would that take? Three years into the women's professional football business, Mathews had already incurred enough debt to scare any solid businessperson out of an investment. And yet, he refused to give up on the idea. The arrival of the Lobos and the continued success of the Troopers tempered whatever misgivings Mathews may have had. If he could somehow figure out the right way to market women's professional football to the masses, convert the naysayers, and capitalize on the Troopers' athletic prowess and dominance—particularly Linda Jefferson—Mathews was positive he could turn the NWFL into a national phenomenon. Like Friedman before him, he pressed on.

In mid-August 1975, the Dandelions played the Lobos at Mesa College in a 6–6 tie in front of a crowd of thirty-five hundred fans. This was a positive turnout for the start of the NWFL's second official season, and the Dandelions' third in existence. For the Dandelions, the core players—Low, Hoxie, Ford, Patton, Beebe, Garcia, and Johnson—returned for the third, 1975 season, even though they often weren't getting paid.

The game between the Dandelions and the Lobos set two important bars. First, it was the first locally televised NWFL game in league history that could be watched live and in real time (and the first in women's football history); prior games that aired on television had been previously recorded. And second, the game was the start of a newfound rivalry for both teams, not due to any bad blood, but because of proximity and convenience.

In 1975, the Dandelions and Lobos played each other four times, more than they did against any other teams in the NWFL. While the regular matchup with the Lobos definitely saved Mathews money on expenses and traveling, it didn't do anything to expand the league as a whole.

Other teams in the league functioned similarly. With no real schedule against different teams in the league or thorough organization, regional games were the easiest to set up and play. The Troopers played the Detroit Demons four times and squared off against the Columbus Pacesetters three times, while the Demons and Pacesetters played each other only twice. The Fort Worth Shamrocks were the only team in the league to venture outside of their region, playing against the Troopers and the Lobos.

The Dallas Bluebonnets were on the verge of folding as a team and would merge with the Shamrocks (they became the Dallas–Fort Worth Shamrocks). Mathews knew the NWFL needed more teams, more games, and more competition—not less. Especially because the Troopers were still dominating.

o———o

By 1975, Linda Jefferson—perhaps the greatest player in the league—had become somewhat of a household name, but only in and around Ohio. Yet a few major magazine stories launched Jefferson, the Toledo Troopers, and the NWFL into the national spotlight.

The first story ran in *Ebony* in November 1973; it was called, "Weaker Sex?—My Foot." The magazine featured photos of Black players from the Bluebonnets, Dandelions, and Troopers—including Jefferson—in a beautiful seven-page spread.

Then came a new magazine called *womenSports*. Founded in May 1974, *womenSports* was created by Billie Jean King and her then husband, Larry King, with the purpose of highlighting women's sports and women athletes in a way that no other sports magazine had done before. The inaugural June issue featured King on the cover and would continue to showcase a diverse selection of women athletes on each cover from that point on.

When *womenSports* covered the Dandelions and the NWFL in November 1974, Barbara Patton, Dandelions linebacker, became one of the first Black women to be featured on the cover of a national sports magazine. King's top editor at the time, Rosalie Muller Wright, recalled, "We were so happy to have the ability to be the first to feature a Black woman on the cover. We thought, 'This is deserving, and let's do it.'"

The *womenSports* article, "Wham, Bam, Thank You, Ma'am," was written by Ron Rapoport and gave readers some background on the league and an inside view of how the Dandelions got started. The article also shared why some of the players enjoyed playing football—"Catching the football in your gut and rolling over, it's almost a sensual feeling," said one—and even how Dandelions head coach Bob Edwards shifted his approach to coaching football for women instead of men. It was a crisp and clean eight-page spread, complete with full-color photos, much like the numerous types of features on men's sports, teams, and players found in the pages of *Sports Illustrated*.

In spring 1975, leading up to *womenSports*'s anniversary issue, the magazine held a national reader poll asking subscribers to vote for the "WomanSport Athlete of the Year." Jefferson, propelled by a publicity surge of Troopers fans, friends, and family across Ohio, won the award in a last-minute push over volleyball star Mary Jo Peppler. "Frankly, it surprised us, too. Linda Jefferson as the first WomanSport of the Year? Over TV superstars like Chris Evert and Olga Korbut? Where did she get the votes?" the intro to her profile read, incredulously. "From Toledo, Ohio, that's where."

The idea for *womenSports* magazine was born in a car, suspended over the San Francisco Bay by beams of steel. Several weeks before she captivated the nation by beating Bobby Riggs in the "Battle of the Sexes" tennis match in the fall of 1973, King sat in the passenger seat and stewed. At the wheel was Larry, driving the couple from Emeryville near Oakland toward San Francisco on the Bay Bridge. As Billie Jean flipped through an issue of *Sports Illustrated*, she complained, which is what she always did whenever she picked up an issue of *SI*. "I can't believe it," she recalled saying to Larry after each turn of the page. "I get *Sports Illustrated* and all I get is men, men, men, men. Don't they ever think about us, and the women and what we're doing?"

King made women in sports a focus for her magazine, which grew to seventy thousand subscribers by 1975. And in June that same year, the magazine featured Jefferson—who rushed for more than one thousand yards in each of her first five seasons with the Troopers—on its cover for the inaugural "WomanSport of the Year" issue.

Perhaps it's serendipitous that *womenSports*, a sports magazine that was owned and published by King, was the biggest media outlet to feature the NWFL and its best player—Jefferson—in a positive light. But the selection was not without controversy.

Staff at the magazine, and King in particular, were reportedly shocked that Jefferson had beaten out well-known, superstar athletes. But the fans and Toledans who had voted for her recognized that they needed to take it upon themselves to drum up interest, since the national media largely ignored the league. "In the absence of a national-media mechanism," a fan wrote to *womenSports*, "we have not gotten the publicity we deserve. This makes it necessary for us to hustle all the more."

According to King, there were concerns that the issue wouldn't sell with a relatively unknown Black woman on the front, but the staff was steadfast: It's nonnegotiable. This is the right thing to do. "Why did we start this magazine in the first place?" said King. "We're supposed to help make a better life for women in sports in every way."

A cover story for any athlete is the key to superstardom. What does it mean to be a superstar? "A star (as in sports or the movies)," as defined by *Merriam-Webster*, is someone "who is considered extremely talented, has great public appeal, and can usually command a high salary."

Linda Jefferson ticks two of those three boxes: she was considered to be the best player in the NWFL, and, fifty years later, it's nearly impossible to talk to anyone involved in the league without her name coming up. Her stats are undisputed: As a member of the Toledo Troopers, the winningest team in pro football history, Jefferson led her team to win all but approximately five games over nine seasons (the exact numbers are disputed). She rushed for almost nine thousand yards. In 1977, the *Toledo Blade* called her "the heart and soul—in fact, the meal ticket—of the Troopers." When she retired from the game, she had scored 140 touchdowns—more than NFL greats Walter Payton, Jim Brown, and O. J. Simpson.

As for having great public appeal, that, too, is undisputed. Jefferson received press attention disproportionate to that of her teammates, was on the cover of *womenSports* magazine, and appeared on *The Dinah Shore Show* and the popular game show *To Tell the Truth*. She was young and good-looking, her white teeth arranged neatly in a nearly straight row, her hair worn in an Afro shaped to perfection. She gave a great interview: assertive and matter-of-fact about her talent and the fact that women should be able to play sports at the same level and to the same fanfare as men.

On the third box—high salary—Jefferson falls short. Despite her talents, her records, and her ambitions as a twenty-one-year-old to eventually become a millionaire, that didn't happen. Within the context of the NWFL, Jefferson may have been considered a superstar. But most of the world did not know who she was, and still doesn't.

Perhaps more importantly, that characterization—of being a superstar—has never sat right with Jefferson. Half a century later, she rejects the label. She rejects, too, the notion that it was she alone who was in the spotlight, even though it was her name and her face that appeared on the press coverage. That's because her name appeared alongside another name, too: that of her team. Any media attention Jefferson got, she saw as being in service of promoting her team.

The way Jefferson sees it, the attention was a testament to her team's skills, not her own. Football is a team sport. Without her teammates, there would be no spotlight for Jefferson at all. Without her line getting the blocks she needed and making holes for her to run through, there would have been no touchdowns scored, no rushing yards racked up.

Jefferson's main blocker was fullback Dorothy Parma, who stood at just four feet eleven inches and weighed ninety-four pounds. Though she was slight, she did most of the blocking for Jefferson. "If Linda gets a touchdown, I feel I've done my job," she said. "I feel just as good as when I score a touchdown myself."

Jefferson's success can also be attributed to the Troopers coaching staff—and her willingness to be coached. After spending her entire life as a star athlete but feeling like no one ever cared enough to invest in her potential, Jefferson felt relieved to have coaches who wanted her to be the best she could be. She soaked up everything she could.

"Linda has speed, quickness, and a lot of natural moves. She makes most of the guys I played ball with at Bowling Green look sick," Troopers defensive coach Carl Hamilton said in 1973. "And like most of the women in this league, she's very coachable because she's eager to learn the game of football."

To say that Jefferson was in the spotlight would have been implying she wanted the attention all for herself. But that wasn't the case. Jefferson was focused on promoting her entire team, the same way Rose Low was when she did interviews and appeared on television shows to represent the Dandelions. Both players wanted to show the world what women's football players could do.

That desire never went away, even to this day. Jefferson only agreed to talk about her time as a Trooper and in the NWFL if her former teammates were promised the same amount of attention as well. Dallas Bluebonnet Barbara O'Brien said the same thing. She was dismayed by the disproportionate amount of attention she received in comparison to her teammates during her playing days. She only wanted to discuss her time as a player if everyone else on her team got the credit they deserved.

o———o

The Troopers' Bill Stout was the kind of coach that transformed a team of athletes with no football experience into seven-time world champions by demanding nothing less than perfection. His practices were known for being brutal, and he didn't pull any punches.

"Goddammit, Pickles!" Stout screamed at defensive tackle Vickie "Pickles" Seel during one practice when she was a little slow off the line. "You stand there with that stupid smile on your face, but you don't *do* anything." Seel was silent for a moment, looking at the ground before finally answering. "You expect me to just go out and *annihilate* her?"

"*Yes!*" Stout thundered, exasperated, because of course that's what he wanted her to do. Annihilate her.

He was the kind of coach who fired all the referees after a home game against the Columbus Pacesetters that his team won because the refs had failed to call enough penalties on his team. Stout felt this only made his job as a coach harder: How can he have a perfect team if the players' mistakes aren't flagged so they can better learn the game? During that game, Stout was beside himself, yelling, berating his players from the sideline, and making a scene during the entire first half. At halftime, the team headed into the locker room, where Stout's yelling continued. Finally, one of the Troopers looked up at Stout and said, "But coach, we're beating them forty to nothing." "Yeah," said Stout, "but you look like shit doing it."

But Stout also believed that a team needed to have a bond, a level of camaraderie and intimacy, in order to play well on the field. When the Burt Reynolds film *The Longest Yard* premiered in 1974, a Troopers coach took the team to see it together. Bonding breeds familiarity, loyalty, and dedication, which pay off during game play. They say that blood is thicker than water, but, said Collette, "the Troopers were thicker than that."

<hr />

Even though the league was only one year old in 1975, there were rivalries galore in the NWFL. This is true of any sports league, but particularly true in the NWFL because some of the teams had played each other frequently as independent franchises.

But perhaps the most brutal rivalry was between the Troopers and the Detroit Demons. One paper described the teams as "football's answer to [the] 'Hatfields & McCoys,'" calling their matchups "something between a grudge battle and a holy war." The teams knew each other well; due to relative proximity they played each other often, and both had been around since before there was even an official league.

They'd had years for animosity to build into full-blown hatred. At least one game ended in the third quarter when the Demons felt the Troopers were "headhunting" and officiating was favoring the Troopers, so they opted to just go home instead of continue playing (to hear the Troopers tell it, however, Detroit went home because they were being beaten so badly). It was even rumored that they taunted each other with dog biscuits prior to games, and that the Detroit team had a dummy with Linda Jefferson's number on it that they would pulverize during practice. "They hated us because we were good at what we did," said Trooper Gloria Jimenez. The Troopers considered "unsportsmanlike actions," like the digs they faced from teams like Detroit and Dallas, to be the behavior "teams of lesser ability" would "resort to . . . in retaliation."

The notorious fight happened on October 25, 1975, during a Saturday night game in Detroit. The Demons were not very good at football but they played dirty and had bad attitudes, which took them further than their lack of skill might have otherwise. The Troopers arrived in Detroit and exited the little yellow school bus that had transported them to the game—and which doubled as their locker room, because there was no locker room for the opposing team in Detroit—to a cold and rainy Michigan evening. They were already in a bad mood, having had an uncomfortable ride up, no changing facilities, and dismal weather. There was tension in the air before the game even started, and that, coupled with the fact that anytime the two teams met "it was ugly and there was usually controversy," according to Jimenez, meant the entire thing was a powder keg waiting to explode.

During the teams' first six meetings—two games per season in 1972, 1973, and 1974—the Demons failed to score a single point against the Troopers. Toledo, for their part, scored 225 points in those six games. Losing to the same team over and over again gets incredibly frustrating—although, so does beating the same teams over and over again. Jefferson told *womenSports* magazine that winning all the time without a challenge was getting old. Of the eight games the Troopers played in 1975, four were against Detroit, while three were against Columbus, and one against the DFW Shamrocks. While it's cool to look back at a nearly undefeated record, people play sports because they thrive on competition.

Running over that competition every time they took the field may have been fun at first, but by 1975 the Troopers were ready for a challenge. And, that October evening, Detroit was ready to give it to them.

One of the meetings between the two teams the previous month had been the closest the Demons had ever come to beating the mighty Troopers: the final score was 20–18. What had changed was that, for the first time in their existence as a team, the Demons had a coach who was invested in teaching them the ins and outs of the game. The team that had started as a gimmick under Sid Friedman may have wrested control away from the promoter out of a desire to play real football, but they lacked anyone to teach them how.

For their first few seasons playing as the Demons, they were mostly self-taught, though the husband of one of the players had tried his best the previous year. But 1975 brought head coach Tom Brown on board; what he found was a bunch of athletes who were hungry to be coached. The result of his guidance was rapid improvement and a team that could finally show their rivals a truly competitive matchup. "It wasn't that they weren't capable," said Demons assistant coach Dan Adair, who joined the staff in 1976, "they just had no one to show them."

That October night, Detroit managed to get on the board, but Toledo was dominant again. The frustration of having been so close the last time and failing to pull out a victory this time likely pushed the Demons over the edge.

At the end of the fourth quarter, the Troopers kicked off with just enough time for one more play. Jimenez punted the ball. The way Demons coach Tom Brown recalled it, the punt was blocked and a fight broke out. Jimenez remembers the team running down the field, and Jimenez and fellow Trooper Verna Henderson zoned in on the Demons player that had the ball. Out of nowhere, Jimenez recalled, Sunday Jones—six feet one, one of Toledo's hardest hitters, known to her teammates as "Dr. Death"—clocked the girl with the ball, knocking her right into Detroit's sideline. Collette remembers trash talking that went over the line.

The Demon snatched off her helmet and hit Jones with it. Several Demons rushed the field. Within moments, both benches had cleared and players were wielding their helmets like weapons, swinging them willy-nilly at whoever was in their path. "It was no little thing," Troopers PR person Ken Dippman told the *Toledo Blade*.

Troopers blocking back, 4'11", 90-pound Dorothy Parma, sat on the chest of a Demons player who weighed almost twice as much as she did. Every time the Detroit player would try to get up, Parma would hit her in the face. Jimenez remembers swinging her helmet at Demons coaches, because that's who was closest to her at the time.

The fight effectively ended the game. The two teams met the next week in Toledo, where the papers promoted the game by regaling readers with tales of the fight the weekend before. In doing so, the papers neglected to mention a single play or even the final score (it was 19–7). The Troopers'

Dippman had to insist that the fight had not been staged for promotional purposes. After all, the teams had parted ways with Sid Friedman because they didn't want to be a spectacle, though the papers were insistent on continuing to make them one.

Toledo coach Bill Stout was known for taking film of every game and making his team watch it obsessively. Every Monday night, the players gathered in Stout's basement to review film and recap the previous game. It was part of what made the Troopers so good; it was also what made it impossible for any player to deny her involvement in the melee with Detroit. "We came to the part about the fight and everybody's going, 'Well, I didn't do nothing,'" remembered Jimenez. "Of course, here he's got us on film and he's already got me on film. I'm swinging at the coaches."

Toledo won those games against Detroit. But their victories were getting harder to pull off, and other teams were becoming more competitive. They failed to shut out Detroit in any of their four meetings in 1975 and didn't score more than twenty-five points in a single game, a far cry from the thrashings they'd given the Demons earlier in their career. An injury to quarterback Lee Hollar's hand also hurt the team because with Hollar injured, other teams knew the Troopers' passing game would be hobbled. It became easy for opponents to guess what the Troopers were going to do: they were going to run the ball, and the person running it was going to be Jefferson. Jefferson was quick and her offensive line was good, but the question remained—How long would it be before a team figured out how to shut her down?

CHAPTER 11

DOWN IN OKLAHOMA

As if fate intervened, the Oklahoma City Dolls arrived in 1976 just in time to inject some drama and excitement into the NWFL and provide serious competition for the Toledo Troopers. They had the size, skill, coaching, and talent—players like Mary BlueJacket, Cindee Herron, and Doris Stokes—to propel them to one of the top teams in the league right from the start.

One player who suited up for the Dolls was twenty-five-year-old Charlotte Shoate Gordon. The elementary school teacher's maiden name would have been familiar to any Oklahoma college sports fan. Her brothers, Rod and Myron, played football for the University of Oklahoma. Rod would go on to spend six seasons in the NFL with the New England Patriots and was inducted into the College Football Hall of Fame in 2013. Gordon knew what it was like both on the field and on the sidelines. She played both ways for the Dolls as an end and a linebacker; she'd also been a cheerleader at OU.

Gordon was born and raised in the small, then-unincorporated town of Fort Coffee, Oklahoma, outside Spiro near the Arkansas border. It is located within the Choctaw Nation tribal jurisdiction, and her great-grandparents, who were Choctaw freedmen, settled in the area after enslavement. It was an agrarian community, located just south of a bend in the Arkansas River, and Gordon lived on a farm with her nine siblings—Gordon was number eight of ten—and their parents, Levester and Lula Shoate. The family all pitched in on the farm, and when they were able to purchase a tractor, which made the job easier, Levester opened a grocery store for the small, close-knit community.

While in junior college, Gordon had received a scholarship to go to college in Iowa. While she was there, she got a call from some of the coaches at OU. They wanted Rod to play for them, and they wanted her help convincing him to go there. Their parents, too, didn't want Rod to miss out on the opportunity to play for Oklahoma. Rod said he would only attend if Gordon did, too, so she gave up her scholarship to come home. By the time the Dolls came around, she had graduated, gotten married, and was working as a teacher. Her friend Doris Stokes recruited her to come out for the team.

Gordon was adamant that she wasn't following in her brothers' footsteps—"I'm setting a precedent," she told the *Daily Oklahoman*. "I don't like to be compared to them. . . . It's not a hereditary thing. I just try to do my best." Gordon also disputed her coach Mike Reynolds's characterization about the disposition of his players as making it hard to adapt to the game of football. "Most of us out here have a natural ability," she said. She stands by that assessment today: "I have a name. I don't go on [my brothers'] coattails. They have gone on mine, but I do my own and they do their own."

o———o

In 1976—only a few months before their first game on that scorching hot night against the Shamrocks (which was highlighted in Part I)—seventy-five women showed up to the first tryout at Moore Junior High School (now Central Junior High School) in Moore, Oklahoma, just south of Oklahoma City. More than a third made the cut, including Mary Blue-Jacket, who stood at five feet eight inches and wore her brown hair in a Peter Pan–style haircut. The field of candidates self-selected after that first day, however, after the coaches had the women run around the Moore Junior High track eight times—only about half of them came back the next day, but that was the point—to see who was committed enough and tough enough to stick it out. If the women thought the running was hard, wait until they got flattened to the ground the first time.

One of the women who showed up to see what this new football team was all about was twenty-two-year-old Jan Hines. She had seen an ad in the paper asking prospective players to attend a meeting at a hotel conference room. Football had been "the love of my life, my whole life," said Hines, and the thought of getting to play professionally was "all I'd ever wanted." Growing up, Hines played football with her cousins—four boys—and received a new football for Christmas each year. "If you played with the guys," Hines said, "you've got to have the best ball." She would carry the ball with her everywhere she went, pulling it out of her backpack as she walked along. If someone put their hands up and said, "Here! Throw it!" she would, and would play catch with anyone who would play catch with her. If somebody wanted to drop everything right then and there to play, the answer was always yes.

At the beginning of June, more than a month before the season was set to start, Hal told the *Daily Oklahoman* that, despite the number of women they had on the roster, there were only "about 15" that they were "real sure of," meaning players they felt they could put in a game. "We'd like to have a full offensive and defensive squad, that's 22 players," he said. "Right now it looks like we might have to send some both ways."

Like other teams, the women on the Dolls came from a mix of backgrounds, though about 30 percent of them were college students. Others were nurses, secretaries, and housewives. "It was hard instilling the killer instinct into some of them," Mike Reynolds said. "It was already there in some of them, but others didn't want to hit their buddy hard. We're getting away from that now, though." The local paper also reported that about three-quarters of the women on the roster were "serious about what they're doing," which they defined as "ready to do blocking fundamentals over and over again until they get it" right.

The women trained three times per week at a junior high school, which was eleven miles south of Oklahoma City. Hines played softball at the University of Oklahoma in nearby Norman and practiced from 3 p.m. to 5 p.m., five days per week. Then, on days that the Dolls practiced, she would drive the ten miles north on I-35 to Moore, where she practiced football from 6 p.m. to 8 p.m.

Some of the players drove long distances for the opportunity to play professional football. Lindy Albertson, an end, drove over 150 miles from Bartlesville, near the Kansas border. "When I leave [practice], I have exactly three hours to drive back home, change clothes, and be at work," Albertson said. She worked in the research department at the Phillips Petroleum Company, working with high explosives and unstable hydrocarbons.

Pebble Myers, who played halfback, drove nearly an hour each way from Alex, a small community south of Chickasha, Oklahoma. She said that even if she had to drive ninety miles each way, she would still make the sacrifice if it meant she got to play professional football.

Myers was a student at Oral Roberts University in Tulsa. Her father, Dwight "Corky" Myers, told her to get in the car one day, that they were going for a drive. She did, and when they arrived at their destination, Myers saw a bunch of women playing football. That's when her dad told her there was a new team getting started and that she should try out. "I never wanted to parade my talents," Myers said, "so Dad decided I should do it." The only problem was that Myers had missed the formal tryouts and would have to be a walk-on.

Hal only needed players that he could count on to fill out his roster and "be real sure of." So he told Myers that if she could beat their fastest player in a fifty-yard sprint, she could join the team. He shut down practice and all the women lined up to watch the race. Myers won the sprint, and from that day forward, she was the Dolls starting running back.

Some of the women came in with a good grasp on the rules of the game, while others had to be taught. Because most of the women were lifelong athletes, however, they were "quick to catch on," something that surprised Mike. Mike continued pushing this narrative for decades. "Most of the girls who were with the Dolls had previously played some kind of sport, but they didn't like to practice and they weren't used to the discipline needed for football," he told the *Daily Oklahoman* in a 2000 interview. "We had to start from scratch. Most of the Dolls had never gotten in a [football] stance or hit anybody before or ever gotten tackled. Once in a while there'd be some crying going on."

Hines disputes this characterization; she was a collegiate softball player—a member of the first softball team at University of Oklahoma, made possible by Title IX. Just about all of the girls had played softball, which meant they could throw and catch and had good hand-eye coordination. "It takes a certain kind of person that can take a hit and get up and do it again," said Hines. Doris Stokes, who played halfback, had played both powder-puff and intramural football in her hometown of Pawhuska, Oklahoma, before joining the Dolls. Safety Cathie Schweitzer was the women's track and field and basketball coach at OU.

Frankie Neal, the young middle linebacker known to her teammates as The Mayor because she was always befriending the other teams and inviting them out for drinks after the games, had an impressive athletic resume. She played basketball, but really excelled in track and field. The day before a regional meet in high school, her coach put a shot in her hand and told her to throw it. The next day, she placed first in the meet; that year, she finished seventh in the state in shot put. By the time she was a senior, Neal set a new state record and won the state title, tossing the shot forty-three feet, eleven inches and breaking the old record of forty-two feet, six inches.

Despite what Mike said, the players didn't need to learn how to be athletes. What the players actually needed to learn were the intricacies of the game, the details that people who watch on TV don't fully comprehend. This was about players learning each position from top to bottom, knowing what their particular job was on the field, and executing their role to perfection. But once the players got those key things down, they were able to effectively make plays on the field.

Most surprising to Myers was that she had to learn how to fall correctly so as not to injure her wrists. The most valuable thing she learned as a running back, however, was how to stiff arm: "To protect yourself, you have to put your arm out and block off the defenders but still hang onto that ball on the opposite side of your body."

"In the past, when I'd watched football, I just looked for the running backs to go do their thing, go score a touchdown," said running back Doris Stokes. But actually playing the position gave her a newfound respect for the offensive line, because she understood that it was the line who made the running back's flashy touchdown possible. "It takes that line to open up and move people in order for you to perform that. I did gain a lot of respect for the sport, for other positions of the sport."

o————o

The Oklahoma City Dolls were the brainchild of brothers Hal and Mike Reynolds. Mike had read a story about the Dandelions out in LA and heard about a women's football team in Dallas. Mike wanted to start his own, and enlisted Hal for help. "I thought it would be a great thing for Oklahoma City," Mike told the *Daily Oklahoman*. So in 1975, he called the Dallas Chamber of Commerce to find out who owned the Dallas team to ask how to start one. From there, Joe Mathews, who at this point owned the DFW Shamrocks and was vice president of the NWFL's Southern Division, was able to help the Reynolds brothers get started.

Mike was a twenty-nine-year-old data processing worker and union leader at Tinker Air Force Base in Oklahoma City, though he lived in nearby Moore. Hal worked as an IBM marketing representative and was known for having a gruffer personality than his more easygoing brother. The two brothers spent "less than the $25,000 'going price'" to start the franchise (Mike later cited the fee at "several thousand" dollars), financed partially by the sale of some of Hal's IBM stock. They enlisted thirty-four-year-old Dee Herron, a former player on a defunct semipro team called the Enid Plainsmen, to bring his football expertise as the defensive coach. Herron had gone to high school with Hal and Mike. Hal served as the head coach, while Mike was the general manager. One of the players said, "The coaches really know how to work with women."

Mike told the *Daily Oklahoman* that there were "several offers from investors" but they "had to turn them down." The Reynoldses didn't want anyone else to be on the hook and lose money if the team didn't succeed. "If this thing doesn't make it—and we think it will, but there's always that possibility—then we don't want any hard feelings from anyone," Mike said. "All our debts will be paid. As a matter of fact, we're paying as we go."

The Reynolds brothers felt confident that Oklahoma City would be ready to accept and support a women's football team, despite the fact that even men's sports had not fared well in the area. The locals were "a public that has not been easily sold on sports teams in recent years," said the *Daily Oklahoman*. "Basketball, baseball, hockey teams have all had it rough in Oklahoma City."

Media interest in the team was high before the season began, because women playing football was still a curiosity. The local papers were writing stories as much as two months before the first game, building up the hype for this new women's football team and the NWFL in general. The *Daily Oklahoman* came out to write a story about the team finally practicing in full pads, noting the players were now "donning the full regalia of a football player." This coverage made it sound like the players were wearing a costume or playing a part instead of dressing like the athletes they were.

Coverage insisted that watching the Dolls play would be a lot like watching men play, and the coaches perpetuated that narrative, too. Mike Reynolds told one newspaper that it would be hard to tell the players weren't men. "They will act just like men when they take the field," he reassured the public.

In the majority of the coverage, Mike and Hal speak for and about the team, with just a quote or two from one of the players. It is Mike, mostly, who is shaping the public narrative of the team. The photo spreads that accompany the stories, however, feature the players. It's an interesting dynamic: the photos of women to sell the team, the voice of men to legitimize it.

For example, instead of asking one of the players what it was like to wear football pads for the first time—pads that were castoffs from a local high school team and were designed for wide, flat chests and not built for bodies with breasts, requiring the players to wrap towels under the pads to protect parts of themselves—Mike told the *Daily Oklahoman* that they're "having to get used to moving around" in the pads and that "there's a lot of difference" between throwing the ball in gym clothes and throwing the ball in full pads.

The preseason media coverage is the reason quarterback Jan Hines's parents found out she was playing in the first place. Hines just wanted to play football, and tried as hard as she could to stay out of debates about whether women should play. They were debates she was familiar with due to being a collegiate athlete—something that, as a woman, wasn't a popular thing to be.

At the time, the attitude on campus was that the women were taking something from the men. "By having to give [the women] equal money and equal sports," in some people's eyes "you're taking something away from the men that was traditionally and rightfully theirs," Hines explained. And that was just softball. Football was even more of a polarizing topic, so she kept her involvement quiet, even from her own parents.

But somewhat unluckily for Hines, her dad worked at the television station as an engineer. Before the season started, a television crew had filmed the Dolls practicing. Hines was not yet the team's quarterback; the original QB was a javelin thrower for OU named Kathy Gerenda, who was away at a track meet. Their second-string quarterback worked in the medical profession and her pager had gone off, so she had to go, too.

When the TV crews arrived, Hines was the only player on the field who knew all the plays. So she went in and played quarterback so the crew could shoot some film for the 6 p.m. news. It ended up being her audition for the role; from that day forward, Hines was the team's starting QB.

By coincidence, Hines's father was in the editing room at the station when they were working on the news hit. He walked by and said, "Wait, stop right there." He asked the man editing the film, "What is that?" The editor responded, "That's the quarterback for the Oklahoma City Dolls." Mr. Hines shook his head. "No," he said. "That's my daughter."

Unaware that her father had already seen it, Hines rushed to her parents' house and changed the TV to another channel, rather than the one that would be airing the segment about the Dolls. She went into the kitchen to make herself a sandwich. Her dad walked in and said, "I hear you're the quarterback for the Oklahoma City Dolls."

Her sandwich fell from her hands to the floor. "How'd you know that?" she asked, feigning innocence.

"I saw you on TV," her dad replied.

She'd been busted. Like the Dandelions' Rose Low's parents, Hines's discovered she was playing football thanks to a television appearance. But her family, like Low's, turned out to be okay with her playing, and they weren't all that surprised. Their daughter had grown up playing the game; it only made sense that she would pursue a professional opportunity when it presented itself.

While her family accepted her decision, Hines's softball coaches at OU didn't. She remembers being called into the athletic director's office at least three times, being asked to give up football. But at the time, athletes weren't on scholarship. The coaches were clear that they couldn't force Hines to quit football, but they wanted her to. She refused.

"You can tell me to do whatever you want to tell me to do between three o'clock and five o'clock [during practices], and on game day. And I promise you'll have priority if there's ever a conflict," she remembered telling them. "But I'm not giving up football. That's my game. That's the only thing I've ever wanted to play my whole life. That's what I'm the best at, and that's what I want to play."

Her family didn't fare as well when a conflict came up—Hines missed her brother's wedding on August 27, 1977. When her brother had gotten engaged, Hines sent along the Dolls schedule and told him, "You can get married on any day except for these." However, his fiancée had a particular preacher that she wanted to officiate the ceremony and the only day he could marry them was on the night of an away game.

Hines felt she couldn't let her team down. So she took the field in Lawton, Oklahoma, against another 1976 startup team, the Houston Herricanes, instead of attending the wedding. At least it was worth it: the Dolls won that game 34–6.

CHAPTER 12

HERE COME THE HERRICANES

The first game the Houston Herricanes ever played together in 1976 was against the Dallas–Fort Worth Shamrocks, who had a full roster of experienced players from the former Bluebonnets and Forth Worth teams. "You ever seen one of those wildlife shows where they have the meerkats and they're always poking their heads up? Looking?" linebacker Billie Cooper said. "Well, that's what we looked like, the first game out the door, watching the other team get off the bus."

To Cooper and the rest of the Herricanes, the Shamrocks looked like real-life giants and were incredibly intimidating. "They were some big women," said quarterback Gwen Flager. "And we didn't have a big team physically."

The Herricanes may have not had the size, but they were a quick and scrappy bunch, hoping to take advantage of their speed right from the kickoff and catch the Shamrocks off guard. But it was the Herricanes who were caught by surprise when the football bounced off the grass and went right through the kick returner's legs. "We were just nervous," Cooper said. "Nervous as all get out. That's part of the experience of the first game." Houston ended up losing the game, but the experience of it only made them want to get better. "We had to learn a lot of things. Some of us were great athletes but there was a learning curve with football," running back Marty Bryant explained. "Gwen didn't just hand the ball off. There's a way to take a handoff. We had to learn the fundamentals— the three-point stance, the one-spot or three-spot—there were so many things we didn't know because we didn't play the game."

The Herricanes didn't let the learning curve deter them. They worked hard on practicing those very fundamentals, perfecting plays, and running the offense. And as their season went on, things like handoffs and calling audibles at the line of scrimmage became second nature.

Flager saw the evolution firsthand from inside the huddle. "Everybody came back [to the huddle] with input. Someone would say, look this position off my left or off my right, this might be a good play to run. It was such a team effort," she recalled. "I remember that. We were kind of that single focus. We didn't have any hotshots, we didn't have anybody that was, oh—throw the ball to me, throw the ball to me. None of that. We were going to have fun doing it [together]."

○————○

The Herricanes had started on a whim. Twenty-five-year-old Marty Bryant was visiting the dentist for a routine checkup. As the shy and reserved Houston, Texas, resident sat patiently in the waiting room, she picked up a magazine from the coffee table and began to skim through it. That's when she noticed an article about a women's professional football team in Ohio. It happened to be the June 1975 issue of *womenSports* magazine with Linda Jefferson smiling bright and wide-eyed on the cover while cradling a football. Bryant was instantly captivated.

"I just always loved sports. I loved basketball, too," she recalled. "And I could run and I could dribble, but I couldn't seem to run and dribble at the same time. I played volleyball, but in school at that time there was not much offered for women. When I saw that article I thought, well, maybe we can play football, too." Bryant wrote down the contact information for the NWFL office in Los Angeles and eventually wrote them a letter. "I asked them if we could have a team in Houston, and what we needed to do to get started and so forth. They wrote a letter back and said, 'yes.'

They said if there was anything they could do to help me get started, let them know." Bryant was ecstatic but slightly overwhelmed. She wasn't quite sure what to do next.

Unlike the founders of the Dandelions, Dolls, and Lobos, Bryant had no potential investors lined up to help raise the necessary funds for a new NWFL franchise, let alone supply her with uniforms and equipment and to cover expenses. It was a very different situation from NWFL franchises that were financially backed by one, two, or even a group of individuals who took care of all of the monetary concerns. Bryant knew that if she were going to see it through, she and her new team would have to shoulder the entire financial burden themselves. Even without being able to come up with the franchise fee, Bryant was given the NWFL's blessing to start a team and begin practicing without being an "official" member of the league, and even to play "exhibition games." That lifted the burden of having to think about how to raise enough money to buy into the league. All Bryant had to focus on at that moment was finding players. And that was something she could handle.

The first thing Bryant did was contact her local ABC news station and the sports desk at the *Houston Chronicle* to announce the first tryout. She spread the word among her friends and softball teammates, who told their friends, and so on and so forth. Bryant also got in touch with Houston sportswriter Anita Martini, who was a trailblazer for women in sports journalism. Martini not only championed women in sports, she was also working hard to carve inroads for women in sports journalism. She was more than happy to talk about the NWFL on her radio show and the team Bryant was putting together.

After the publicity blitz, about twenty-five or so women showed up for the first official meeting and tryout. Bryant was encouraged. One of the women was Billie Cooper: a spunky short-haired Texan with a background in marine biology who worked at a local Houston chemical plant. Before Bryant had written the letter to the NWFL asking for permission to start a team, she mentioned the idea to Cooper during softball practice one day. "She came up to me and was like, 'I'm thinking about getting a football team together,'" Cooper recalled. "'Are you in?' And I go, 'Oh—absolutely I'm in. Sign me up.'"

The tryout, Cooper added, was a chaotic scene from the start, and some of the women who showed up seemed as if they were there for the wrong reasons. "I thought, what the heck did I get myself into? I don't know why some of the people came out. I'd watch them like, oh my goodness—you're over there fixing your hair. And you're wanting to try out for a football team? You want to run and get sweaty?" Cooper said. "So people kind of weed themselves out, you know what I'm saying?"

There were others like Cooper who were there for football and the chance to actually play in competitive games. Twenty-six-year-old Gwen Flager read about the tryouts in the newspaper. She was working as an assistant apartment manager in Northwest Houston at the time and was curious to check it out.

"You know, I had played as a kid. We played touch football in junior high," Flager said. "But I didn't know any women who had ever played full contact." She didn't know what to expect, but it didn't take long for Flager to warm up to the idea. As soon as Bryant explained to the group what her hopes were for the team, Flager immediately thought—*I want to be a part of this, I want to play, I want to have this experience.* She didn't care what position she played, or even if she got to play at all.

Flager felt deeply that something special was happening and she didn't want to miss out. She was also still relatively new to Houston, having moved there right after graduating from the University of South Alabama, and wanted to meet new people in a comfortable setting. There, in Memorial Park, among Cooper, Bryant, and other like-minded women athletes, Flager felt strongly that she had come to the right place. Seventeen women in all, including Bryant, Cooper, and Flager, committed to the team right then and there. Others mulled it over after the tryout, then joined as well.

The group came up with the team name Herricanes together, throwing the "Her" into it because they knew when people saw the name they would instantly know it was a women's team. Then, they purchased uniforms and equipment on their own dime. Cooper remembers the visit to the sporting goods store as if it happened yesterday. "It was after hours," she said. "We didn't want to be in there trying on equipment with a bunch of customers. We tried on our helmets. And a lot of the helmets were way too big [for us]. So we had to get junior high helmets." They went with what Cooper described as "standard boys-issue equipment," and the total amount cost almost one hundred dollars per player. If they wanted to play, they had to pitch in and pay their own way.

Bryant knew coaches from the community, and they volunteered their time in order to help the Herricanes get their bearings and learn offensive and defensive schemes. They taught them football techniques such as proper tackling and blocking form. By fall 1976, the team was ready to compete and play games.

Head coach Richard Perry had a background in football, and his coaching style reflected that of a disciplined player. Glaring behind a seventies-style handlebar mustache for his headshot in the Herricanes' first game program, Perry's nonstop intensity was over the top—especially for Cooper. "He was brash and talked to us like little kids sometimes, like junior high school boys," she said. "He struggled dealing with grown women. Grabbing us by the facemask didn't go over very well. I mean, you gotta remember, all of us were in our twenties. And some of us, pushing thirty. You had to treat grown people differently than you do junior high school kids. I mean, I coached. And I understand that. Treat grown people with a little bit more respect, a little more dignity. You can't take their dignity away. If you take their dignity away, they quit playing for you."

Assistant coach Mike Smith contrasted Perry not only in coaching style but also in personality. Smith had a full head of dirty-blond hair that stuck out in all directions and a genuine smile that filled his whole face. During practice, it was easy to see the difference in their approach to teaching and coaching women's football. "Mike was a sweetheart," said Cooper, who worked with Smith on defense. "Richard, I think, was overwhelmed. It was a lot to handle." In the beginning, Perry did everything for the team: he not only coached the offense, he also took care of arranging travel accommodations, booked games, put together a comprehensive playbook, and spent extra time teaching the ins and outs of the game. And he did it all during the free time he had away from his full-time job. The stress, Cooper believed, got to him. "He worked his ass off, but he didn't want help."

Cooper had a full-time job herself and tried to help out as much as she could—even with finances. "We really struggled [financially], I'm not going to lie to you," she said. "I had the same shoulder pads and helmet every year. It never changed. I had new stuff, some of the [other players] did have hand-me-downs. When women quit or couldn't play anymore, they donated their equipment." Ticket sales, what little there were, produced the funds to keep the team afloat. "Our fans looked like bee-bees rolling around in a barrel. There were not a lot of them," Bryant added. "But there were enough of them that we had money to pay for officials and for an ambulance. We made enough money to do that."

Although the Herricanes didn't make enough money—after transportation, stadium, and referee costs—to provide each player with the NWFL "standard" twenty-five dollars per game, it didn't dampen morale or deter participation. Like every other team in the league, the players played because they loved football. They didn't care if they were paid or not. They just wanted to play. Whatever extra money players made individually from their full-time jobs or side gigs often went into promoting the team. Cooper once sprung for a set of bumper stickers and passed them out to her teammates to sell. They printed T-shirts and other memorabilia, hoping to bring in some additional cash to help offset travel and stadium costs. The Herricanes scrimped, saved, and sacrificed as a team in order to play, and it only brought them closer.

"The team was all about doing it together. None of us could have done it by ourselves," Bryant said. "Just seeing each other, picking each other up. And it carried onto the field. Someone makes a bad play or a fumble, you know—everybody picked them up like it was okay. It was the camaraderie. Everyone was very supportive of each other."

Cooper saw the Herricanes as one big extended family. "I just thought the world of them," she said. "Like any family, you have bickering. But you kind of kiss and make up. I just loved that feeling of family I had with the teammates. Because they understood the trials and tribulations that you were going through at home, at work, different things like that." For Flager, the team provided a "brand new bunch of friends" she could hang out with and get to know better. During the week, the Herricanes practiced at Memorial Park and played games on the weekends.

"Everybody pretty much worked full time," Flager said. But they were all equally dedicated to practicing, learning the plays, and playing football to the best of their abilities.

Their level of commitment, especially when they were playing for free, is perhaps surprising. But to Flager and the rest of the Herricanes—and to all the women in the NWFL—it made perfect sense. "It was just so simple," she said. "We just wanted to play football. It's not any more or any less than that."

o————o

The Oklahoma City Dolls and the Houston Herricanes weren't the only teams to join the NWFL in 1976. The San Antonio Flames also reorganized as a team (they had been the San Antonio Roses from 1974 to 1975) and participated in the Southern Division. But for every team in the South—and the LA Dandelions out in the West—the Oklahoma City Dolls became their toughest opponent. After winning their first three games—including taking down the formerly unbeatable Troopers—the Dolls became everyone's stiffest competition despite being new to the league.

"The farthest trip we ever took was to Oklahoma City," said Beebe, the Dandelions' punter. "[They] kicked our butts. They were some big girls." Low described the Dandelions' run-in with the Dolls with a bit more theatrical flair. "When we got to Oklahoma City, holy smokes, those were some of the biggest women I've seen in my life," she laughed. "And they killed us. We were mortified when we saw how big they were and we knew it wasn't going to be an easy game. They killed us."

Cindy Turner played quarterback for the Tulsa Babes, a team that formed in 1977 and also participated in Southern Division play. She affectionately describes the Babes as the women's football version of the *Bad News Bears* because they never won a single game during their two-year existence as a football franchise. And because of their proximity, they played against the Dolls quite often and, in turn, *often* got pummeled. "The Oklahoma City Dolls were tough. We had the determination [to try and win], we just couldn't get it done," she said. "I remember that I was running for my life a lot."

The first time the Herricanes faced off against the Dolls, on September 25, 1976, they lost 56–0 on their home turf. And like most of the other teams in the NWFL, Houston was in awe of the Dolls' size and skill. "The first time we saw Oklahoma, I thought—Oh my God, they're built like Volkswagens," said former Herricanes general manager Robin Massey. "It felt like David and Goliath. And we were David." But that game lit a spark in the pits of the Herricanes' stomachs, and from that moment on, they considered the Dolls their biggest rival and challenge—even if the Dolls did not see them the same way. To the Dolls, the Houston team wasn't a threat; they were more concerned about the Troopers.

That dynamic was solidified one week later, when the two teams met again on October 2, 1976, this time in Oklahoma. The Herricanes were "decimated by injuries and operating with just 23 players," according to the local Oklahoma City paper. The Dolls creamed the Herricanes 50–0, but Houston felt they didn't play fair. Houston head coach Richard Perry complained that the Dolls had resorted to "dirty tactics and sandlot football." "Three of our girls were hit in the mouth and [Aurora] Sanchez was intentionally stepped on," causing an apparent "cracked ankle" injury. For the Dolls' part, coach Hal Reynolds disputed the accusation. "We had hard tackling," he told the *Daily Oklahoman*. "The more pursuit you have, the better your team is. Their girls were slugging and kicking. If there was any dirty play, we didn't encourage it."

Even after the lopsided losses, the Herricanes were determined to get a win against OKC, no matter how many games or seasons it took—off-the-field friendships be damned. "Frankie Neal and I were pretty close, but I was going to tackle her butt if she got close to me," said Cooper. "I liked most everybody that I played against. I don't make nice with people who are jackasses. Now if you get out there and you play hard and you tackle me hard, I'm going to give you kudos. You knocked the snot out of me—awesome. Next time, I'm going to knock the snot out of you."

o———o

As evidenced by their blowouts against Houston and their takedown of the formerly unbeatable Troopers (as discussed in Part I), the Dolls were having an incredible inaugural season, though the media was still determined to condescend to them every chance they got. "The novelty is gone. It's like the week after Christmas now for Mike Reynolds," Dean Bailey wrote in the *Daily Oklahoman*. "All the bows and colorful wrapping have been disposed of, and you're left with whatever was inside. For Reynolds, it was a women's professional football team." They still hadn't lost a game, though, and the players were gaining confidence every time they took the field. But during the middle of the season, a conflict between coaches would cause the team to lose two of their biggest assets: Coach Herron and his wife, Cindee.

It was during a game against the Shamrocks in which the entire team was getting drenched in the rain. As Cindee remembers Herron telling it, Hal stood next to quarterback Jan Hines, holding an umbrella over her head. Herron was a good-natured guy, according to his wife, someone who played Santa Claus every year for charity events, but as a former player and current coach, he took issue with one of the players being treated differently than the rest. He expressed his disagreement to Hal, accusing him of treating Hines like a "prima donna." Hal fired Herron, Cindee said.

Mike Reynolds has a different version of the story. He said that Hal and Herron were disagreeing about which play to call—Herron was insisting on a play that would have Cindee run up the middle, but Hal thought it was the wrong call. Eventually, Hal relented, and Herron's play didn't work. Hal muttered something under his breath about knowing he shouldn't have listened to Herron. "Dee came unglued and wanted to fight," said Mike. "I had to jump on his back to keep him from going berserk. All Dee wanted to do was pulverize Hal, and I'm holding Dee back."

Mike said the game was over within a play or two—the Dolls' first-ever loss, and their only loss that season—and "Dee knew he was gone. And he deserved to be gone." The Herrons didn't even take the bus back to Oklahoma City following the game, and Cindee walked alongside her husband. She'd been one of the team's key players. But the Herrons would later make a return to the NWFL, and do it on their own terms.

○———○

After their crushing loss to the Dolls to open their sixth season in 1976, the Troopers won their next ten games, as well as their division.

Meanwhile, the Dolls steamrolled their own schedule, losing only that one game the rest of the season, to the Dallas–Fort Worth Shamrocks in the middle of a downpour, who they then beat in a playoff game to win the Southern Division.

That meant that the Troopers would get what they'd wanted all season: a chance at redemption. Toledo and Oklahoma City would meet in the 1976 NWFL championship game. The way it worked was that the challenging team was the home team and had to pay the other team's travel costs. Even though finances were tight, there was no way to take a multi-day bus trip to Toledo. The Dolls flew into Detroit and then drove to Toledo, where the Troopers paid for their lodging.

The Dolls' attitude was, "If they want to play us, they're gonna have to fly us up there," Hines recalled. And so they did. Because Toledo was also eager to settle the score. "We wanted that game," said the Troopers' Collette. "And Coach [Stout] pulled out all the stops and was going to make sure that we had that game. It was a bloodbath."

But as much as the Troopers wanted revenge, the Dolls wanted to make their own statement. It was an "'I beat you once, I'm gonna beat you again' kind of thing" for them, said Collette. "I mean, it was a *game*."

It was, indeed, a close game. The game was declared a tie, 13–13, and the teams shared the 1976 title. But the record book doesn't tell the whole story.

"I'll tell you exactly what happened," Collette said. "It wasn't a tie."

The game is burned so permanently into Collette's memory that she can recall the date (December 11, 1976) and the weather (below freezing) without being asked. The field of the University of Toledo's Glass Bowl Stadium was covered in snow, and the turf had to be cleared off before play could begin. Collette describes it clearly: "I'll never forget this day as long as I live."

What's not in dispute: that Jefferson scored all of the Troopers' points and rushed for 137 of the team's 140 rushing yards. That the Troopers scored two touchdowns, missed the extra two points after their first touchdown, and made the one-point conversion after the second touchdown. That Dolls' fullback Frankie Neal scored both touchdowns and Mary BlueJacket missed the 2-PAT on the second touchdown.

What is in dispute: the result of the 2-PAT after the Dolls' touchdown in the first quarter. Referees ruled it no good on the field, which Collette still insists was the right call. According to Hines, though, one ref ruled it good while another did not, and she remembers the ball clearly going through the uprights.

The Dolls believed that BlueJacket's kick was good, and they filed a dispute with the league. "Obviously the call had an effect on the outcome of the game, or I wouldn't have filed the protest," Dolls GM Mike Reynolds told the *Daily Oklahoman*. "It was very obvious to us [the coaches] and the players that the kick was good."

According to BlueJacket, she remembers the ball going through the bottom left part of the upright. And she's not entirely surprised that the call was wrong on the field; officials were used to NWFL players missing kicks and this one was close. It was her first year as a kicker, and "I really didn't have my technique down," BlueJacket said. "So either 50 percent of the time I was going to hit, the other time not."

This would not be a problem for BlueJacket in the Dolls' second season—she changed her technique and was nearly 100 percent on her kicks after that. BlueJacket hadn't started out as a kicker but during a practice one day before the season began, she saw a ball on a tee and kicked it "just for the heck of it." The ball went flying and one of the coaches turned around and demanded to know who had kicked it. Just like that, BlueJacket became the Dolls kicker. She was mostly left to her own devices when it came to learning how to kick, since none of the Dolls coaches were experienced in the technique of kicking a field goal.

"My main mistake the first year is I was taking one step and kicking," she said. She was right-footed and so would take one step with her left and then kick with her right, leaving her off-balance and preventing her from getting the accuracy she needed to consistently get the ball through the uprights. After that first season, BlueJacket began taking two steps before her kick: right, left, kick. From then on it was right down the middle, elevated. Good.

But that would come later. In that first NWFL 1976 championship game, all BlueJacket had was her kick that had barely cleared the uprights, the one that she and the official behind her knew was good but that the two referees under the goalposts called no good, and the confusion and controversy that would result.

Collette occasionally thinks of that championship game. The story did not end after the Dolls officially challenged the final score. According to Steve Guinan, a Troopers historian who has written a screenplay and a book on the team, how the game went from a Troopers' victory to a tie related to video footage, which has since gone missing. Guinan has spent years trying to recover that footage, to be able to see for himself what the NWFL commissioner saw that compelled her to anoint cochampions.

Due to the snowy conditions on the field that day, the refs couldn't establish a proper position to clearly see whether the kick was good or not. Guinan says the PAT was waved off on the field, but the Dolls—and some of the Troopers—swore they saw the ball go through the uprights. Dolls GM Mike Reynolds filed his dispute, and video footage surfaced that was apparently undeniable. (A crew from The Oklahoma City NBC affiliate—then WKY—had traveled with the team to Toledo, and it was their footage that showed the successful PAT.) So undeniable that the commissioner felt she had to do something.

At the time, there was no protocol for replay, because in the 1970s it wasn't yet a thing (the NFL formally adopted instant replay in 1986). The NWFL commissioner felt she had to take action, and that was to declare the Troopers and the Dolls cochampions. Had the call on the field been correct, the Dolls would have won the game, but without a clearly outlined protocol for how to proceed, the league officials did what they felt was right.

"I don't accept that," said the Troopers' Jimenez. She is still adamant. "I feel that we won. The end of the game, we won on the scoreboard. I don't think you can just turn around . . . and go, well, it's a tie now."

Hines believes that the refs rigged the game for the Troopers, since they were local officials who knew the players by first name and had followed their history-making ascent atop the NWFL. She places no blame on the members of the Troopers themselves.

The league agreed with that assessment—the championship game was officiated by the same crew who reffed a game between the Troopers and Demons earlier that season, which the Demons chose to end three minutes into the third quarter because, according to Demons coach Tom Brown, the Troopers "were headhunting" Demons players, "beating up [the Detroit] quarterback in the middle of the field," and "the officials didn't do anything." It was that same Toledo-based officiating crew that the NWFL later banned for their work during the championship game between the Troopers and the Dolls.

After a cochampionship was declared, the Dolls were given a small trophy. But Troopers coach Bill Stout paid out of pocket to have a duplicate trophy made, which looked identical to the one the Troopers received.

According to Collette, she asked Stout about what happened years later. They went to dinner shortly before he passed away in 2012, and Collette's story is a little bit different. "I went, 'Coach, don't you remember? I was the outside linebacker. I was there, I watched the ball get kicked over the upright—outside,'" Collette recalled telling him. "Oh, I know," he told her. So why did it end up being called a tie? "He says, 'I don't remember, I think I just got tired of . . . them whining about [it].'"

Collette doesn't much care what the history books say, though. She knows the Troopers carried the field. "In my eyes, in my heart," she said, "I know that we won." Just don't tell that to Hines. When asked if the Dolls won that game, she's clear: "Oh, absolutely."

CHAPTER 13

MEDIA MISCUES

Rose Kelley and Janice Merritt both stumbled onto the Herricanes by accident. Merritt just happened to be driving around Houston's Memorial Park and saw a group of women in football gear. The twenty-five-year-old teacher was struck with a mixture of curiosity and envy. Growing up in a family of nine, she had played football with her three older brothers and missed it. "I pulled over and I think Billie [Cooper] was the first one I talked to," Merritt recalled. "And she told me a little bit about what they were doing and asked if I was interested. I said, sure." As for Kelley, it was the Herricanes who first took notice of her as she was jogging through Memorial Park. Kelley had the size the Herricanes were missing on defense. "They asked me, was I interested in playing," she explained. "It was up my alley and I said yes. I went over and I had to try to make the team. That first hit, they said, 'She gonna make it.' I'm not bragging, but I was a good defensive tackle."

Even though Kelley came from a family of thirteen, the Herricanes became an instant, extended family to her. She felt valued and appreciated, not only for her size and strength but for who she was. The football field became a place of acceptance, love, and appreciation for women like Kelley who, as a large, Black woman, often felt ostracized and unwelcome in a society that held such staunch standards for how women should look, act, and live. When they were in their uniforms and pads, nothing else mattered but the game.

"Those are my best friends. Those are my sisters. I call them my sisters," Kelley said. "I loved playing because in this world, they don't give women the opportunity to do things that guys do or make money. We didn't get paid, but the community was like we got paid because it was joy. Women don't have a lot of opportunities to prove they can do what a man can do."

The Herricanes may not have won a lot of games in 1976, but Cooper believed the learning experience they gained from those losses was worth it. Throughout that first season their roster was constantly in flux, with some players quitting and new ones coming into the fold. But that was okay, Cooper insisted. The ones that left weren't meant to be there, and they filled those empty spots with people who really wanted to be part of the team.

Brenda Cook was one of those players. She desperately wanted to be a part of the Herricanes and what they were building. Cook was in her early twenties when she saw an article about the team in the *Houston Chronicle* and showed it to her husband. She had read about the Oklahoma City Dolls before and promised herself that if Houston ever got a team, she would try out. Back in high school, Cook had gotten a taste of organized football when she played in a couple of powder-puff games. "That's when I just fell in love with playing it," she said. "I said, 'Man—these guys have been keeping this a secret forever.'"

Cook lived about an hour outside of Houston but worked downtown in the city. She would drive into work in the morning, get out at five, and then mill around Memorial Park until practice started at six. After practice, Cook would head off on the hour-long drive back to her house. Most nights, she wouldn't get home until nine. "It was a full day," she said. But she loved every minute of her time as a Herricane because she got to do something she had never been able to do before—play organized football.

"I can't deny that I really loved running with the ball," she recalled. "But you know, there was really no outlet for girls sports in high school. And I knew I could run in high school. Never had the opportunity. There were no track teams at my school. So I always felt like that was something that I missed. This gave me the opportunity to do something with my running, to compete with my running. That was a big drive. I really enjoyed that."

Twenty-four-year-old Jane Schulte heard about the Herricanes after their first season from a friend and was asked if she wanted to join the team. Schulte showed up at a team meeting and as soon as she walked through the door, Flager's eyes lit up. At quarterback, Flager had taken her fair share of hits during the Herricanes' first season and knew the team needed some extra size on the offensive line and a new center, since last year's center had gotten injured. "When I walked in, Gwen Flager looked at me and said, 'That's who I want for my center,'" Schulte said. "She immediately tagged me."

Schulte wasn't a "big girl" by average center standards and figured she was best suited for linebacker. But she was muscular and strong, and Flager wasn't about to let her play any other position besides center. So that's where she ended up. One of her first games against Dallas, Schulte snapped the ball and was instantly steamrolled. "They had a big old girl that played and all I remember is hiking the ball and ending up on my back, looking at the sky. I saw stars after that." After a few games, Schulte fell in love with the position and developed a special, symbiotic relationship with Flager. "I think part of it was that I had the protector mentality. That's what I was there to do, to keep Gwen from getting sacked," Schulte recalled. "We had a pretty good line when I played with them. And we did a really good job. She didn't get sacked very often. I was glad that we could do that."

○———○

The Herricanes were able to overcome some of the pitfalls they experienced as a new sports franchise in 1976 with the help of their volunteer general manager, Robin Massey. Massey was good friends with Herricane founder Marty Bryant. She grew up around the corner from Bryant and they often hung out together with their sisters. When Bryant started the team, Massey was more than happy to offer moral support. At first, she sat back and watched things unfold, offering assistance only when asked to help out. But when she realized the Herricanes needed a little bit more organization,

Massey eagerly stepped in. "I wasn't working full-time. My sister was a player, so I knew a lot of the players," she said. "I just jumped in there. I didn't know what I was doing but I didn't let that stop me."

Richard Perry, the Herricanes head coach, didn't return after the first season. The stress, Cooper believed, finally got to him. And his coaching methods not only exhausted the players, but also weren't effectively helping them learn and grow on the field in the way they wanted to. Flager, who described Perry as being "rough around the edges," said there were times when he would run a play instead of explaining the ins and outs of what made the play work. "It could be that he was unable to coach an inexperienced team of women," she explained. "Of course, he did volunteer his time and helped the best he knew how."

"I think Rich wasn't advancing the team the way they wanted to be," offered Massey, whose husband, Robert, took over as head coach after Perry left. Together, the Masseys assisted the Herricanes in any way that they could. "He began working with the team. I arranged stadiums, and bus transportation, hotel rooms and assigned rooms. At one point I got tired of that and just said, here are the keys girls—you figure it out," Massey recalled with a laugh. "I've always been an organizer, so as far as organizing the everyday business of the team, that was easy for me. One thing I loved about the girls was their enthusiasm and dedication. These girls went out there and did full-contact football just like the men do and they weren't being paid. They endured the pain and all kinds of injuries. And they still came back every Monday. I thought that was amazing. They kept coming back so I kept coming back."

One of the main things Massey tried to accomplish during her time with the Herricanes was to share and promote the team as much as she could, and get the players the attention and recognition she felt they deserved. With all of the dedication and sacrifice they put in, it was the least she could do, she thought. And the best way to get the word out about the Herricanes was through the media.

Unfortunately, throughout the entire history of sports, the media has consistently treated women's sports leagues, teams, and players poorly: as less than, a novelty, or, in some cases, altogether nonexistent. Even today, with so many proven and talented women in the Women's National

Basketball Association (WNBA), National Women's Soccer League (NWSL), National Women's Hockey League (NWHL), gymnastics, golf, and tennis, for example, sufficient media coverage is severely lacking from mainstream and popular sports media outlets. And this shortage runs from player profiles and feature stories to magazine covers and television documentaries. According to the Tucker Center for Research on Girls & Women in Sport, 40 percent of all sports participants are women and girls, yet women's sports receive only 4 percent of all sport media coverage.

"The fact is, too often, women's sports is treated in mainstream sports media as a curiosity. A sideshow. A heartwarming tale, an inspirational story, a talking point," professor of digital media production and online journalism Brian Moritz wrote on his sports media blog, Sports Media Guy, in 2018, in 2018. Moritz is right. When looking back at newspaper articles in the 1970s, that is exactly the way the NWFL was largely covered by the media. Newspapers, especially in the sports department, predominantly employed male editors and reporters who weren't willing to take women's football seriously. What was written, printed, and portrayed about women's football came from the male point of view—often skewed as less than because of the men's preconceived notions about women and sports in general. But at the time, women's football—including the Herricanes—had to take what they could get.

Massey was relentless in her pursuit of media coverage and support. She drew up countless press releases and sent them to every media outlet she could think of, including all the major newspapers in the Houston area and beyond, smaller weekly newspapers, radio stations, and television stations. She even did "backup" calling to see if every press release she dutifully sent was received. "I remember calling one major news station to see if they had gotten my press release," Massey recalled. "And [the news director] said, 'Yeah, I threw it in the trash can.' So I kind of knew where he stood on it. We got minimal coverage."

○——○

Bob Mathews in LA, and Sid Friedman in Cleveland before him, both understood implicitly that, more than anything else, relevant and consistent media attention and coverage were an integral part of the success of their women's football ventures. But the two differed on one crucial aspect: content.

Friedman was thrilled with any and all kinds of coverage, serious or otherwise. Articles that painted the girls in a joking light or that were satirical in nature didn't bother him. For Friedman, as long as his teams and his players were mentioned in the pages of the newspaper then that's all that mattered. Being the seasoned promotional agent he was, publicity—good or bad—was publicity.

Mathews saw things differently. He desperately wanted the NWFL to be respected, and his team—the Los Angeles Dandelions—to be taken seriously by the media. He wanted women's football to stand on its own, and for the league to move beyond the "gee-whiz-look-at-the-girls-play-football" stage and into a spectator attraction viewed for its own special qualities. And he wanted reporters to cover the players and the games like they would any other sport: fairly and without comparing them to the NFL. In order to accomplish that goal, Mathews avoided turning the league into a battle of the sexes or a spectacle for male viewers like "women's wrestling or roller derby." He firmly believed that women could become professional sports stars in their own right, and in football, in particular. We see that today with the popularity and success of Megan Rapinoe of the United States Women's National Soccer Team (USWNT), Serena Williams in tennis, and Candace Parker and Sue Bird in the WNBA.

Mathews was ahead of his time in that regard, but not many people cared to listen back then. The majority of the sports media landscape wasn't ready to comply or embrace women's football or the players in earnest, and coverage of the NWFL varied from potshots and satirical articles to a few legitimate features on the teams and certain players. There was no consistent game coverage for most teams, other than a box score or a brief recap of a game here or there. As the years wore on from the official start of the league in 1974, the curiosity and novelty of women's football fizzled and sports editors and reporters deemed that it was no longer a newsworthy, "page-turning" topic.

This must be viewed not as simply a lack of coverage. Rather, this is the example of a crucial flaw for all media, where failing to report on women in the sports world sends a message about the kind of world it believes should exist. Instead of helping to fan the flames of interest, sports media on the whole—by largely ignoring women's football or not taking the NWFL seriously—was a willing participant in snuffing out those very flames. As a direct result, newspaper articles written about the NWFL, teams, or players appeared sporadically, if at all. The history of this important league was being erased as it was happening, bringing the legacy it could someday have into question.

When newspapers did run stories about the league during its heyday, the majority of them were written with feigned interest or mocking intent. The *Detroit Free Press* once described the Detroit Demons as playing "bloody bad football" for a crowd who "after seeing one game, never returned."

The *Fort Worth Star-Telegram* also ran a feature on a game between the Detroit Demons and the Dallas Bluebonnets the prior season, and sportswriter Paul Rowan wrote a decent recap of the contest, complete with quotes from players and some fans. But whatever good intentions he may have had in writing a respectful article, his words were sullied by a large, offensive editorial cartoon that was placed directly in the middle of it. The cartoon featured a voluptuous woman dressed in a tight-fitting football uniform, with her hair done up and makeup on her thin and pointy, seductive face, and the "measurements" 36-24-36 printed across her chest in place of a regular jersey number, while another average-looking player stared at her with what could be interpreted as either envy or lust. The cartoon—a gross, sexist, stereotypical representation of women football players in every light—had absolutely nothing to do with the content of the article, not a single word. It was placed there simply to incite laughter and mock women athletes for the fun of it.

And yet, it wasn't an outlier. Male reporters, sportswriters, editors, and columnists often took what they saw on the football field as an invitation to poke fun at the players in headlines and in print, challenge the women players' football knowledge, comment on their looks and body type, or directly inquire about the players' breast equipment.

"How do you protect your breasts was a favorite question," Dandelion Susan Hoxie recalled. "Back then there was a theory going around that if you got hit in the breast, it would cause cancer. Or if women ran long distances, their uterus would fall out." According to Houston Herricanes quarterback Gwen Flager, one male reporter felt so emboldened that he got up right underneath center during practice as he was filming a segment for a local news story. "I bet the Houston Oilers wouldn't have let him do that," she said. Another time, a reporter came up to her to ask a question and said blatantly, "Can you call a play? Call a play." Flager was so taken aback, she didn't know how to respond.

The sexism in the media was not helped by the hyperfeminized names that some of the teams had. "Some dolls say 'mama' when punched or prodded, but not these dolls," read a story in the *Daily Oklahoman*. "I don't know why they called us the Dolls, but at least it wasn't the Dandelions," said Mary BlueJacket. "Who would want to be called a Dandelion?" Not to mention, "the Babes."

o————o

Absurd questions, teasing headlines, zingers, and unbridled focus on the women's ability, physicality, and looks were commonplace, especially as women's football appeared in the public eye. "What's this? Mascara above those two big brown eyes peeking out from behind the facemask on that gold helmet? Polished nails on that dainty hand extending from that dirt-caked jersey?" read a piece written by Glenn Esterly for the Women's News Service wire. "Don't worry, though, the Boys in the Band haven't invaded the locker room, it's just [Dandelion] Charlotte Raff," he added, throwing a side of homophobia in with his sexism, in a reference to the 1968 play *The Boys in the Band*, which was about a group of gay men and featured a cast of largely out gay actors. A 1974 story in the *Fort-Worth Star Telegram* called a game between the Shamrocks and Bluebonnets "a hen party with helmets, a gabfest with cleats."

Gail Dearie, who played for the New York Fillies in 1972, was eagerly plucked from the tree of Fillies and put front and center by the media not just because of her looks. It was also the social conundrum she appeared to encapsulate—a feminine beauty, married mother of two, who was athletic and tough enough to play tackle football. Dearie welcomed the attention because it essentially provided free advertising for the Fillies.

And, although she was gracious during interviews, she was not blind to the media's intentions. That's why she often answered their off-color questions with a splendid mix of confidence and sass.

"I enjoy a bit of Jekyll and Hyde. One night I might play a great game," Dearie once quipped to the *New York Daily News*. "Then the next night, if a man whistles at me, it's fun to know I can probably kick a football further than he can."

Dearie admitted to feeling guilty about being singled out from her teammates. She never asked for it, she said, and it was a line she was forced to straddle because the media put her in that position—the same position that many women athletes still face today, not just in the press but on social media—where she was judged by her looks first and her athletic ability second. The opening paragraph in a 1974 feature story about Dearie in the *Daily Register* says it all: "Take a hand-span waistline, soft blonde hair, the whitest of teeth and deepest of eyes, high cheekbones, a silky voice, a darting mind, grace and wit . . . and you have that improbable young woman, Gail (Mrs. Donald H.) Dearie, a professional football player." Dearie was described by her looks first, mental capabilities second, and her athletic achievements last, with her husband's name mentioned alongside her own, as if he had anything to do with them.

"Long ago, I came to grips with the fact that I am who I am," said Dearie, who now lives in Florida. "I have athletic ability. I have, if you want to call it 'looks' or something. You don't have to play that down because you want to be feminine. My husband will always say, look—she was the forerunner of women feeling unashamed of their athletic ability."

Bluebonnets quarterback Barbara O'Brien suffered a similar fate. Her good looks and feminine appearance made her a press favorite, including having her name featured in the headline of a *New York Times* piece on the league. The hyperfocus frustrated O'Brien, who understood football to be a team sport and wished that other Bluebonnets players received some of the recognition. One paper called her a "lass." When her teammates did receive their own recognition, it was often to contrast their looks with O'Brien's—particularly when it came to Bobbie Grant, known as Super Sugar. In photos run alongside each other in the *Dallas Morning News*, 5'9", 165-pound O'Brien—who is white—is shown kicking the ball with the caption, "Barbara O'Brien can't punt a lick without lipstick," while 5'11", 265-pound lineman Grant—who is Black—is shown standing on the sidelines above the words, "Go ahead! YOU tell Bobbie Grant her seams are crooked."

Often when Grant was featured in the media, the coverage was fat-shaming and cruel and always mentioned how much she weighed. In one photo, Grant is shown from behind while she sits on the bench, perpetuating the "headless fatty" trope—a term coined in 2007 by Dr. Charlotte Cooper to describe the dehumanizing trend of press photos of fat people's bodies that crop out their faces. Under Grant's photo it says, "EVER HEAR OF WEIGHT WATCHERS? Most of Dallas' defensive front wall Sunday was occupied by Bobbie Grant. Ms. Grant, looking like the 'before' half of a Weight Watchers ad, packs a tidy 265 pounds on her 5'11" frame." In another, she's called the "female Bubba" (a comparison to NFL lineman Bubba Smith) while shown jogging alongside teammate Willie Johnson, whom the caption calls "a svelte 130-pounder."

Johnson was small, at five feet three inches, which meant reporters focused on how little they thought she looked like a football player. The mother of three is quoted as saying the exercise helped her slim down, and she is referred to as "dainty" and "a pretty little thing." The preoccupation with women's weight is a theme that appears throughout coverage of the league. A 1982 article about Columbus Pacesetters player Pam Jansons assures the public that playing football has not made her big and bulky: "Her weight is nearly the same as when she began playing" although she "took off some weight but put back on muscle." The piece also goes out of its way to describe Jansons as a "tall, lithe young woman" who "moves with a grace that could make you think [she] would be at home in the latest fashioning evening gown, with a copy of *Harper's Bazaar* under her arm."

These characterizations reveal deep and century-long anxieties about women who played sports, a fear that they were hypermasculine and that athletics would make them undesirable to men. These paternalistic fears were rooted in homophobia, which ties into another trope that filled media coverage of the league. While players like Dearie and O'Brien dealt with the societal paradox of being both aesthetically pleasing and a good football player, others dealt with the assumption that because of their athleticism, they must be lesbians. "Being small has kept me from being labeled a dyke," Dandelion Sue Davidson told the *Los Angeles Times* in 1974.

Even so, most of the girls aren't big, "butchy" types. They're not amazons. You do find maybe a little more lesbianism in girls' sports in general, but it's negligible. People blow it out of proportion because they're already looking for it; they want to label you. Women athletes on and off the field are usually a little more aggressive than non-athletes, and aggressiveness is generally thought of as a masculine trait. So, if being aggressive is being masculine, then, OK, we're more masculine than the average woman. But we're talking about massive stereotyping, the kind of thing we, in 1974, should be getting away from.

"Men assumed we wouldn't be any good, that we weren't going to hit hard. Women assumed we were a bunch of butch, lesbian women," recalled Dandelion Susan Hoxie. "It was assumed that all female athletes were lesbians. I had a terrible time dating because guys assumed it would be a waste of time. It was part of the perception, especially if women were playing football." To Hoxie, the stereotype was ridiculous and didn't make sense. She once told NBC News: "Football's no more any less feminine than getting down on your hands and knees and scrubbing the kitchen floor, cleaning greasy ovens or changing the baby's diaper."

Hoxie's teammate, Joyce Johnson, thought it was good that the media focused on some of the more feminine-looking players, because then it took away from the speculation about their sexuality, she reasoned. "Yeah, they are going to focus on the more attractive people in their mind. Which wasn't a bad thing," she said. "Then people didn't think it was just a whole group of, to put it one way, lesbians out there banging heads. We had everybody. We had straight, gay, moms, grandmas, you name it we had it. Everybody just wanted to play. It wasn't to prove a point or anything like that."

It seemed no matter how many times Johnson and others emphasized that all they wanted to do was play football, the media had a hard time believing them. They couldn't understand how the women of the NWFL could put so much time and effort, with little to no pay or recognition, into a brutal endeavor like football simply because they loved it. And it blinded them from writing the kind of stories the players and the league deserved.

Instead, the media focused on other things, like the feminist movement that was so popular at the time and its direct impact on the growth of women's sports. According to Andrew D. Linden, an assistant professor of sport studies at California State University Northridge whose research focuses on football and social movements in the 1970s, many of the players did not particularly identify with the women's movement that was going on at the time.

"The sportswriters were just trying to sell their paper and some of them made fun of it. We were just athletes who wanted to play ball," Dandelion Rose Low said. "We weren't out on a mission for women's lib or anything like that, we just wanted to play." Even still, the second-wave feminist movement did, in fact, pave the way for these women to be on the gridiron.

Essentially, the NWFL existed because the timing was right. "It's Billie Jean King becoming a cultural icon [with] the Battle of the Sexes in 1973. Title IX passed [in 1972], the fight for the passage of the Equal Rights Amendment was constantly in the press," said Linden. This push for gender equality in sports was unprecedented, and opened the door for a league like the NWFL.

o———o

Not all of the stories and articles written about the NWFL throughout its existence came from a place of skepticism or mockery. Though few and far between, there were some thorough game recaps that focused specifically on the plays of the game itself and discussed which players stood out and did well. There were also a few features that dared to go deeper than the surface questions of whether the women were making a feminist statement or how they were going to protect their breasts when they played.

Victoria Billings of the Copley News Service wrote about Barbara Patton of the Dandelions. At the time the article ran, Patton was thirty-two years old and well into her second season with the team. As a working mother separated from her husband, she was known for bringing her two young children with her to practices and games, as well as being outspoken and jovial with the press. Billings painted Patton in true form as both a professional football player and a dedicated mother. "Critics say the Dandelion players would meet their match in a boys' junior varsity team from high school," Billings wrote. "But Barbara Patton says pound for pound women can be as mean as men. When she storms onto the field against National Women's Football League rivals there's one thought on her mind. 'I want to kill them,' she says." The article was picked up by a handful of different newspapers around the country, from the *Cincinnati Enquirer* to the *Alabama Journal*, and readers across the nation were unwittingly introduced to one of the most charismatic players on the Dandelions squad.

A 1974 background piece on the Detroit Demons and their quest for legitimacy in a historic sports city like Detroit is another exemplary article. Written by Nancy Woodhull of the *Detroit Free Press*, the article delved into the Demons' humble beginnings as the Detroit Fillies—a team that was assembled a few years prior, during the latter part of the Sid Friedman era—and the dispute between the team's previous owners and players that ultimately led to the Demons taking over their own team, and expressing their desire to be taken seriously. "This year, the Demons cling tenaciously to their new jerseys (second-hand [Detroit] Lions' practice shirts) and a new coach, Chuck Moeser, husband of a linebacker," Woodhull wrote. "The women say they are wiser now, that backers won't have any say in how the team is run."

Houston sportswriter and television commentator Anita Martini, who had helped Marty Bryant get the word out about the Herricanes' first tryout when the team started, was an ardent media supporter throughout the Herricanes' tenure. As a woman in sports media, Martini knew the obstacles they were up against firsthand, and like the women of the NWFL, she too broke down barriers. In October 1974, after a National League championship game between the Los Angeles Dodgers and the Houston Astros, Martini became the first woman in sports media to enter a male locker room to conduct a postgame interview with the players. In a 1975 interview with *Sports Illustrated*, she expressed her disappointment at not being offered a national broadcasting in baseball job due to sexism in the sports media industry. "What burns me is the networks are looking for women to accomplish something their men haven't done yet," Martini said. "I'm not capable of doing a perfect game, but neither is any man."

And in 1978, *Houston Post* sportswriter David Casstevens wrote an extensive feature about the Houston Herricanes. He attended practice, then traveled with the Herricanes on their team bus to one of their away games. Casstevens went all in on writing a thoughtful, unbiased, captivating piece, portraying the Herricane players as legitimate athletes. "Sitting on the bus after the game, waiting to leave the dark, deserted stadium, the Herricanes didn't care about their routine aches and pains and sprains," Casstevens wrote in the concluding paragraph. "Or the fact that they'd have to be back at their jobs come Monday morning. They had won. That's all that counted."

What made Casstevens's feature stand out from other typically reported pieces on women's football players was twofold: he respected them and took their women's football endeavor seriously, and he didn't assume to know anything about them simply from their appearance. His transparent approach showed in the article as well as to the players he interacted with during their road trip. "He was utterly awesome," Herricane Billie Cooper remarked.

o———o

During their second season of existence in 1977, the Herricanes were never asked to supply the franchise fee they hadn't paid to the NWFL the year before. Which was a blessing, because they had barely enough money to function as a team as it was. Still, they continued to participate in league play and became a true team in every sense of the word, not just on the gridiron but off the field as well. Bryant believed that riding together on the bus to away games gave everyone an opportunity to get to know each other better, connect and bond on a deeper level. She said it sometimes felt like a scene from *A League of Their Own*, the 1992 box office hit featuring the women of the All-American Girls Professional Baseball League. They played cards, talked about their lives and

troubles, slept, read books. Everyone on the Herricanes came from different sports backgrounds, including soccer, rugby, softball, and others.
Some were married, some were not. Some had kids, some did not. Some
were younger, others were older. "I never saw anyone doing each other's
nails or anything like that," Bryant joked. "It was just all kinds of women
coming together for a common goal."

For Schulte, the best part of being a Herricane was spending time together after the game ended:

> We'd sit around and either celebrate our victory or drown our misery, you
> know? I actually enjoyed the long bus rides the most. Because that's where
> I got to know people. I was not much of a sleeper on the bus, and we'd take
> off at midnight on a Friday night, make that trip up to Oklahoma [City], or
> Tulsa, and learn about how different their lives were from mine. Talking to
> people who weren't like you, didn't grow up like you. Me being a kid who
> grew up in a country town, you know, I didn't know about other ways of
> life. And so it was quite an eye-opener for me, in some cases. It made me
> realize how many different kinds of people there are in the world.

It's important to remember that the league was viewed through the
lens of the people writing about it, not those who were living it. Most of
those writers were men. The questions they asked the players were not
neutral; they were a reflection of their ideas about sports and who should
be playing them, about women who broke societal rules. It's why so many
of the women were asked if they were "libbers," why their marital status was asked after and reported back in the press, why reporters wanted
to know what their boyfriends or husbands thought about them playing football. Some reporters even wholesale made up quotes. Jan Hines,
the quarterback for the Dolls, remembers newspaper articles including
quotes attributed to her that she never said, from reporters she'd never
spoken with. She never pushed back, though, because they were just so
grateful to be getting any press coverage at all.

Knowing this context brings up larger questions about the history we
think we know. If Hines were not around to correct the record, as researchers and archivists, we would assume that the information reported

in the papers was accurate. But aside from the box scores and game recaps, which the reporters generally did well and got correct since they were sports reporters with the skills to write a good gamer, it's hard to know which other parts of the stories are true. The people writing them were largely not equipped to cover sports through a political or feminist lens, or to understand the ways in which their biases colored their work.

History is generally told by the people in power or through the lens of the status quo; the stories written about the NWFL are no different. We don't always know what the players really thought about their experience because their quotes are so shaped by the leading or loaded questions being asked by the reporters—if the quotes are true at all.

Tulsa Babes quarterback Cindy Turner once had a particularly prickly encounter with a reporter from the *Tulsa World* before a game. "[He asked], 'Why are you even doing this?' I looked at him and said, 'Have you ever played football?' He said no. I said, 'Don't ask me another thing about it.' It really ticked me off," Turner explained. "Another thing he asked me—if I thought I could hit as hard as a man. I said, no I couldn't. Then he asked me, 'Why are you doing it then?' I said, 'Because I like football. I like sports.' It wasn't a feminism thing, it wasn't us trying to show that we could do what the guys could, because we knew we couldn't. But we were having fun. We liked football. Whoever was out there liked football. We weren't trying to prove anything to anybody, except ourselves. We liked the game, that's it."

A 1974 story in the *Cincinnati Enquirer* by sports reporter Jack Murray insulted the athletes while making sexist quips and jokes about sexual harassment. "Instead of throwing a frying pan at the wall, these women and teenage girls let off steam on the playing fields," Murray wrote of the Columbus Pacesetters. He called them "unladylike," printed a quote from a man in the stands insulting his wife by saying the only thing women can do better than men is argue, mocked the assistant coach's wife for not knowing the names of the positions, spending several paragraphs on her misspeaking, before ending the story with a quote about a male photographer trying to enter the locker room: "I think he's got evil ideas," one of the women said. "That's okay. We'll tackle him if he tries anything."

Several papers also sent reporters to practice or scrimmage with teams, again turning the game into a gimmick. The idea, of course, was that any male reporter embedding with a team would be dominant, and that any female reporter putting on pads would show that the play was so easy that anyone could do it.

Judy Fossett, a reporter for the *Sunday Oklahoman* magazine was allowed four plays worth of playing time at left tackle during the Oklahoma City Dolls' first game against the Shamrocks, a position Hal felt would allow her to "get some real action without a lot of technical skill and without getting hurt too bad." Afterward, Fossett declared that "Playing football is better than winning Miss America." In a 1972 article in the *Toledo Blade*, two male journalists recounted their experience scrimmaging with the Troopers: "George Plimpton has it all wrong—if you want to find out about professional football, you don't play with men, you play with women."

Much like the way mainstream media coverage of women's sports functions today, when it came to drawing attention to on- or off-the-field drama, plenty of outlets were more than happy to write about the NWFL and the teams whenever there was negativity to report. General Manager Robin Massey and the Houston Herricanes felt this firsthand.

In early 1978, a Houston male soccer team launched as a new franchise under the name Hurricanes. The *Herr*icanes were not thrilled. "When we formed our team, we did everything we were supposed to do," said Massey. "We filed protection on the name—did everything an organization should do to protect us financially. Then a couple of years into it, a professional soccer team came in and took our name." The Herricanes told the new Hurricane team that although the two names were spelled differently, they could still be mistaken for the other. They decided to take the male soccer team to court, to cease and desist using the name and to get them to change it to something else. And they hired two female lawyers who agreed to take on the case pro bono. Once the lawsuit was announced, the media leapt on it.

In February 1978, the Associated Press ran a blurb about the lawsuit, and it was picked up by countless daily newspapers across the country under a variety of satirical, condescending headlines, such as "Madder

Than a Wet Herricane," "Mad at Hims Over Name" and "Silly Season." "The Herricanes want the professional men's soccer team to give up the name Hurricane," the blurb read. "In effect, the state district court claims the women had the Herricane name before the Hurricane team formed last month."

It wasn't a "claim." The Herricanes had already been established as a women's football team for two years before the men's soccer team came along. But the AP and other media outlets didn't bother to acknowledge that important tidbit of information.

One month later, the Herricanes got their day in court. And after the long task of presenting sides, the judge ruled. "[He] sided with the men's team," Massey said. "His reasoning was that nobody would surely confuse a women's football team with a man's soccer team. Needless to say, we weren't happy." The Herricanes were denied exclusive rights to a name they had already been using for the better part of two years.

Ironically, on the same day she returned home from the courthouse, Massey found a bill in her mailbox from a sporting goods store. It was for the cost of thirty jock supporters.

"I thought, well isn't this something," she said crisply. "We're already being confused with the male soccer team. I called [the store] and said, I'm sorry but the women's football team doesn't use jock supports. And I wish I had gotten it a day earlier. I would have taken it to court with me and we might have won the case."

The outcome of the court case discouraged the players, but the Herricanes moved on. Massey said the media coverage from the name lawsuit was the most press they had ever received. It was a slap in the face for a women's team in a women's league that wasn't getting the consistent press they needed to help draw in fans and bring attention to women's football. And it showed in the empty stands.

CHAPTER 14

TALES OF REDEMPTION

"First the good news: Lawton is apparently going to have a professional football team," read the 1977 story in the *Lawton Constitution*. "Now, girls, the bad news: instead of those rugged, virile, hairy-legged bruisers whom we enjoy watching on television, these players are going to be wearing perfume."

The Lawton Tornadoes' plan was to spend a year getting in game shape and enter the NWFL at the start of the 1978 season. In order to do that, the already established and very dominant Dolls would need to help them drum up interest. Members of the OKC team traveled to Lawton in August that year to attend the first organizational meeting of the Tornadoes, where more than thirty interested women showed up to find out more about the league and the soon-to-be Lawton franchise. At that point, midway through their 1977 season, the Dolls were 6–0.

Later that month, the Dolls were back in Lawton to play a game against the Herricanes at Cameron Stadium in front of twenty-five hundred fans to give people a sneak peek at women's football. They would remain undefeated when the game was over. The *Lawton Constitution* noted that the Dolls put in a "very workmanlike performance" and "did not fumble the pigskin all evening"—though they did draw 70 yards in penalties in the first half alone. The major difference was in the running game: the Dolls rushed for 270 yards while the Herricanes managed only 93. Oklahoma City won by a final score of 34–6, with Houston's only points coming on a touchdown pass from Flager to receiver Janice Merritt. Houston's determination to finally beat OKC only grew as they failed yet again to come away victorious.

The Dolls' thrashing of the Herricanes on Lawton's turf was a preview of what fans could expect when their Tornadoes took the field. The Tornadoes poached some of the Dolls' top talent, including Pebble Myers, Cindee Herron, Cathie Schweitzer, Melissa Barr, and Terri Talley. Lawton's first game was against the Shamrocks, which they won; in just their second game, they met the Dolls on the Tornadoes' home turf. Playing against their former team was tough for some of the players, though, and the Dolls were victorious in their first meeting—a theme that would continue during the Tornadoes' two seasons. They never managed to pull out a win over the World Champion Dolls. Cindee Herron credits Dolls quarterback Jan Hines with much of the Oklahoma City team's success.

o———o

The formation of the Lawton team would also offer a chance for redemption for a family who felt the Dolls had done them wrong. Dee Herron missed coaching football after he'd been suddenly and unceremoniously fired from the Dolls midgame during their inaugural season (or quit, depending on whom you ask). He'd only gotten to do it for half a season, which hadn't been nearly long enough to satisfy him. His wife, Cindee, missed it, too. She'd been elated when she scored the Dolls' first touchdown in the NWFL, stunned to receive the game ball after they'd taken down the supposedly unbeatable Troopers. Having to leave in the middle of the season because Hal Reynolds had a temper tantrum had been a disappointment for both Herrons. So when their phone rang one day in 1977 and Pebble Myers, their former Dolls' teammate, was on the other end with a proposal, the Herrons were immediately interested.

Myers had been a star running back for the Dolls, coming within a few yards of matching Linda Jefferson for rushing yards one season. But after the 1977 season with the team, she didn't want to return because tensions among the players had become too much for her. Herron was a good coach, the best one she knew, and there were a few other women who had gotten fed up with the Dolls, too, but didn't want to give up playing. Plus, the commute to practices was long for some of the women and was beginning to wear on them. (Though to hear Mike Reynolds tell it, Herron poached his Dolls players by feeding them the lie that the Reynolds brothers were making money off of them.)

Myers's dad, Dwight "Corky" Myers, had invested money to start a new team in Lawton, Oklahoma, about an hour and a half southwest of OKC. Lawton was a military town, with Fort Sill Army Base located there, and the owners hoped to bring in fans from the community. They'd be called the Tornadoes and would wear black and goldenrod uniforms (owner Neil Laughy said they considered the name "Lawton Ladies" but thought they could too easily be confused for sex workers). They would enter the Southern Division, alongside the San Antonio Flames, the Houston Herricanes, the DFW Shamrocks, the Tulsa Babes, and, of course, the Oklahoma City Dolls. Were the Herrons interested in coming on board to challenge their old team? You bet they were.

The Tornadoes finished their first season with a 4–4 record, and over fifty women came out for the 1979 team, nearly double the number they'd had the first year. By 1979, interest in the league was dwindling, though not from the players. Throughout the NWFL's run, there were always women eager for a chance to play football; it was the fans and owners who gave up on the venture. During a game between the two teams that season in Taft Stadium in Oklahoma City, the crowd was described as a number "large enough to cause a mild traffic jam but probably not enough to turn a profit" and estimated at around five hundred to one thousand people. It was the second game of the Tornadoes' second season—they'd beaten the Herricanes to open it—and the Dolls won handily 30–6. It was the Dolls' tenth straight win, having come off an undefeated 1978 season, and the Tornadoes were no match for them.

Myers, one of the best running backs in the league, played only one season for Lawton. She got hurt in a dog pile on the field when someone twisted her ankle while her leg was sticking out from the pile; her knee gave out and effectively ended her football career. Without money pouring in, the male owners of the Tornadoes decided to fold the team.

o———o

Throughout their entire tenure as a team, the Herricanes had one main focus when it came to the football field: beating the Oklahoma City Dolls. For four long seasons, the Dolls had pummeled and pounded the Herricanes game after game, and tossed them around the field like rag dolls.

But as the Herricanes gained more experience and grew stronger together as a team, they began to put up a fight. By the 1979 season, the Dolls weren't steamrolling the Herricanes on their way to multiple touchdowns as easily as they had before. They'd also lost some of their veteran players, like kicker Mary BlueJacket and halfback Doris Stokes. "OKC was the strongest team, and we always had problems with them," said Jane Schulte. "I always got up a little bit more when we played that team, because I'd think—*Are we going to beat them? Is this the year? Is this the time? Is this the game?*"

The Herricanes knew the only way they could win against Oklahoma was if they could keep the Dolls offense from doing what it did best: scoring a ton of points. That meant the Herricanes had to play tough and stout defense from start to finish and keep Dolls running back Frankie Neal in check. It was a lofty task, considering the Dolls were known for their offensive prowess and ability to run up the score on opponents. But it wasn't impossible. The Troopers had bested Oklahoma more than a few times. And while the Herricanes weren't as good as the Troopers, they weren't as bad as the Tulsa Babes, either. They knew they had enough talent on their roster to get a win against their longtime rival. But they'd need to play a perfect game.

In early September 1979, it finally happened. The Herricanes beat the Dolls in a gritty, low-scoring battle in the end-of-the-summer heat that left every single player on the field thoroughly exhausted. "It was blooming hot in Oklahoma for that game," said Billie Cooper. "We played at night but it was still hot. There was no breeze. You could feel your warm breath coming in and out of you."

For Cooper and the rest of the Herricanes defense, it was the hardest-fought defensive game they had ever played. "They were double-teaming me and I couldn't get loose," Cooper explained. "I hit Jan [Hines the quarterback] and knocked the ball loose [on one play]. That gave us a lift."

The Herricanes' goal was to keep the Dolls' offensive attack in the center of the field and box them in so the running backs and receivers couldn't break to the outside for a long gain. And it worked.

The Dolls were baffled by the Herricanes' level of physical play. "Every time we knocked them down, they got pissed," Cooper laughed. "They couldn't break a run or complete a pass, and they were getting frustrated."

When the whistle blew, signaling the end of the game, the scoreboard read 7–6. The Herricanes had finally done it. Not only had they beaten the Dolls, they had held them to one of the lowest-scoring games in the history of the Oklahoma franchise. It was the Dolls' first loss since the 1977 NWFL title game against the Troopers.

"I remember it was one of the best wins for our team," said Flager. "We had been so badly outscored by [the Dolls] our first year, losing by at least fifty points each game, that this felt like we had come into our own as a viable team in our division. While we had won other games, this was the big one. I suspect that the credit for the win needs to go to the defense. They played their best to keep [the Dolls] to six points."

The elation of such a grueling and hard-fought win was short lived. One week later on September 22, 1979, the Herricanes played the Dolls again and this time it was for the Southern Division Championship.

The game plan was the same for the Herricanes—play tough defense and keep Oklahoma out of the end zone. But the Dolls had adjusted their own game plan and knew how to attack the Herricanes' defense scheme differently this time around. It was a back-and-forth game, with both teams trading a pair of touchdowns. Following a Herricanes punt early in the fourth quarter, the Dolls marched sixty-nine yards down the field and took the lead, 21–14. They added another touchdown and put the game away, 28–14.

The Dolls walked away with yet another win, and the Herricanes just walked away. It would be the last game they would ever play together as a team. The financial problems that had dogged them since the start of the franchise in 1976 had finally caught up with them.

"[We] were paying for things game to game," explained Robin Massey. "The gate fees from one game had to pay for the next stadium. We were barely able to get a bus and a hotel for the away games. And oftentimes, the girls paid for their own meals. Other teams had the same problem. When we'd go to San Antonio or Tulsa, we'd see the same things. They were going through the same struggles as we were."

The hope, Massey said, was to get to a point where the team made enough money to be able to give some back to the players or at least cover their meals on road trips. But throughout her time as general manager with the Herricanes (until 1978), that never happened. The Herricanes eventually ran out of money, and after the 1979 season, they ceased operation.

"We did not end the team very well," said Cooper. "They just kind of said, we're folding because of the money situation. We never had a last gathering. Never had that closure. I understand that the money situation was tough, because it was—very, very tough. It cost a lot of money to transport, set up games, even at home. To give you an idea, one stadium was $2,500 a night. I don't know about you, but back then $2,500 was a lot of change."

"I think the only thing the Herricanes could have done differently is find a millionaire to support them," said Peggy Hickman, who played for the Herricanes from 1977 to 1979. "It was really all about not having the money to continue. If we would have found the money and the backing, we would have all wanted to be out there." Herricane Brenda Cook agreed. "It would have been so much better if we could just show up and not have to worry about paying for the bus trip," she said. "Even though the practices might have been tough, when you are doing what you enjoy doing, it's possible. You don't see it as being a pain. That would have been better if we didn't have to worry about the finances. That would have been nice, if we could have had a sponsor or two."

When Marty Bryant first started the Herricanes in 1976, she never envisioned the team would last as long as it did or that it would become a family. The experiences they shared together, both on and off the football field for four seasons, left an indelible mark. And if they had had the financial means, the team might have lasted longer than that it did.

"There wasn't enough money to function on, to pay for fields, anything," Bryant said. "It wasn't that we didn't want to play anymore. The team was interested. Financially, it was not feasible." She was envious of other teams that had more money to operate, like Oklahoma City, though appearances were deceiving; the Dolls weren't much better off financially than the Herricanes. It wasn't for a lack of trying. The Herricanes worked tirelessly to find sponsors and bring in more funding. But companies weren't investing in women's sports, let alone women's football.

There was nothing more the team could do but disband. Bryant and the rest of the players moved on. They had no idea that other teams were wrestling with the same dilemma—keep struggling along or fold—or that the NWFL was in a financial hole itself and was beginning to come apart.

Brenda Cook, Brant Hopkins, and Baby Murf, Houston Herricanes
January 1979, Safety Valve, published monthly by Houston Natural Gas Corp., original photo
provided by Brenda Cook, Houston Herricanes

PART V

THE DOWNFALL OF THE NWFL (1979–1988)

WHEN WE PLAYED OUR LAST GAME, WE DIDN'T EVEN KNOW IT WAS OUR LAST. IT WAS SAD.

—JAN HINES, OKLAHOMA CITY DOLLS

CHAPTER 15

CRACKS IN THE FOUNDATION

"**Y**ou look at women's tennis, the WNBA—put women in front of it and all of a sudden it's a whole other demon. And nobody wants to support. You can't get sponsors, you can't get investors, you can't get underwriters—like, why not?" Herricane Gwen Flager mused. "Obviously, things have changed, but good gravy it's been forty years and we're still banging on that door. If we had had Nike or even a sporting goods store in town to back us, gosh anybody, one of the football players on the [Houston] Oilers, anybody, to say, yeah—let's support these women. Where would we be? None of that was available."

Money and sponsors, or lack thereof, was a consistent problem for the NWFL. In 1975, a year after the league initially launched, the founders raised the franchise fee to $25,000—up $15,000 from the original fee of $10,000, which San Diego Lobos owner John Mulkey Jr. had just paid that spring—in order to raise additional capital. Bob Mathews and the other owners were hoping the league would continue to expand. "We are hoping to add a team from San Jose; there is a new one starting in San Antonio, Texas, and Philadelphia and Chicago are getting ready to organize teams," Mathews told *Élan*, the East Los Angeles College magazine, in 1976. "We eventually plan on 27 teams across the country, which includes 12 on the West Coast."

But those additional twenty-seven teams never materialized. The teams that the NWFL already had barely had enough money to function themselves. The model of having a holding company that owned the team and supporting it with a booster club ultimately proved unsustainable for the Toledo Troopers. And they were not the only team supporting themselves with ad sales and raffle ticket promotions.

And yet, this holding company model is the one that many women's teams today continue to have to rely on. Many of the women currently playing in semipro, full-contact football leagues in the United States hustle for sponsorships, beg for community support, and still end up paying out of their own pocket in order to play the game they love.

Each team goes about it differently. Collette, who scraped by for years to play for the Troopers and now co-owns the Toledo Reign of the Women's Football Alliance, says the team's players get sponsors, and they also host fundraisers. "One is called 'Fan Shirt Club,'" she told Bustle.com. "We design T-shirts for friends and family, and they get $5 off their player's fee for every shirt they sell." Reign players also work the county fair in exchange for money to go back toward their team fees.

In the seventies, Stout and the Troopers were convinced that if they could hang on long enough, be good enough, and tell enough people about their on-field product, eventually the money would come. They were depending on Title IX and society catching up with what they were doing, trusting that the public was on the verge of being ready for something progressive like a women's football league. In 1977, the *Toledo Blade* predicted that "the struggle for women's grid proponents is on the eve of being erased." "Big bucks will come, in time," wrote Pam Royse in a 1978 game program. "But until that time, it's up to all women not to sell themselves or women's football short."

But Stout and his team are also an example of what NWFL teams were up against. The Troopers had done everything right in setting up a holding company and an organizational structure, were quite literally the best team in the world at what they did, and had a lot of support from the local media. The *Toledo Blade*'s Tom Loomis was a major supporter of the Troopers, as was legendary Toledo sportscaster Orris Tabner, who was even on the Toledo Troopers Board of Directors. And they still couldn't sustainably finance a team. Sheer will and determination alone are not enough to run a football league if you can't get fans in the seats and large entities to bankroll the cost.

o———o

As professional and as legitimate as Bob Mathews tried to make the league appear when he first helped launch the NWFL in 1974, even then, there were signs of instability lingering just below the surface. In reality, Mathews and the other founders were unprepared to take on such a groundbreaking endeavor. And this was because—just like Sid Friedman before them—they were too focused on grand, long-term goals, instead of taking the necessary baby steps to make the NWFL viable and sustainable in the short-term. They were essentially trying to sell a house on curb appeal alone, without fixing it up on the inside, and there were too many cracks in the foundation.

Those cracks—poor organization, insufficient funds, and lack of media and fan support—only grew wider and more apparent as time went on. "Being an athletic director [now], I think they needed some women in the room to figure it out," Dandelion Rose Low said of the league. "I don't think they had the knowledge because they were businessmen and not athletic administrators. So, they didn't have that mindset."

From the very start, there was a lack of communication within the league itself. Other than the first executive session meeting held in September 1974, there's little to no information that indicates the league ever convened as an organization again throughout its entire tenure. It's as if the NWFL launched not so much as an official organization but as more of a general umbrella with each team functioning individually, under each team or owner's guidance.

"What made this league unique was that [the teams] were all locally franchised owned under individuals, who all came together under the NWFL umbrella," said Neal Rozendaal. "When you had the NWFL concept, you could have teams across the country and nationalize it. Anybody, anywhere who wanted to start a team essentially could. But that didn't necessarily benefit them."

Teams without an owner, like the Houston Herricanes, winged it as a group. After joining the NWFL in 1976, Marty Bryant said she never interacted with the league at all after she initially contacted the NWFL office about starting a team. She went about the business of getting a team together and setting up games on her own. And without regular communication from the league as a whole, keeping every team abreast of updates, information, and decisions was impossible. No one team knew what the other teams were doing, unless they played each other.

A consistent league-wide schedule is another crucial aspect of any sports league, so fans and media can make plans to attend games and keep track of their favorite teams. Yet, the NWFL didn't have one.

Mathews ambitiously released a "schedule" after the executive session meeting in 1974 before plans were actually in place to hold those games. It listed a slate of seven games to be played throughout September and October with a forthcoming list of November and December games to follow, yet most of the October games were never played at all. In 1975, the league "intended" to play a forty-game schedule and appointed a "special schedule" committee to help set up those games and bring that goal to fruition. Only about half of the games were played.

The league "needed a strong league headquarters somewhere," Demons coach Dan Adair says now, when reflecting on why the teams didn't ultimately succeed. "Each team ran things their own way. Had there been a centralized league office with people in there that knew how to do marketing, that knew how to do proper scheduling, fundraising . . . we might have been able to give this thing a go."

Without an organized schedule of any kind and no real guidance, NWFL teams played sporadically and were forced to publicize those games on their own dime. Some teams played more games than others, often repeatedly playing against a particular opponent that was closest to them geographically on the map. In 1975, the Los Angeles Dandelions played the San Diego Lobos at least four times, and the Toledo Troopers regularly squared off against the Detroit Demons and the Columbus Pacesetters.

Some players didn't even know that certain teams existed outside of their geographical radius and, even fifty years later, didn't know how many teams had been in the league at all. Mathews's explanation for this was he tried to "organize round-robin competition for local teams" to generate enough interest in the NWFL and women's football as a whole. Once that was accomplished, he had hoped to increase travel between teams located farther away and eventually hold a national championship game.

Although the NWFL did eventually have its first league championship game in 1976, the game wasn't based on any kind of playoff format where multiple teams had a shot to win the title. The Troopers and the Dolls were clearly the two best teams in the league. Both dominated the teams they played during the season, were full of talented players, and were two of the better-run organizations. As such, it only made sense to have them square off in the first official league championship game. The Troopers could also afford to fly the Dolls to Toledo, where the game was held.

Travel costs overall were a big financial impediment for the league. It cost the Dandelions almost twelve thousand dollars to bring the Bluebonnets to California for a game, which is why one time the teams decided to meet halfway and play in Albuquerque. And since it was far too expensive for the Dandelions to travel from Los Angeles halfway across the country to play the Troopers in Toledo, the Troopers—who averaged a paid attendance of thirty-five hundred to thirty-eight hundred fans—offered to help shoulder the cost of the trip. But the financial burden was one of the main reasons the Dandelions never actually played the Troopers, even though the two teams tried their best to make it happen.

Without the financial means necessary to fund the league, the NWFL was working on a shoestring budget. Every team owner in the league lost money, and teams without an owner had to raise funds themselves for travel, uniforms, equipment, and other necessities.

In 1977, the Columbus Pacesetters attempted to take control of their future by purchasing the team from SKW Enterprises, the Toledo corporation that owned it (SKW also owned the Troopers). The players and coaches formed the Ohio Professional Athletes, Inc. and pooled their money in order to make the purchase. Linda Stamps, who founded the team back in 1974, told the *Marion Star*: "I am sure we will have a better crack at determining our own direction by building our strengths, eliminating our weaknesses, and backing a winning team."

The move by the Pacesetters to buy their own team fits into a larger theme of players trying desperately to self-determine. The Detroit Demons had wrested control of their team away from Sid Friedman in order to join the NWFL when it launched, giving them the ability to dictate how the team would be run. But it came at great cost to the players; in 1975, even with a team budget of just $15,000, they lost $4,000. The next year, 1976, they operated on a $24,000 budget—one player put $8,000 of her own money toward that, while quarterback Bea Guzman threw in $6,000. They ended up losing $13,000 that season, even though it was their first with a winning record and five dedicated coaches on board to help them improve.

The Herricanes had always been player-owned, but it came at the expense of financial support or security. In the 1980s, a former Demon named Mary Lohrstorfer owned teams in both Battle Creek and Grand Rapids (and later, the Lansing Unicorns), single-handedly financing the NWFL in the state of Michigan through car washes and T-shirt sales. Stout and a bunch of other men had been in control of the Troopers' financial situation, making those players subject to the whims and decisions of their male owners.

It was the women on the field who set the records and won the championships. But they never saw any financial benefit from their talent. And they lacked even the agency to be able to make decisions about how the team would run—or when it would end.

o———o

Without television deals or steady media coverage on par with men's football to help spread and create interest, the flame of curiosity in women's football was starting to wane in California. Mathews was forced to reconcile with the fact that his ownership of the Dandelions franchise may have run its course. But the reality of his situation didn't stop Mathews from doing everything he could to try and save even more money than he was already trying to save.

To keep the team afloat, Mathews changed the Dandelions' status from professional to semiprofessional for the 1977 season, in order to get out of paying workman's compensation insurance, which had risen dramatically in cost in a single year from twenty-five hundred to sixteen thousand dollars. The move drives home how desperate Mathews must have been: He'd always been one of the owners most invested in his players and had a lot of respect for the women. He wouldn't have scrimped on insurance if he could have avoided it.

The Dandelions were not only playing without pay, they were now putting their bodies on the line without a safety net. If they got injured, their hospital or doctor bills would not be covered. Low, who was still with the Dandelions as one of the team's original members, was unaware of this but said she would have continued to play regardless. "I guess back then workman's comp did not have much meaning to me. All I knew was that I had medical coverage through my parents, and was just happy to play. I was so blessed not to have sustained any major injuries. Just bumps, bruises, and a few sprains."

Mathews's last-ditch effort to shore up costs by opting out of workman's compensation didn't end up making much of a dent in his expenses. And after losing money season after season, the Dandelions never getting a chance to really compete for an NWFL title, and investing his time and effort for five years in a row, he finally relented. Mathews sold the team at some point during or after the 1978 season to LA businessman Russell Molzahn. Mathews also relinquished his role as president of the NWFL.

Just like that, the aspirational vision Mathews once held for women's football and the future of the sport had vanished. After five years, he felt he had given all he could to the Dandelions and the NWFL. He had invested time and money, and tried his best. There was nothing more to do but walk away from both his team and the league. And that's what he did.

Most, if not all, of the original 1973 team moved on from the Dandelions as well. Johnson and Hoxie had left a few years prior, and Low—who had finished college and was ready to pursue a career in physical education in fall 1978—hung up her cleats, set down her helmet, and continued on with her life. The remaining Dandelions kept on playing under

Molzahn. But Molzahn was reportedly unhappy with the NWFL and how it functioned. There was the lack of a cohesive schedule and communication, as well as the inability to travel to play teams in the Eastern and Southern Divisions due to lack of funds. These failings frustrated Molzahn so much that he decided to break away from the NWFL and tried to start a spin-off league of his own.

Molzahn attempted to reorganize a women's football league primarily located in the California region, called the Western States Women's Professional Football League (WSWPFL). This was a strategy to address the financial constraints associated with travel, and also to combat and prevent the lack of communication issues that existed within a larger, more expansive league like the NWFL. If Mathews had given Molzahn any parting advice on running a franchise or an entire women's football league, Molzahn didn't listen or take it to heart.

"On paper, the WSWPFL was going to consist of the Dandelions, Hollywood Stars, Long Beach Queens, and Southland Cowgirls in California, and the Mesa American Girls, Phoenix Cowgirls and Tucson Wild Kittens in Arizona," wrote Neal Rozendaal in the *Women's Football Encyclopedia*. "Whether any of these teams actually got off the ground is unclear; no concrete evidence exists that any of these teams truly made the jump from planning stages to competitive play."

o———o

It's easy to look at the NWFL and point out all the reasons it didn't succeed. What none of that takes into account, however, is the usual trajectory of a professional sports league.

A bunch of men decided to start women's football teams in the hopes that they'd see a quick return on their investment. The only thing is, that was a preposterous idea from the start. It didn't make sense, not because the players were women, but because the initial decades of *any* professional sports ownership are financially bleak. The difference is that, historically, male owners have been willing to pour millions and millions of dollars into losing men's teams year after year. Meanwhile, men have shown themselves unwilling to make the same kind of "losing" investment in women's teams.

"There's just this tremendous gap between the emotional investment of the owners in men's sports and the emotional investment of owners in women's sports," said David Berri, coauthor of *The Economics of the Super Bowl*. "The [mostly] men who own these teams don't see women athletes the same way they see men athletes, and that's really the basic issue. So that's why we see the behavior where they're like, 'Well, I didn't make money in the first 10 or 20 years so I think it's a failure.'"

For example, the NFL began in 1920 and in the first decade of its existence, there were over forty teams. *Ninety percent of those teams failed.* "The NFL was a financial disaster the first ten years," said Berri. "Nobody wanted to watch professional football. And this is in a world where college football had been around for at least four or five decades and was actually quite successful."

A telling example of the way men are willing to invest in men's sports, even when they're losing money, is the NFL's Pittsburgh Steelers. The Rooney family formed the team in 1933, thirteen years into the NFL's existence, right in the middle of the Great Depression, in a league where almost everyone who had ever tried to start a team had failed. Not only did the Rooneys keep investing in this team, the team—like most others before it—was a total failure. It didn't win anything for forty years. For four decades, the Rooneys poured money into the Steelers and never got anything out of it. Even at a time when men's sports owners only cared about wins and losses over turning a profit, they didn't even have that. By the fall of 2020, however, the franchise was worth roughly $3 billion.

"Early on in men's sports history, the only thing that mattered [to the owners] was winning. They didn't care about profits," said Berri. "But when you look at the way we talk about women's sports, all they care about is profit. As if this is all just to make money, and that's not realistic that it would do that." The fact that most NWFL teams had crowd sizes in the thousands in their first several years was actually very good, and on par with what many NFL teams attracted in the first few years of their existence.

The reason it takes so long for a professional sports team to become financially successful is that, in order to have people invested in a team or a league, they need to identify as fans of that franchise. Simply creating a new team and telling people it exists is not enough to create that identification. You could take a college football player that people loved to root for when he attended a university, for example, and put him in a Chicago Bears uniform as part of the new National Football League. But if people have no connection to this new team or the new league, their allegiance will not follow that player. They don't know what a "Chicago Bear" is, so why would they want to watch one?

Contrast that with colleges and nations, which Berri says "both have built-in fan bases." A college can put on a sporting event and attract a crowd because the student body already exists, the alumni exist, and people are already emotionally attached to the institution. A nation can hold a sporting event and people are already emotionally attached—it's why the Olympics are so popular. Or consider the US Women's National Soccer Team, which has millions of fans and viewers, but when Megan Rapinoe puts on her OL Reign jersey and takes the field as part of the National Women's Soccer League, the fan base doesn't necessarily follow her. When you create an entity that never existed before and say, "This is the Chicago Bears" or "This is the Dallas Bluebonnets," people don't have any emotional attachment to that.

Most fandom is inherited from parents. It takes generations to build that out. It's really hard for adults to change their fandom; asking an adult to change who they root for would be equivalent to asking them to change their political party or change their religion. These things all have a similar emotional experience and attachment—people talk about religion or politics the same way they talk about sports. Rooting interests can often be irrational, based on habit and nostalgia, and it takes time to change someone's allegiance. This was time that the NWFL, like most women's sports leagues throughout history, was never given.

○――――○

Before Mathews sold the Dandelions, the writing was already on the wall. By 1977, they were a veteran outlet in the NWFL. But things were not as dandy as Mathews had hoped they'd be by his team's fifth season, and part of the reason for that was because he never fully learned how to use the press and the Dandelions' proximity to Hollywood to his advantage.

All the dreams and expectations that he had for his women's football team hadn't come to fruition, and, by now, Mathews was having a hard time convincing himself that they would. He wrestled with the blunt reality that his inability to lure enough fans to games on a regular basis was the main cause of his team's financial woes.

This failure was in spite of a few creative promotional attempts, which included everything from having his players appear in a commercial, on talk shows and game shows, in print ads, and other marketing gimmicks. Back in 1974, the Dandelions appeared in a Plymouth Duster car commercial featuring actress Judy Strangis from the television shows *Room 222* and *Electra Woman and Dyna Girl*. Low, Hoxie, Johnson, and others all appeared in the commercial, which featured a group of women practicing and playing football. The Duster, a fashionable sports car with a moonroof, could hold a lot in its expandable trunk—football equipment, too. It was only a thirty-second spot, but the players had fun doing it and were hoping it would lead to other things.

"The producers of the commercial wanted women playing football in the background," Susan Hoxie recalled. "They had seen us and wanted some of us to be extras, so a bunch of us signed up." For two days of work, Hoxie and the others were paid $120—more than they made in an entire season playing for the Dandelions. "We were hired because we were professional football players," Hoxie added. "But they had us doing stupid things like wearing different colored jerseys, some with helmets and pads, some without. And they had us hitting each other in really odd ways."

Hoxie still enjoyed it. It was the easiest money she ever earned, and spending a couple of days in North Hollywood Park with a few of her teammates, eating catered food and "soaking up the rays," made for a memorable experience. Seeing herself on television wasn't too bad, either. "In the beginning [of the commercial] there are two women in the background with white jerseys on, hitting each other with their arms essentially. The one on the left with the number 26 jersey on is Rose [Low]. I can't be sure, but I believe the other is me."

Being in California and so close to Hollywood, Mathews could have easily brokered additional commercials and numerous guest spots on television shows for the Dandelions, possibly even a movie. It could have been a promotional gold mine for the team by helping to foster interest and increase their visibility.

But Mathews had drawn a hard line in the sands of legitimacy and was too careful not to cross it. He had weighed many offers from local radio and television personalities who wanted to set up exhibition games between men's teams and the Dandelions but declined them all. Mathews wanted to maintain the integrity of women's football, and not turn it into some sideshow—even for publicity. "In order to get public acceptance, we are going to have to keep it straight," Mathews told the *Independent Press Telegram* in 1975. "We're trying to appeal to young families that enjoy football. Our biggest support is eventually going to come from college-level women who are becoming more and more involved in sports. The older people are a little bit against women playing football."

A circus act–like exhibition against an all-men squad was one thing, and Friedman had definitely used that novelty approach to his advantage before. But using the power of Hollywood to market your product to the masses would have been completely different and extremely beneficial for Mathews. This was especially true because the Dandelions were struggling at a time when most of the country didn't even know that women's football existed, and, yet, interest in women's sports was on the rise. Throughout his entire time in Los Angeles as the Dandelions owner, Mathews never considered the latter as a consistent promotional tool.

Eventually, Hollywood reached out on its own accord. But this was only after the NWFL had already begun to fall apart, and the majority of teams had folded. An advertisement looking for former Dandelions and San Diego Lobos players to be extras in a television movie ran in the *Los Angeles Times*. Former Dandelions Anne Strohecker Beebe and Joyce Johnson both replied to the ad and were chosen to participate in the film. They soon discovered that the movie, *The Oklahoma City Dolls*, was loosely based on the real-life Dolls team they had played against in the NWFL. For Beebe and Johnson, and other former players, it was a chance to experience something new and relive their pro football days, even if it was only to pretend. They also got to meet actress Susan Blakely, who played the lead role as the quarterback.

Dolls owners Mike and Hal Reynolds had signed a contract with Godmother Productions to make the film, which Columbia Pictures was in charge of shooting. Prior to the film contract, the team had been for sale, but the Reynoldses had no prospective buyers. Mike told the *Daily Oklahoman* that they could have sold the team if they had included the movie contract in the sales price but they "were not willing to do that." How much money they got for the rights to use their team's likeness is unclear, but the contract included "a set amount plus the lowest percentage you can get of the gross." This was because the real hope was that the movie would be such a success it would become a television series, which is where the real profit would be. The brothers were promised the movie would be serious about showing the women as legitimate athletes, and a production crew reportedly spent six weeks in Oklahoma City doing background research.

But the movie itself was not an accurate portrayal of women's football players, the Dolls, or how fiercely they played football on the field. In fact, many members of the actual Dolls team were furious about it—the male owners had sold their likeness, only for it to be made a mockery of and net the women no financial profit to boot. Kicker Mary BlueJacket called it "a sorry movie" and "thought it sucked." "It pissed me off," Charlotte Gordon said, and her teammate Doris Stokes agreed. Their biggest gripe was that it didn't feature any of the players themselves and that it wasn't true to their reality. As Stokes said: "They could have researched it better."

Instead, the movie fused together a Hollywood-esque mix of women's liberation with women's naivety about sports and football. This resulted in a lighthearted tale about a group of female factory workers who were tired of the inequality on the production line and decided to prove their worth by forming a women's football team. Ironically, Blakely had to have a male stunt double stand in for her during game scenes (Dolls owner Mike Reynolds in a wig). If the producers had taken the time to investigate the real backstory of the Dolls, they would have found a dozen or more plotlines and intriguing individual stories to go on. And maybe a few former NWFL players could have stood in for Blakely and thrown the ball around instead.

Had the media as a whole fully dedicated some time and resources and dove into the individual backgrounds of the players, they would have discovered countless narratives about players, what their motivations were, why playing football was so fulfilling, and what it offered them. And had they dug into the formation of the teams and the rivalries that developed on the field, they would have unearthed so much more. There are so many incredible stories about women's professional football and the NWFL that were never told, that rightfully belong in the women's sports history books alongside so many others. But due to the lack of dedicated coverage, articles, honest attention, and recorded words, the history of women's football and the NWFL remain invisible, unacknowledged, and predominantly unknown in today's sports world and beyond.

It has also made telling the league's story challenging. While the early years of the league and the teams received a lot of press coverage because of the novelty of women playing football, that coverage eventually dwindled as the fans in the stands did. The teams' beginnings are well documented but their endings are not, nor are the later years of the league.

Women were still taking the field, but the newspapers had stopped caring enough to write about it. If there's no one there to tell the story, did it ever happen at all?

CHAPTER 16

ONE LAST GASP

In the late 1970s, the NWFL was slowing down, though some teams soldiered on. The new decade, however, would serve as a dividing line between the five years it spent as a relatively robust league and the later years that players spent fighting tooth and nail to bring it back to life, refusing to give up on their dreams of playing professional football.

Throughout the league's existence, there were also a handful of teams that came and went as quickly as they had begun due to financial problems and lack of players. The Lawton Tornadoes, Tulsa Babes, and San Diego Lobos lasted only two seasons. The California Mustangs, San Antonio Flames, and Philadelphia Queen Bees barely lasted one full season (the Mustangs rebranded as the Earthquakes, and then reemerged later as the Pasadena Roses, but also didn't last). After the 1978 season, the NWFL lost a longstanding team in the Dandelions and with them, the Western Division. Even so, the league still had the top two marquee teams in the country: the Toledo Troopers and the Oklahoma City Dolls. As long as they continued to dominate and play each other competitively, the attraction and allure of the NWFL was still alive.

In 1977, the Troopers averaged three thousand fans per game, and nearly six thousand showed up in OKC to watch the two teams face off.

That year, Jefferson's sixth season as a Trooper, she gained 1,824 yards on 101 carries, averaging 18.1 yards per rush, which the *Toledo Blade* called an "unheard of figure." She scored thirty-five touchdowns. The two marquee teams faced each other in back-to-back NWFL championship games in 1976 and 1977, with the Troopers winning both contests (though '76 was disputed), and were expected to go at it once again for the 1978 title. Sometime during the latter part of the 1978 season or after, without the Dandelions or any other team located on the West Coast, the NWFL reorganized into two divisions—Northern and Southern—instead of the three they had established back in 1974.

Despite the reorganization of the divisions, interleague play didn't change much and the team rivalries—a key component to the success and appeal of any sports league—that had been previously established, except for the Dandelions and Bluebonnets, remained intact. The Demons and Troopers, and the Herricanes and Dolls, were some of the more heated matchups in the league. But the Troopers and Dolls matchup was on a different level, akin to some of the most significant rivalries that exist in all of professional sports today. The players respected each other but, whenever they played, fans on both sides knew they were going to see a tough, competitive football game.

This particular rivalry made it easier for the NWFL to justify the third consecutive championship game between the Troopers and Dolls without playoffs. The 1978 championship was a slugfest, and the Dolls emerged victorious after shutting out the Troopers for the first time in Toledo's storied franchise history, 8–0. The Dolls 1978 season was one for the history books and rivaled even the Troopers' best years: Hines says they averaged thirty-five points a game and allowed just eight points all season.

Even though they lost the championship game, Troopers head coach and league president Bill Stout had to at least feel good about the NWFL's overall standing heading into the 1979 season. Some of Sid Friedman's original All-Star football troupe, the Cleveland Daredevils, reformed into the Cleveland Brewers and were ready to join the NWFL as an expansion team. And the Troopers and Dolls were still the draw of the league.

There were nine teams expected to take the field for the 1979 season: the Columbus Pacesetters, Middletown (Ohio) Mavericks, Cleveland Brewers, Toledo Troopers, Dallas–Fort Worth Shamrocks, Houston Herricanes, Lawton (Oklahoma) Tornadoes, Oklahoma City Dolls, and Atlanta Angels (it is unclear whether the Angels ever took the field). Former Columbus player Paralee Adams, who had been with the team since the beginning, was now part of the coaching staff; she'd begun coaching the year before, making her what many people suspect is the first woman to coach professional football.

But the tides of power were shifting. The Troopers weren't running over everyone and beating teams off the field in overwhelming fashion, as they had grown accustomed to doing. The Columbus Pacesetters shocked the league by handing the Troopers just their third loss in team history, 35–12. And when the 1979 season came to a close, it was the Pacesetters, not the Troopers, who won the right to play the Dolls in the championship game.

"It was a stunning loss, and it took much of the excitement out of the league championship game, which now pitted Oklahoma City against Columbus," wrote Neal Rozendaal. "In fact, Toledo's absence from the game sapped so much interest out of the contest that the 1979 NWFL championship game was canceled entirely" when the Pacesetters declined to play the Dolls, citing travel costs. "The fourth NWFL title game never took place, a sign that the league was in serious trouble."

While the lack of a championship game at the end of the 1979 season most certainly impacted the NWFL's momentum and perhaps even stalled it altogether, it wasn't the main catalyst for the downfall of the league. Championship game or not, no sports league can survive without sufficient funding. And the NWFL had been operating at a loss since its inception. It didn't matter if a team had an owner or was player-funded: owners never saw a return on their investment, and player-funded teams like the Houston Herricanes were scraping by. Without a sponsor, the financial burden fell directly on the players' shoulders.

After the 1979 season, the dominoes fell one-by-one. Without enough teams in the Southern Division, the Dolls had no one nearby to play, so they had no choice but to fold. Their owners, Hal and Mike Reynolds, thought they might make more money if they got into the oil business.

"When we played our last game, we didn't even know it was our last," said Hines. "It was sad." The Dolls' four-year record was 32–3–1, posting 1–1–1 in NWFL championship games. While the Troopers are remembered as the best ever, it's also important to recognize how good the Dolls were in the few short years they played and how much talent the world missed out on as a result of a lack of support and financing for the franchise.

That left the remaining teams in a tough spot. But the final punch that knocked the NWFL out came when the Toledo Troopers announced that they, too, were folding. In 1980, the owners put the team up for sale, but no buyers materialized. Following the 1979 season, the league that once had fifteen teams in three divisions failed to have a single team from the Western or Southern Divisions take the field again.

Without enough women's football teams to field a league, no financing, no real media support, and no fans, the NWFL looked as if it was over. But there were signs of life for the fledgling league yet. It turned out, 1979 wasn't the end of the league. Instead, it was a turning point.

o———o

While most of the original teams were reaching the end of their runs in 1979, some new teams were forming. The Columbus Pacesetters were still hanging on, and a team from Cleveland, the Brewers, joined the league that year.

The Brewers were started by head coach Joe LaRue, who played semi-pro football and coached Pee Wee football. LaRue invested more than twenty thousand dollars in the team. Any money that came in was reinvested back into the team in stock. "If we expand or start making money, the stock will go up," he said. "If not, it goes back into the organization." After the required two years with the team, most of the players invested in the stock option plan for financing the team, which LaRue was hopeful would help the team grow; it meant that the players put the five dollars they earned per game back into the team.

LaRue estimated that it cost $35,000–$40,000 to run an NWFL franchise, and each game cost between $1,000 and $1,500. In addition to his players raised funds by selling swag, raffle tickets, and advertising in their programs.

Equipment was also expensive. To minimize injury, they used "the same thing as the [NFL'S Cleveland] Browns," which cost up to three hundred dollars for a single player's uniform and gear. The helmets cost at least a hundred dollars each. The first season, some players would use plastic cups to protect their chests, slipping them into nursing bras and cushioning them with falsies. But the cups pinched a lot of players so they stopped using them.

Bill Ballow, who coached against LaRue in Pee Wee, enthusiastically signed on to coach offense for the Brewers. Ballow, who sported a head of dark hair with a dark beard to match, had gone to two USA Daredevils games when they were owned by Sid Friedman and had hoped to get involved with the team, but they'd folded before Ballow had the chance.

Rounding out the coaching staff was defensive coach Ken Kane, who played high school football and knew about the Brewers because his sister, Kathy, was on the team. Kathy Kane had spent her life playing as many sports as she could. Kane had cerebral palsy and was partially paralyzed on one side of her body, giving her limited use of her right arm. When she played softball, she caught and threw the ball with her left hand.

Football was a harder fit for Kane, and she didn't see a ton of action in her first two years on the team. But by her third season, the team decided to switch her from one side of the field to the other, allowing her to get more use out of her left side. As a result, Kane saw a lot more playing time. Her teammates also knew how to cover her right side and help play to Kane's strengths.

Like the other teams, the Brewers fielded women from a variety of backgrounds and occupations, including an ex-nun. Of the twenty-eight or so players, four were married. Most had college degrees, and the average age was twenty-four. The oldest player on the team was thirty-nine-year-old grandma Carol Foss, who trained horses for a living. Foss was 6'1" and 170 pounds and one of a handful of players who played both ways for the team—as a center and defensive lineman. The divorced mother of two got her daughters into the game, too. Her ten-year-old would come to every game to cheer her mother on while her oldest daughter, twenty-one, played on the team for a time but couldn't afford the cost of a babysitter for all the games and practices.

With new teams came new rivalries. Forget the Troopers and the Dolls or the Dolls and the Herricanes; now it was time for the Brewers and the Pacesetters. By this time, the Pacesetters were the veterans of the league. They'd been around since the beginning and were known for their passing game, led by quarterback Lee Anderson.

The Brewers went 4–2 in both their first two seasons, with all four losses coming against the more experienced Pacesetters. The 1981 season was a mess, with three of the six teams folding during the course of the season (including the Cincinnati Mavericks, who played two games), leaving just the Cleveland Brewers, Columbus Pacesetters, and Battle Creek (Michigan) Rainbows—who had formed in 1980—standing. During one game, the Pacesetters' public address announcer quit midgame, citing bad officiating.

Like most teams before them, the Brewers struggled to get support, especially in those early years, when getting coverage in the paper was nearly impossible. "They wouldn't even put our scores in the paper," said Brewers fullback Judy Muldoon. Their games drew just three hundred to five hundred spectators, but the team called them "quality fans." Their biggest follower was seventy-seven-year-old Harry Kovac, who diligently attended each home game. When he passed away in 1982, his family attended the team's playoff game in his memory and the Brewers dedicated the game to him.

The team used to play Sunday afternoons, but that forced them to compete for viewership against the Browns. So for their third season, the team switched their home games to Saturday nights. With the change came a change of venue, too—from Baldwin-Wallace University in Berea to Cleveland's John Marshall Stadium.

o———o

The 1982 season began with the Brewers determined to finally beat the Pacesetters. They'd spent the offseason preparing, participating in a conditioning program at Vince's Gym on Cleveland's West Side. They showed up three nights a week to put in two to three hours of conditioning, hoping to increase their stamina and prepare their bodies to withstand the game without injury.

During their first meeting, Columbus won 14–12. With forty-eight seconds left in the game, Muldoon, who also kicked, went for an extra kick that would have tied the game. It went right up the middle, but fell a foot short.

The second time the teams met, it wasn't even close. The Pacesetters won 35–0.

For the first time in their four years of existence, the Brewers decided to opt in to the NWFL's playoffs, which were optional because they cost more money than teams had budgeted for the regular season. They beat Battle Creek in the semifinals, which meant they would be facing their nemesis, the Pacesetters, for the championship. No one could have foreseen the way the game would play out; it would become the second disputed championship in the NWFL's relatively short history.

By the time the 1982 championship game was said and done, double overtime would be played, the executive director of the league would issue his resignation, police escorts would be called onto the field, and a championship would be challenged and then revoked. With it would come the coveted victory the Brewers had been after. But the way the championship came would leave a bad taste in everyone's mouth. Coach LaRue would liken winning the 1982 championship in the way his team did to "kissing your sister."

The October 10 game ultimately came down to bad officiating. Regulation play ended with a tie score: 12–12. By the time double overtime was over, the Pacesetters would be declared the champions with a final score of 18–12. But the Brewers were mad as hell. "The officials called a terrible game," Muldoon said. "Whenever we got close enough to score, they'd hit us with thirty yards in penalties. They even threw [coach] Bill [Ballow] out of the game when he called a timeout to protest."

Tensions ran high on the field. The Brewers felt they'd done everything right—sacking the quarterback, intercepting passes—and couldn't catch a break from the refs. Ultimately, a police escort had to be called to walk the officials off the field. Muldoon added: "It got so bad that Dan Dorman, the executive director of the league, resigned."

After the game, the Brewers coaches filed a formal protest in a letter to league commissioner Norm Richardson, who was also the coach of the Pacesetters. The league held a hearing on neutral territory, in Battle Creek, Michigan, the home of the only other fully operating team in the league at that time. Richardson was not there, and more than two dozen other representatives for the league were present.

The hearing found that Columbus, who hosted the game and was therefore responsible for hiring the refs, had used an unsanctioned official. League rules stipulated that officials must be sanctioned by the Ohio State High School Athletic Association or another statewide governing body. As a result, the Pacesetters would have to forfeit their championship. The Cleveland Brewers were named NWFL Champions for 1982. "I hate to win a championship like this," said LaRue. "But I think it's only fair that Columbus not keep the title. When you get hit for more than 260 yards in penalties, something has got to be wrong."

○———○

In 1982, while only three teams from the Northern Division played a full schedule—again the Cleveland Brewers, the Columbus Pacesetters, and the Battle Creek Rainbows—several other teams, in Cincinnati, Toledo, Oklahoma City, and Grand Rapids, were reorganizing and trying to get something off the ground.

In 1983, Toledo did just that when they debuted the Toledo Furies, made up of some players from the former Troopers' roster. Returning players included Eunice White, Mitchi Collette, and Gloria Jimenez.

It was a rough transition because three seasons had passed since the last time the Toledo team had taken the field. During that time period, many of the players retired, and the Furies included a lot of rookies with no football experience who had to learn the game from scratch, just like the Troopers had over a decade before. That made the team's championship in 1984 all the more sweet (though they wouldn't receive their championship rings until 2019—thirty-five years after the fact).

The Grand Rapids Carpenters joined the league in 1983, too. They were owned by Battle Creek Rainbows owner Mary Lohrstorfer, who also played defensive end for the Rainbows and served as the president of the NWFL. "The more people realize that it's serious, the more they take you seriously," Lohrstorfer told the Associated Press.

The Rainbows began the 1983 season without a coach, and by the time they reached the final game of the season, they didn't even have enough players to field a team. For two games, including the season finale, the Carpenters and Rainbows joined forces and played as one team against the Pacesetters, and only the Carpenters would return for the 1984 season. Players were doing anything and everything they could to keep the league alive.

The Carpenters' uniforms were hand-me-downs from the Rainbows, who had received them from the long-defunct Detroit Demons, who had been gifted them by the Detroit Lions back in 1974, a decade earlier. A testament to how few resources the teams had is the fact that those secondhand practice uniforms were used for ten years across three teams.

In 1984, in an attempt to drum up enthusiasm and exposure, the Brewers and Pacesetters traveled to Dover Township, New Jersey, to play a game that was mostly financially fronted by the Toms River North Booster Club. The power balance between the two teams had shifted, with the Brewers no longer strictly in pursuit of the Pacesetters. It was a rout—Cleveland beat Columbus 34–0 in front of the measly three hundred people who had braved the bad weather to watch the teams play. By this point the league had six teams and the local paper reported they planned to add two more the following year, and hoped to expand to New Jersey one day.

Despite the fact that women had been playing professional football consistently for a decade at this point, coverage of it continued to lag behind. "I think it's weird," Fran McGough of Tom River, New Jersey, told the *Asbury Park Press*. "But I am very surprised at how good some of them are." The coverage of the teams playing in the 1980s continued to treat the players like novelties or boundary breakers who were doing something unheard of, ignoring the decades of evidence to the contrary.

In 1985, Lohrstorfer tried to get the Rainbows restarted as a team in Kalamazoo, Michigan, but it's unclear if that team ever came to fruition. The Carpenters defeated the Furies for the 1985 championship, but by the end of that season, whatever foundation these teams were trying to build effectively crumbled. The Pacesetters continued to play until 1988 and the Furies until 1989, when players decided to form a flag football team instead ("for some ungodly reason," Collette said).

The NWFL—finally, painfully—was over. Women's professional football went on hiatus for nearly a decade and didn't return again until 1999.

o———o

The original intentions of Bob Mathews and the founders of the NWFL were genuinely good. Even so, they severely underestimated the importance and monetary value of consistent sports media coverage, unconditional support of women athletes, and the capitalization of unique promotional opportunities. Without those key factors, it's hard to grow a women's league and make it viable, even today. And even though everything seemed to be trending in the right direction in the 1970s, with Title IX and Billie Jean King's success and fight for fair pay in tennis, the hurdle was just too high for women's football to get over.

Regions like greater Ohio and greater Texas, where they tried for so long to make women's football work, were home to two antagonistic cultural truths. These would collide, empower, and, ultimately, destroy the NWFL.

The first truth is that a football-centric culture already existed in these regions. This culture created the interest from potential players and also sustained a desire to field local teams. This culture is likely why the Troopers took the field in Toledo early on in the wave of growth in the women's game in the 1970s, and lasted for nine seasons. This is also why the former players fought so hard to field another NWFL team after the Troopers folded, successfully assembling the Furies in 1983. This culture explains why the only team in the NWFL to exist from its inception to its ultimate demise, the Pacesetters, hailed from Columbus, and also why other Ohio cities, like Cleveland, gave it a go.

In theory, the on-field interest in the region was there and so, too, should have been the spectator interest from the fans. "You need a city where there's already a large base of women athletes and a liberal enough attitude to accept the sport," said Trooper Nancy "Eric" Erickson, a thirty-five-year-old rookie in 1973 who had played professional baseball with the Kalamazoo Lassies in 1952. "You can't set up a team in Podunk where the dignified ladies will look down their noses at women football players."

But, on the other hand, was the second cultural truth: the sexist belief—not exclusive to the two regions, but certainly vibrant there—that the women's game was the lesser game. Comparatively progressive or not, it turned out that the public did still look down their noses at women playing football.

Why go to a Troopers game when you could watch Ohio State or the Cincinnati Bengals play? The NWFL games weren't airing live on TV, so the only way to watch was to attend a game in person. And those games lacked the game day experience and lure associated with collegiate and professional men's football. Not only that, the quality of this supposedly professional league was on par with a very good high school team, not a professional one. As such, it was hard to secure and keep spectators when Ohio had so much other quality football to offer its fans.

While there were NWFL teams all over the country, the ones outside the Rust Belt seemed to be the outliers rather than the rule. The teams with sticking power, or the places where women's football continued through the 1970s and '80s or persists into today—Ohio, Michigan (Texas and Oklahoma to some extent)—were in the Rust Belt.

Many of the women who took the field for the NWFL were products of the culture they had grown up in. In the Rust Belt and the working-class South, where most of the teams hailed from, there was a particular brand of womanhood—both straight and queer—that valued toughness and an ability to hang with the boys.

The Rust Belt is not entirely clearly defined, and some people have different answers when asked where it is. But, loosely, it is a portion of mostly the Midwest that extends down from Buffalo in Western New York, along the Great Lakes to Chicago and up toward Milwaukee, and comprises largely cities and towns that were built on steel and industry and manufacturing. Toledo, for example, is known for its glass production, a fact that Troopers game-day programs proudly proclaimed. Rust Belt cities were largely devastated in the 1970s, during the NWFL years, as the result of a steep decline in manufacturing. In the years following that period, many Rust Belt cities lost large numbers of their populations; anywhere from 80 to 90 percent of the manufacturing jobs in many of the cities vanished in the mid-twentieth century.

Detroit was perhaps hit hardest, with the loss of jobs in the automotive industry, population decline spurred by white flight to the surrounding suburbs, and huge amounts of municipal debt. Toledo was not hit as hard as Detroit but still lost many of its major corporations, which kept the city afloat by providing jobs to its residents, as well as providing money to the city for infrastructure and support services.

For example, in 1960, Toledo was home to six Fortune 500 companies—more than the average city of its size, with two others in nearby communities. The city peaked with seven Fortune 500 companies from the late 1960s until the early 1980s. In 2020, only Owens Corning remained. Former mayor Carty Finkbeiner told the *Toledo Blade* in 2013 that, at one time, Toledo factories produced "three of the best-known products on the planet": Jeep, Toledo Scales, and Champion Spark Plugs. Only Jeep is still in Toledo.

For the NWFL teams in the region, they crumbled alongside the economies of their hometowns.

Billie Cooper and Rose Kelley at the 2019 Houston Herricanes reunion
Brett Coomer/© Houston Chronicle. Used with permission

PART VI

THE LEGACY OF THE NWFL

IF IT WEREN'T FOR THEM, WE WOULDN'T BE HERE. YOU HAVE TO STAND ON THE SHOULDERS OF SOMEBODY TO REACH THE ULTIMATE HEIGHTS, ESPECIALLY AS WOMEN. . . . THEY MADE ME BOLD. I'M SO BOLD BECAUSE I KNOW I AM LIVING ON THE LEGACY OF SOMEONE ELSE.

—ODESSA JENKINS, COFOUNDER AND CEO OF THE WOMEN'S NATIONAL FOOTBALL CONFERENCE (WNFC)

CHAPTER 17

UNWITTING ACTIVISTS

One evening, in the summer of 2019, Billie Cooper straddled the line between excitement and anxiety with as much dexterity as she had during her playing days. She checked her hair, pulled her maroon mesh practice jersey over her head—now faded and snug from forty years in a closet, the number 86 peeling off in places—and tucked her scrapbook under her arm. The sixty-four-year-old walked steadfast through the parking lot, approaching the door of Harold's, a restaurant in the Heights neighborhood of Houston, Texas, where the reunion was taking place. She followed the signs that directed her to the second floor and climbed the stairs. The din of elated chatter and the tone of familiarity drifted closer to her ears with each step she took.

For a moment, she was back on the field again. She could smell the sweet scent of grass and mud. She could feel the weight of her shoulder pads, the beads of sweat gliding down her flushed cheeks in the late-summer heat, and the heaviness of her warm breath as her chest heaved. She could hear the crunch of the helmets, the calls of the quarterback, and the hollers from her teammates on the sideline. She remembered how it felt to frustrate offenses and level opposing players with such force that it knocked the football from their hands. Cooper laughed to herself. She was often double-teamed to try and prevent her from busting up a play or getting at the quarterback. But that was part of the challenge. That was part of what she loved about the game, about being a member of the Houston Herricanes of the National Women's Football League—the first professional women's football team in the city.

It had been one of the most meaningful experiences of her life, playing football. But what Cooper had held onto the most for all these years was the family she had made, and the love and respect between her and her teammates. The Herricanes began in 1976 and had disbanded abruptly in 1979, without having one last meeting or a final gathering as a team. For Cooper, there was never any closure. And now, four decades later, she was about to see everyone again thanks to the reunion—which had been organized by another former player's daughter, who was in the middle of making a documentary about the Herricanes and their time together. Cooper took an extended breath.

How would it feel to see them? Would she remember everyone's names? Would they remember hers? Would she even recognize their faces after all this time?

As she ascended the final step and turned left into the banquet room where her former teammates awaited, the questions swirling around in Cooper's head dissipated. When she finally entered the room, a re-laxed smile broke on her face. It was as if no time had passed at all. She'd aged, of course, and so had everyone else, but the familiarity that only comes with being someone's teammate was ever present. There was Gwen Flager, the quarterback—even at sixty-nine, she had the same stature and self-assured presence she'd had all those years ago. There was Rose Kelley, the best defensive lineman on the Herricanes roster, who possessed the same booming laugh and wide smile she'd always brought with her to practices and games, until she got on the field and flattened opponents to the ground. And Marty Bryant, the quiet and reserved running back who started the team on a whim.

"Are you staying out of trouble?" someone asked.

"No!" another gleefully responded.

As she looked around at the faces of the women she'd known so many years ago, Cooper felt the familiar adrenaline rush she would get whenever the ball was snapped before a play. These were the same women with whom she had broken barriers, done all the things girls weren't "supposed" to do, during a time when women were seen as secondary and less than. The women whose accomplishments had long been forgotten, who had been erased from Houston sports history—if they'd ever really been recorded there at all.

Before long, Cooper was holding court—as she is wont to do. Her big personality and Texas drawl filled the space, spreading out and touching everyone there. She sat at a table and opened her scrapbook, her former teammates squeezing in behind her, craning their necks to see, their heads taking up every inch of space above Cooper's shoulders.

It may be true that most people had never heard of the Houston Herricanes, that the team had been left out of the history books. But just like a tree that falls in a forest makes a sound, even if no one is around to hear it, the Herricanes existed, even if no one else remembers them.

Standing together with the rest of the women in that room, Cooper knew for certain it hadn't all been a dream. It had been real. And they had lived it, together.

o———o

Cooper is sixty-six years old now and is retired. The 2019 Houston Herricanes reunion reconnected her to her long-lost football family. They celebrated a little taste of notoriety when the reunion was covered by the *Houston Chronicle* and the *Washington Times*, and the story circulated on social media. They're also looking forward to whenever the documentary about their team, *Brick House*, is completed. Since the reunion, Cooper has stayed in touch with some former teammates and kept busy. "People think that I sit around and don't do anything all day—you know, watch TV and eat bonbons," Cooper joked. "I'm busier now than I was when I worked. Anybody that needs help, I'm there to help them out—whether it's land clearing or Costco or something like that. In my spare time, I mess around with a couple of dogs. And I do a lot of travel."

Cooper's teammate and quarterback Gwen Flager uses her hands to write plays for the stage now instead of executing them on the gridiron. Flager worked as an attorney for many years before she retired and began a whole new second career as a playwright. In 2018, one of her plays—*Shakin' the Blue Flamingo*—won a local competition in Houston at the Queensbury Theater. Flager, now seventy-one, and her wife, Ruthann, have been together for over thirty years. They got married in 2008.

"She knew about my time playing football," Flager said proudly. "I still have my jersey. In hindsight, forty years later, I don't know that we realized the impact of what we were doing. It certainly wasn't a political statement, it certainly wasn't a cultural or social statement. We just wanted to play football. Now people had different ideas about that. But that's what we wanted to do and it was remarkable that we accomplished that. Not everybody was favorable to it."

A lot of things have changed. By the time the NWFL officially became a league in 1974, there was already a major momentum shift happening in the realm of women's sports and athletics. The passage of Title IX in 1972 had effectively launched a national movement, giving women who had long felt, and rightly so, like they were on the outside looking in when it came to sports a chance to not only participate but to show they belonged on the field, the court, the ice, in the gym, along with everyone else.

Title IX stipulates: "No person in the United States shall, on the basis of sex, be excluded from the participation in, be denied the benefits of, or be subjected to discrimination under any education program or activity receiving Federal financial assistance." As a result, money poured into junior highs, high schools, colleges, community centers, and so on, to expand recreational and competitive sports programs for women. This also included better equipment and facilities. And for the first time, women could go to college on an athletic scholarship.

Monumental changes happened across a variety of institutions on a national scale. In 1973, New Jersey became the first state to allow girls to play Little League baseball after the National Organization for Women sued on behalf of a girl named Maria Pepe. Twelve states, including California, integrated noncontact sports in high schools and colleges by 1974. In Washington, at least thirty thousand girls were participating in youth basketball programs—none were playing ten years prior. And at the University of Miami, when athletics scholarships were introduced, over four hundred women applied for a total of fifteen available grants.

Every step taken, whether at the youth, amateur, or professional level, no matter how small, was one more step forward in the advancement of women's sports. Of course, there was ongoing resistance. But the tide continued to shift regardless. Complaints were filed; court cases won. And despite the discrimination many women athletes faced before Title IX and even after it was enacted, they pushed forward. They courageously laced up sneakers, skates, and cleats. They played hockey, participated in competitive gymnastics, raced horses as jockeys, and drove race cars. Billie Jean King fought for equal pay in women's tennis, Nina Kuscsik became the first woman to win the Boston Marathon, and Marcia Frederick became the first American to win a gold medal at the World Gymnastics Championships.

While the expectations of change weighed heavily on some minds of NWFL players, others in the league had never even heard of Title IX, knew that it had been passed, or even recognized consciously at the time that there was something deeper at stake. A lot of the women who played professional football never saw it as a defining moment in the history of women's sports, or a legacy-in-the-making endeavor.

"To be honest with you, I didn't think of it like that," Cooper confessed. "I don't know how the others felt. We were a team, we were a family, and we were playing a sport that we grew up playing in the neighbor's yard and not able to play on a real field. We knew we were getting to do something that we weren't able to do as kids. But we didn't get to the point where we thought, *Hey—this is a groundbreaker.* We didn't think that way."

○────○

Whether the players considered themselves to be part of the women's lib movement or not, the media was determined to connect those dots for them. The press was quick to associate them with it, but the players were just as quick to distance themselves.

"Most of us don't give a damn about women's lib," one Demons player told the *Detroit Free Press* while swigging a beer in the locker room. The women may have been clear that they just wanted to play football, but a 1973 newspaper article included the subheading "Now Even Pro Football 'Liberated.'" The players were asked incessantly if they were "libbers," and the existence of the teams in the first place was largely credited to (or blamed on) the feminist movement, most likely because associating something with feminism was a surefire way to discredit or trivialize it.

While it's true that the NWFL coincided with the women's liberation movement of the 1970s, led in part by Rust Belt native Gloria Steinem, it also didn't feel particularly resonant or urgent to a lot of the players. Particularly for the working-class women of the NWFL, the goals of the women's lib movement did not resonate for them. Some of the women were wives and mothers but the majority were not. Moreover, the feminist movement at the time focused a lot on reproductive choice and abortion access, along with advocating for women's ability to work outside the home.

For mothers who did take the field, however, football was often a distraction and an escape from the responsibilities at home. When Constance d'Angelis played for the Troopers in 1971, 1972, and 1973, she was "a full-time student in sciences at the University, a single mom, on welfare, and going to school on a Pell Grant." The second-string halfback (behind Linda Jefferson) and starting middle linebacker was on the pre-med track at the University of Toledo and saw football practice as "a relief from the stress, studying, and feeling of responsibility." Joanne Mathis, a thirty-year-old mother of four who suited up for the Detroit Demons, said in an interview published by the *Times* of Shreveport, Louisiana, "All the frustrations you get at home with the kids you get to take out on your opponent."

Other women found their football careers cut short by pregnancy and the demands of family. Dolls player Charlotte Gordon took the field to begin practicing for the 1977 season, but shortly after that, she discovered she was pregnant and stopped playing. Her teammate Doris Stokes played three seasons, but did not return for the team's final season in 1979, which is the year she got married. Troopers coach Bill Stout also lamented the loss of players to pregnancy. "We lost a great player last year," he told the *Blade* in 1977. "She got pregnant. You don't have to worry about that with men."

But many of the women might have felt disconnected from the women's movement for another reason: their class status and/or racial identity. Working-class and blue-collar women were often left out of the movement by the middle- and upper-middle-class women at its forefront due to stereotypes about the roles they desired. A 1980 study in the *Sociological Quarterly* found that "the perception of working class women as especially traditional and domestic" led to their support for feminism being underestimated because it had "been assumed that they lack the personal discontent with traditional roles on which the movement is based," but that those stereotypes were largely untrue. The study also found that working-class women who worked outside the home were more likely to be open to the ideas associated with women's liberation and feminism.

"In the women's movement . . . the articulation, study and theories of advancement toward gender parity—has been crucial to social progress. Of equal import and less acclaim, though, is what working-class women . . . do for the cause," writes Sarah Smarsh in the *Guardian*. "Their worlds often resist the container of politicized terminology that is often the exclusive province of college-educated people. But working-class women have seen the most devastating outcomes of gender inequality."

The majority of the NWFL players already were working outside the home, many of them in male-dominated industries—as working-class women had always done. Betty Young of the Dallas Bluebonnets climbed telephone poles for a phone company, a job she held for decades and one where she was always the only woman. Many of the Troopers worked for UPS, D. A. Starkey of the Bluebonnets was a mechanic, and Mary BlueJacket of the Dolls worked in the warehouse of a grocery distribution company. Many others were teachers, a large number of them physical education teachers, bringing their love of sports to their careers.

For these women, the big-picture fight of the women's lib movement didn't seem to impact their daily lives. Not only that, the mainstream women's lib movement lacked lesbian visibility and often solidarity. Betty Friedan, author of *The Feminine Mystique*, famously referred to lesbians as the "Lavender Menace." There was particular disdain among many feminists toward butch women, whom they wrongly viewed as wanting to emulate a heterosexual kind of hypermasculinity. For many of the queer women in the NWFL, they didn't have a male partner at home oppressing them. In that way, these women had divested from patriarchy in their personal lives and were already succeeding in industries they were told women couldn't work in. Indeed, their lived experience was entirely different from the one the messaging of the women's lib movement largely spoke to. Their entire existence was already about subverting the expectations put on them by a patriarchal society, making it hard to see the value or necessity on a personal level.

There is also the fact that the most visible leaders in the women's liberation movement were organizing in Washington, DC, or in big cities like New York. That, too, made it hard for the women in America's heartland to place themselves within the movement. As Smarsh points out, the determining factor in terms of who gets to show up and protest is often economic agency. Not only that, what significance did an argument about the value of housewives and the role of mothers have to a lesbian welder in Ohio? Not much.

Black women of the NWFL may have felt left out or unrepresented by the mainstream women's movement, as well as left out of the larger Black liberation movement that was steeped in sexism. For these women, Black feminists were forming their own women's movement, one that was what we would today call "intersectional," to use a term coined by Kimberlé Crenshaw in 1989. In *How We Get Free*, Princeton professor Keeanga-Yamahtta Taylor writes, "Black women's experiences cannot be reduced to either race or gender but have to be understood on their own terms." This new movement was being forged at roughly the same time as the NWFL, from the National Black Feminist Organization in 1973–1976 to the Combahee River Collective (CRC), which was founded in 1974. The CRC has ties to Ohio, too: it was started, in part, by lesbian twin sisters Barbara and Beverly Smith, who were born in Cleveland; Beverly's entrance into activism had been through the racial justice movement in her home state. The third author of the CRC manifesto, released in 1977, was Demita Frazier, who grew up in Chicago, another Rust Belt city.

And then there is the case of internalized misogyny, which all women have to some extent and which often requires an intentional effort to unravel. This was reflected in some of the players attempting to legitimize the league by promising they would look just like men when they played the sport, or the surprise the women often expressed that the teams weren't full of catty drama. As women who had spent their lives being

"one of the boys" or "not like other women," as well as breaking stereotypes by sheer will and determination, it was easier to distance themselves
from the larger women's movement than it was to align with women who
seemed so different than they were. All of these overlapping and inter-
secting identities and issues would have impacted whether or not the
women of the NWFL openly identified as "libbers."

But you don't have to think of yourself as a feminist in order to be one.
There are a lot of reasons women might want to distance themselves from
feminism, many of them valid. "In some people's eyes you were a cult
hero. And in other people's eyes you were just the biggest heathen ever,"
said Dolls quarterback Jan Hines. "And I just didn't want to deal with any
of that, so I just didn't."

When the women are pushed, today, about why it was important for
them to play, they often talk about concerns that align with the feminism
they might not name. These concerns include their frustration at the lack
of opportunities they received, how little resources they were given, how
much they were doubted and discounted. The players speak of a desire
to prove that women can do anything men can do, an unwillingness to
be restrained by societal expectations, and a determination to refuse to
allow those barriers to stand in their way. "You know, we were letting our
voices be heard back then," remembered Bluebonnets quarterback Barbara O'Brien. "And not backing down from some of the comments and
responses to us, and [we] just did what we wanted to do."

Those are the beliefs of feminism, that all genders deserve equal rights
and equal access and that no one should be discriminated against or
pushed out of spaces on account of their gender. "Working-class women
might not be fighting for a cause with words, time and money they don't
have, but they possess an unsurpassed wisdom about the way gender
works in the world," writes Smarsh. "For these women, the fight to merely
survive is a declaration of equality that could be called 'feminist.' But
here's the thing . . . right or wrong, they don't give a shit what you call it."

During her years on the Troopers, Constance d'Angelis didn't have
much to her name, as a college student and a single mom on welfare. "As
I look back on this experience, I realize that I lived at a time where massive changes in mindset and legal status were emerging. I was just trying

to survive," she said. "At the time I was playing football, I had no idea about any of this. I just wanted to play football—real football, with full gear and able to knock heads."

Before becoming a teacher, Linda Jefferson worked in an assortment of jobs and broke barriers for Black women at many of them. She was the first Black woman and one of the first three women to work for Dundee Cement, as well as the first Black woman to work for UPS in northwest Ohio.

Some players did associate with an explicit feminist identity at the time, like Julie Sherwood, who practiced with the Columbus Pacesetters before going on to become their longtime trainer. Sherwood grew up in a white, working-class family in Ohio and was a lesbian who was not out to her family but found acceptance on the Pacesetters. She attended the Ohio State University, and it was there that she discovered the new Women's Studies Department, giving her language and theory for her personal experiences. Sherwood said that even if the players on the team wouldn't have used those words, playing on the Pacesetters "was kind of seen as the feminist thing to do. . . . It was a way to get attention to do outrageous things, and football was right up there with one of the most outrageous things you could imagine."

Even still, to admit openly to feminism "was to condemn yourself to be trivialized." And Sherwood saw the efforts of the media and others to attribute playing football to being a feminist statement as an attempt to minimize and trivialize the reality of what the women were doing.

Bluebonnets quarterback Barbara O'Brien also said she identified with the feminist struggle. O'Brien worked as a lineman at AT&T, and the company was just starting to hire women to do those jobs. "The men there just hated it, they hated the women that were in there, and they were giving everyone heck about it," O'Brien remembered. "The guys would try to knock me off the pole. . . . I didn't last long there because of all the harassment by the men. Because they were, at the time, trying to move women up quickly in the organization, and [the men] would say horrible things and accuse you of sleeping with bosses to get a better job."

O'Brien's lived experience on the job showed her exactly why the fight for equality was necessary. And her time on the Bluebonnets taught her that she did not have to settle for the status quo. O'Brien was not the only woman whose time in the NWFL provided her with skills that allowed her to succeed or assert herself in the workplace. In 1975, after she completed her degree, Trooper Constance d'Angelis was offered a job in the technical division of Owens Corning Fiberglas. The company had never hired a woman outside of secretarial and support jobs; d'Angelis was the first. "The world was changing," she said.

The year after d'Angelis was hired, the company held a Fitness Festival and twenty athlete employees were invited to compete. Again, d'Angelis was the only woman. The employees were divided into relay teams to compete in swimming, running, and an obstacle course. D'Angelis said her "teammates were more competitive than cooperative" until she won her relay. "After winning or placing in my assigned 'legs' of the relay and gaining points for our team, there was a shift in attitude," she remembered. Her athletic achievement, being able to prove herself against men, also earned her the respect of one of her idols. "What I remember most is that [NFL coach] Don Shula was the keynote speaker at the awards banquet," she said. "He called me up onstage. There's nothing like being recognized by your hero."

Being a quarterback for the Dolls afforded Jan Hines leadership qualities that she took into her off-the-field career, too: she worked as a line worker at Western Electric in Oklahoma City and was promoted to a supervisory role due to the assumption that she could lead a team, because her bosses knew she had played quarterback. She would eventually ascend to the level of director at Lucent Technologies, "just a hair short of vice president."

Some of these women would come to identify with feminism later in life, even if they didn't at the time. For Trooper Olivia Flores, her desire to play was rooted in "want[ing] something more for [herself] than what [her] parents could have possibly envisioned," though she didn't yet have the words to look at it in the context of seeking liberation from oppressive gender roles and structures. Today, she feels differently, and attributes her political identity as a feminist to her experience on the gridiron.

Whether or not the women of the NWFL identified with the word "feminism" or with the larger movement for women's liberation, they were unwittingly part of it, simply by living their truths. In that way, they are like countless other women throughout history who never set out to change the world but did so anyway, just because they had the courage not to take no for an answer or accept the role that society told them they should hold. Laurel Wolf may not have seen herself as "a radical, liberal flag waver" when she took the field with the Troopers in 1979. Still, she played a sport she'd been told her entire life was not for her.

Football "empowered women," said Pacesetters player Linda Stamps. "One of the things many of us loved about the game is the sense of 'power over'—you tackle someone, take them down. You don't get that experience anywhere, metaphorically or in real time. As a woman, you're normally sitting there with your legs crossed, waiting for the next pinch on your ass."

o———o

After the 1975 season, Susan Hoxie left the Dandelions and joined the army. She had fulfilled her mother's wish and then some—trying out for the team, making the team, and playing professional football for three seasons. "I'm proud of it," she said, now seventy-one and a retired paralegal living in Colorado Springs, Colorado. "It was like I was some kind of pioneer or something. When I grew up there were only three careers we could have: nurse, teacher, or secretary. I never dreamed of playing pro football and yet I did, if only briefly."

One of the most memorable moments from Hoxie's pro football career was when a little boy asked for her autograph. It has remained close to her heart all these years later. "[I] was astounded," she said. "I was a football player and it didn't matter if I was male or female." Hoxie played in one more game for the Dandelions in 1976, against the Oklahoma City Dolls. On a weekend pass from the army, she joined her teammates on the football field for two plays for the very last time.

At some point in 1976, during the Dandelions' fourth season, Joyce Johnson tore her ACL and the injury abruptly ended her professional football career. But she stayed on with the team as the unofficial trainer, showing up for practices and games, taping up her teammates before kick-off, and getting ice for those who were injured on the field of play. "Many of us became pretty good friends," Johnson said, looking back on her decision to stick around. "So it was a fun way [for me] to stay connected." In spring 1977, she graduated from college and was teaching by 1978. For Johnson, it was the right time to move on from football altogether.

Now sixty-eight, Johnson is a retired physical education teacher, coach, and former athletic director. She still resides in California, in Laguna Niguel, and while she fondly remembers her time in the NWFL, the experience wasn't something she considers to be life changing. "The way I look at it—it's hard to explain," Johnson said. "It was just a chapter in my life. When that chapter closed, I just continued on with my life. Once I got into coaching and teaching, that was the next chapter. And I never even thought about football. I never even told people about it. I still, to this day, don't ever tell—hey, did you know I played pro football back in the 1970s?"

Still, Johnson has plenty of reminders of her professional football years. She eventually had to get a knee replacement, thanks to that torn ACL she suffered with the Dandelions. And then there are the boxes and boxes of mementos she has in storage. Within them, old pictures of the Dandelions, game programs, schedules, and articles. "It's a chapter of my life that's fun to look back at. I'm the type of person who documents stuff all the time. I have boxes of stuff full of chapters of my life."

Rose Low held onto the Dandelions a little tighter than Johnson, and most of her other teammates. The now sixty-eight-year-old stayed with the team from its inception in 1973 to her last season in 1978, then taught physical education and eventually became an athletic director of a high school for twenty-plus years. Low credits her time as a professional football player for opening her eyes to possibilities and doors she never thought possible. "It was just such a rare opportunity for women to play any professional sport, let alone tackle football," Low said. "I know there were a lot of young eyes watching us, and hopefully we were good role models for them."

As the team captain, Low was often asked to be the face of the team when requests for speaking engagements and television appearances were made. She did so graciously, and made sure to talk about the team as a symbiotic unit first and foremost—never wanting to mention a single player above the rest. "[I] always tried to cheer on everyone and appreciate their role on the team. Everyone contributed. Not everyone got to play in the game, but everyone was needed and had a role in practice that contributed to our success."

Even after the team disbanded and NBC News asked to take a trip down memory lane in 1993 to revisit the team, Low happily obliged. After the spot ran on the local NBC affiliate, Low wrote NBC News Archives and asked them for a VHS copy. She recently had the program and footage transferred to DVD, and made several copies for her former teammates.

"Many of my teammates did not see or know of the existence of the video footage that I was able to track down. I feel a responsibility to try and get copies to as many of the girls as possible. We are no longer spring chickens, so they can share it with their children and grandchildren," Low explained. "I want all of the Dandelions to be proud of us for being bold and for becoming a good team of football players. There are very few people now who even know who we were. So, I am glad that we saved the evidence that we did exist and hope that we made a difference."

With the passage of time, Low has realized just how much of an impact being a Dandelion made on her life and its direction, and her appreciation of the experience has gotten exponentially deeper. "The achievements and special times we shared are priceless," she said. And even if the women of the NWFL are never inducted into the Pro Football Hall of Fame—as her former teammate, Barbara Patton, once surmised would happen—Low knows they were all a part of something special.

Patton's own son, Marvcus, who she brought to practices with her, followed in his mother's footsteps and played linebacker in the NFL from 1990 to 2002 for the Buffalo Bills (and later, for the Washington Football Team and Kansas City). Marvcus credits his mother for teaching him everything he knew about football, and being an inspiration. "She was a mother and father to me, so even at the time and to this day, I don't remember myself having any problems not having a father in the home," he explained in an interview at the Bills practice facility in the early nineties. "I'm definitely proud of my mother, just for the fact that she [played football] and she allowed me to play the game. I'm definitely very proud of her."

During the time that Marvcus played in Buffalo, the Bills went to four straight Super Bowls and lost each one. Naturally, Patton had something to say about that. After one of the losses, she said she "pointed out a couple of things to [Marv Levy] and told him the next time they lose another Super Bowl, that I was going to come down and help him coach."

Though Marvcus never made it to the Pro Football Hall of Fame, perhaps his mother still has a chance. The lack of recognition of the NWFL raises a legitimate question about the women who played. They are a significant part of football history—particularly the Troopers and their near decade of domination—and should be honored as such in Canton, Ohio, as the women of the AAGPBL have been in Cooperstown, New York.

Linda Stamps, one of the founding members of the Pacesetters, contacted the Hall of Fame in the 1980s about archiving the league's materials, much of which have now been scattered or lost to time. "I spoke with someone in the archives," she said. "They wouldn't even take [the materials], much less display anything." They gave her "a polite brush off."

Imagine a display featuring pictures, memorabilia, and information about NWFL teams and players that would serve as a reminder to football fans young and old that the NWFL existed, and a tribute to all of the women who played so that their stories live on and are not overlooked and forgotten. Imagine what a moment it would be for Patton and Marvcus to witness together?

o———o

Bluebonnet Toni Gibson's son was inspired by her football career, too. He played through high school and always wore number 32, just like his mom.

After two years of playing football, Barbara O'Brien hung up her helmet at some point during the 1974 season. She'd had three concussions and wanted to focus on sports that wouldn't hurt her body so much. Lucky for O'Brien, she was a natural athlete and had plenty of options. In late 1974 and early 1975, she competed against twenty-four other female athletes for the title of the world's first Women's Superstar at the Houston Astrodome.

The competition required contestants to face off in seven of ten possible categories, including bicycle racing, navigating an obstacle course, and rowing, among others. Athletes could not compete in their specialty, which gave O'Brien confidence despite having to compete against Billie Jean King in several events, and as an amateur in a field full of professionals. "She may be a good tennis player," O'Brien told the *Dallas Morning News* at the time, but "I may just turn out to be better in everything else."

The groundbreaking competition aired on ABC. O'Brien came in third place in the first round, which scored her a spot in the finals. She ultimately came in seventh place, winning fifteen hundred dollars in prize money. Two years later, in 1976, Linda Jefferson took part in the competition and came in fourth.

After giving up football, O'Brien focused her energy on golf. She played as an amateur on the pro circuit. In 1989, she started the Barbara O'Brien Invitational Golf Tournament, which began as a daylong tournament with eight to one hundred lesbians competing; in 1991, she opened it up to include men.

In 1983, O'Brien did something that would allow her to do one of the things she loved most: cultivate community. She opened Desert Moon, a new Dallas lesbian bar, which would operate for a decade. Her love of sports shaped the events and groups Desert Moon hosted, including golf and tennis leagues. It also brought the inception of the Bluebonnets that night in the lesbian bar full circle.

O'Brien found a passion for running charity golf tournaments to raise money for social justice causes. Her first tournament raised funds for the Genesis Women's Shelter, a Dallas-based domestic violence organization. In 1983, she hosted the first Life Walk for AIDS, which raised $186,000—a huge deal at a time when the disease and those battling it were incredibly stigmatized. In 1996, she received the Kuchling Humanitarian Award from the Black Tie Dinner, which "honors individuals who have made extraordinary gifts of their time and talents on behalf of the LGBTQ community."

A lot has changed for female athletes in O'Brien's lifetime. "I was in a school that had nothing to offer for women," she said. "I was so glad to see Title IX happen. I just wish it had happened a little sooner, you know, for a lot of us that loved sports."

For her part, Gibson still can't believe she got to play football and share a stadium with the Cowboys. Her place in history is not lost on her, either. "It was a privilege for us," she said. "It was kind of like the first time that women got rights, we got rights that we were all athletes and we could go somewhere and play." Her teammate CoCo Manson was just seventeen when she first suited up for the Bluebonnets, and the experience shaped the rest of her life. "For the first time in my life I felt like I was doing something valuable, something important," said Manson. "I remember the first time a little girl in Detroit asked for my autograph. It was just amazing, the feeling it gave you, that some little girl was looking up to what you were doing."

The Dolls were equally important to Jan Hines. She describes her time with the team as "the best four years" of her life, and she is now retired and living in Virginia. Many of the Dolls, if they're not directly in touch with each other, still run into each other in the community. Charlotte Gordon spent thirty-four years working in education, eventually getting her master's degree and moving up to work in administration. She was the principal of a school that was attended by the children of her former teammate Terri Talley.

Pebble Myers was a coworker of Gordon's husband. Cindee Herron lives a few houses down from halfback Glenda Cameron, and even though their stints on the Dolls never overlapped, their shared history has created a kinship between the women. Gordon and Doris Stokes remain close friends and even played on a seniors basketball team together. Stokes worked in education for forty-three years, as well as coaching as many sports teams as she could. She then got into refereeing, and played for the Senior Olympics.

In 2000, Cathie Schweitzer became the first woman athletic director at Springfield College in Massachusetts. She held the position at the Division III school for fifteen years, during which time Springfield won fifty-nine conference championships and produced twenty-four individual national champions and eight team national champions. In 2020, the school announced that she would be inducted into the Springfield College Athletic Hall of Fame.

○———○

As for the Troopers, they are the team who has been best remembered and most honored. There are talks of a documentary film, called *Perfect Season*, a forthcoming book by Troopers historian Steve Guinan, and rumors of a screenplay. In 1983, the Troopers were recognized as the "winningest team in professional football history" at the Pro Football Hall of Fame. They were also the first team to be inducted into the Women's Football Foundation Hall of Fame in 2014.

Mitchi Collette has remained a fixture of the Toledo women's football scene, carrying the torch for the history of the sport in Ohio. Linda Jefferson went on to become a teacher, working in the field for thirty-five years. She has remained a local celebrity around Toledo and, more than forty years on, still gets recognized in the grocery store.

CHAPTER 18

WHERE DOES WOMEN'S FOOTBALL GO FROM HERE?

I t's not hard to draw a connection from the NWFL to the women's football leagues of today. In fact, there is a direct thread that runs to the owner of the Toledo Reign of the Women's Football Alliance (WFA), Mitchi Collette. Follow it backward to the 1980s, when she suited up for the Toledo Furies, and to the decade before that, when she was a member of those powerhouses of women's football, the Toledo Troopers. That thread, running through Toledo, goes even further back to the 1930s, and one of the first organized attempts at women's football.

We don't have to search and hypothesize to understand how and why the NWFL is significant in the current day. One reason, among many, is that people like Collette are living history, still impacting the game, half a century later.

Looking back at the timeline of women's football, the formation of the NWFL was inevitable. History has clearly shown that women have been interested in watching and playing organized football since the sport was invented. The timing of Title IX and the growth of women's sports in the 1970s, as well as the public's curiosity in women's football fostered by Sid

Friedman years before, provided the perfect launchpad from which the NWFL took flight.

This is why it should come as no surprise that today, women are still as invested as they ever were. In February 2020, NFL commissioner Roger Goodell announced the league had reached a record total of 187.3 million fans. Almost half—47 percent—are women, which accounts for roughly 88 million.

While the number of girls participating in youth football and at the high school level has increased exponentially over the years, there are still not enough players to provide a legitimate pipeline to any of the amateur or semiprofessional women's football leagues that exist today. Women's soccer, hockey, basketball, and tennis have enough participants at the youth, high school, and college level that top talent rises through the ranks and players feed seamlessly into their respective professional leagues. Women's football has never had that luxury.

The lack of infrastructure for the women who played in the NWFL showed on the football field. Most of the players essentially learned the game in their early twenties and thirties. As a result, the skill level between teams in the league was incredibly skewed—some were great and had natural athletic skills to fall back on; others were awful. While the quality of coaching was definitely a factor in the disparity between teams, some of it was just luck. The teams drew participants from whatever pool of players showed up for the tryout in their location. Some teams were forced to take lesser-skilled players simply to fill out their roster.

There was no official draft to facilitate spreading talent around the league, either. This is mirrored today in a league like the Women's Football Alliance, where some teams are dominant and others are on the fringe. The Troopers and Dolls were the most dominant teams, and while the popular narrative is that a team like the Troopers was really, really good—and it was—it also often lacked meaningful competition, which most certainly had an impact on the team's overall record. The Troopers won a lot. And that could be frustrating. In the 1975 *womenSports* piece, Linda Jefferson talked about the Troopers getting bored of beating the same teams over and over again. It became redundant. It is fun to win, but it's not always fun to walk all over everyone.

Good competition is healthy for everyone involved in the sport—the fans, the players, and the league itself. But without the proper infrastructure in place to help build, weed out, and spread the talent around the NWFL, the level of play suffered. And that's one thing the women's football leagues of today want to change.

Most girls who play against boys at the youth level don't continue doing so in high school. And in college, women like Toni Harris playing a full-contact position on a men's team are extremely rare—they are the exceptions rather than the norm. For those who want to continue playing, there's no alternative. There aren't enough girls playing football to field entire high school teams for competitive play, let alone at the college level.

The best case scenario for high school and college women is to try and make a men's team, or participate in intramural or recreational flag and two-hand-touch football teams. Eventually, as adults, they can try out for one of a handful of women's football leagues—a single, well-funded, functional women's professional football league does not exist.

The fact remains, without a youth, high school, and college system in place, women's professional football will always be a step behind other women's sports when it comes to growth, due to a lack of participants.

But again, the interest from players is there, as it has always been.

When Neal Rozendaal compiled *The Women's Football Encyclopedia* in 2016, he did so because he was already immersed in the sport and amazed at the level of commitment of the players. His wife played for the Washington, DC, Divas and he did some content writing for the team. When researching his book, he spent two years collecting data and stats from all of the different women's football leagues that existed between 1999 and 2015. He also spent time researching the NWFL and the history of women's football in general.

"The NWFL showed there could be interest in the sport. There could be legitimate rivalries, and there were some women who achieved some fame or celebrity. No one had ever really known if women's football could do that before," said Rozendaal. "I know when they restarted [women's professional football] in the 2000s, a lot of teams looked to the NWFL basically as their forefathers, so to speak, to what it is that they do today. To me, I think their legacy is that they started a movement that really has continued to this day and will continue in the future. These women really are pioneers. And they are really beloved in the current women's football landscape."

Odessa Jenkins is the cofounder and chief executive officer of the Women's National Football Conference (WNFC), an amateur women's football league with professional aspirations. She harkens back to the days of the NWFL as the source from which all future women's football leagues have sprung.

"If it weren't for them, we wouldn't be here," she said. "You have to stand on the shoulders of somebody to reach the ultimate heights, especially as women. Because so much of the promises of the world aren't really made available to you as women. You have to fight harder to get the things you want. When I tell people that women have been playing football for fifty years, they're like, 'what?' They made me bold. I'm so bold because I know that I am living on the legacy of someone else."

Like many of the women in the NWFL who came before her, Jenkins played football growing up. And her love for the game never went away. As an adult, she played running back in multiple different leagues for ten seasons—including the International Federation of American Football (IFAF), the Independent Women's Football League (IWFL), and the WFA. And even though thirty-plus years had passed since the NWFL's heyday, Jenkins found that some of the same roadblocks and issues that were prevalent in women's football in the 1970s still existed.

"The way we traveled wasn't nice. And there didn't seem to be a lot of cohesiveness between the teams," she explained. "There could be one team spending thousands on their brand and another team treating [the league] like a recreational team where they wore different colored helmets and nobody really cared. There were no sponsors. Players had to pay for every single thing. Owners and teams had to pay for every single thing and also pay the league. And the league wasn't really bringing anything back. There was no evolution."

It's disheartening to Jenkins that similar issues still exist after all of this time. But it's not surprising, she admits. The system that propped up and incentivized men's sports over women's sports for years is the same one that operates today.

But Jenkins believes the world is changing. And she's right. Women's sports leagues are growing and the fan base is expanding. They are attracting sponsors, investors, television deals, and so forth, and the Women's National Basketball Association (WNBA) and the National Women's Soccer League (NWSL) are at the forefront of the movement.

In 2020, a group of high-powered women investors—from actress Natalie Portman to soccer legend Mia Hamm—announced they had the rights to start a new NWSL team in Los Angeles. Viewership in the WNBA in 2020 was up 19 percent for opening weekend, a trend that has continued for the past five years, and up 68 percent for the season overall. The National Women's Hockey League (NWHL) also expanded to six teams in 2020, launching a team in Toronto. These markers point to the fact that women's sports are not only growing, but are worth investing time, money, and energy in.

Jenkins has a similar dream for women's football and the WNFC. She wants the league she helped start to not only succeed, but to evolve over time and become self-sustaining. She wants it to thrive and make money, and she firmly believes it can get there with the right business and marketing strategy in place. This strategy involves bringing in sponsors and big-money investors—something that the NWFL was never able to do. "I started working on my five-year plan of bringing in sponsors, bringing in money, elevating the sport in 2018," Jenkins said. "When I started, there were no major sponsors. No real television deals. One year later, I jumped out there with Adidas and the Riddell sponsorship. And the national cable deal. Now, with just that little bit of effort from our team and our league, there are things happening in women's football. Yeah we are not making millions, and our players aren't getting paid yet, but we are closer to professionalism than we've ever been."

What Jenkins learned most from her playing years, the leagues that came before her time, and the NWFL specifically, is that league executives and team owners failed to operate like a business. For a long time, women were content just to have the opportunity to play. They didn't complain about getting paid pennies or not getting paid at all, lack of proper equipment, and poor travel accommodations because they took what they could get at the time. But times have changed.

"I think the women in the seventies lacked that foresight because they just wanted to play football," said Jenkins. That desperation and willingness to do anything to play was also reflected in the only women's football league that's ever had any mainstream success: the Legends Football League (LFL), originally known as the Lingerie Football League. Mention professional women's football, and even if most people don't know about any of the number of full-contact leagues that have sprung up over the years, they'll often know about the lingerie league. What started in the early 2000s as a pay-per-view alternative to the Super Bowl halftime show became a league five years later and almost immediately landed a TV deal with MTV2 as well as countless sponsorships. The league had eight teams in 2019, which was their tenth and final season, and different rules than both the NFL and the other women's leagues. Their uniforms were also drastically different, which you might be able to guess based on the name of the league: instead of playing in full pads, jerseys, and pants, they wore underwear and bras. Yes, the league consisted of women, in their underwear, tackling each other.

There were shades of Sid Friedman in the LFL, in attempting to have a successful women's football league by resorting to entertainment and the exploitation of the athletes. The matches even began as halftime entertainment, as so many women's football games had early on in history. The difference was that these hypersexualized athletes, who were willing to play in their underwear if it meant getting to play the sport they loved, were more successfully exploited as a "performance act." It is likely not a coincidence that the only women's football league to garner any television deals or mainstream sponsors required the athletes to be minimally clothed for the enjoyment of a presumed straight male audience.

But today's players are no longer willing to do that, as evidenced by the fact that the LFL rebranded itself as the X League. "The barriers have been broken to play football. So that's not my goal," says Jenkins. "What I am working on is for women to have the ability to sustain a league that will be around for the rest of our lives. We have to take some chances, just like every other business does. I will do whatever I can to help get it there."

Today, there are at least four legitimate, functioning women's football leagues in the United States: Jenkins's WNFC, Women's Football Alliance

(WFA), United States Women's Football League (USWFL), and Women's Tackle Football League (WTFL). Since the NWFL folded, there have been a dozen or so other leagues that have come and gone.

In order for women's professional football to succeed and not repeat the mistakes of the past, Jenkins believes that one unified league should take the reins. "There will always be side leagues, but I think there needs to be one pro league. We can be dreamers, but we have to be smart. Because women in sports don't get nineteen chances to get it wrong."

Molly Goodwin, the fifty-year-old owner of the WFA's Boston Renegades for the past several years (working closely with her business partner Michelle McDonough and general manager Ben Brown), agrees that a single professional league is the best way to grow women's football. But that's also easier said than done. For the current women's football community, whether they can come together and unify into one league is the million dollar question.

Goodwin believes it's going to take a lot of compromise, focusing on the goal at hand and agreeing on a set of ground rules across the board that everyone can comply with. "In the twenty years that I've been involved in football, we still have the issue—similar to what the NFL and the NBA had in their beginning years—that there are multiple leagues," she said. "And I think that we are all fighting for the same resources."

The complicated situation of multiple leagues existing within one sport is not uncommon and has often been a precursor to the success of some of the most popular sports leagues in the world. The NBA and the American Basketball Association (ABA) competed for market share, audience, sponsors, and players from 1967 until 1976, when four ABA teams finally joined the NBA to form one league. The NFL and the AFL operated separately for ten years from 1960 to 1970, when they merged together to form the football powerhouse the NFL is today. And when the WNBA officially launched in 1997, the American Basketball League (ABL) had already begun playing games in the fall of 1996. But with the weight of the NBA behind the WNBA, the ABL folded two years later, and the WNBA has been evolving and expanding ever since.

Having one league with the ability to soak up all of the fan attention, lure sponsors, pique the interest of investors, and grow exponentially, and doesn't have to share or split necessary resources, has become the blueprint to success. Over time, these things tend to work themselves out. But it's been almost fifty years since the NWFL first made its appearance. And there's still no clear path ahead.

"From our team and what I've seen over the last five years, we've seen a lot of turnover in terms of ownership," Goodwin said. "I think it's because you have these owners who have been doing it for ten to twenty years and have been putting their life savings into it, and it just hasn't evolved enough for them to stay involved with it." She suggests, "We have to think about it differently. We can't wait for the league to build that infrastructure and help provide that innovation. I think each of our teams, particularly the ones that have been successful, have to take it into our own hands to help build out other teams and build best practices, build pipelines together. We can't wait for some other change agent to come in. We have to be that change agent."

Goodwin made it clear she doesn't want the NFL coming in to help start a women's league, even though this blueprint has worked out well for the WNBA over the past twenty-five years, with the NBA as its initial backer, launchpad, and financier. "I actually don't want the NFL coming in here and trying to take over our teams or our league. Because that would usurp the owner that's put in all this time and money, and actually knows and cares about [the organization] in a way that [the NFL] never will," she said. "I think we have to be careful that if we do bring in a large investor or group of investors, that it's people that we know that are going to care about us. And that we're not going to just come second to the NFL, but really make our league the priority—whatever that league looks like."

Goodwin's concerns are valid. Even now, the NBA has yet to become fully invested in the WNBA as more than just a "sister" league but as its own, successful, thriving entity. It's also unclear whether much could be expected from NFL support. The Dallas Cowboys supporting the NWFL's Bluebonnets was ultimately unhelpful aside from making the women feel validated; the Houston Herricanes wished their NFL counterpart, the Oilers, had stepped in. But there's no guarantee it would have changed anything beyond giving the team an air of legitimacy in the eyes of the public, which it definitely could have used. Even Sid Friedman had tried the NFL connection with beloved former players as coaches, which still did not legitimize his teams or bring in hordes of fans or sponsors.

It's a conversation currently happening in the women's hockey community, too, with players, coaches, and owners disagreeing on whether the NHL should step in and help start a league, or whether a league that allows players more independence is the way to go. The Professional Women's Hockey Players Association (PWHPA)—made up of some members of the US National Women's Hockey Team as well as college standouts and former players in the National Women's Hockey League (NWHL)—is hoping the NHL will step in because they believe it's the best path forward for the growth of the sport.

But NHL commissioner Gary Bettman has said the league will not get involved as long as a pro women's league already exists. And the NWHL is still going after six seasons and isn't looking like it's going to fold anytime soon. Still, PWHPA board member Alyssa Gagliardi told The Athletic in January 2020, "I think we look at the WNBA model and see the success that's had and the longevity that's had, and I think that is something that is definitely appealing. But it's really just about trying to create something, whether it's the support of an existing league like the NHL or not."

It's an important consideration, and looking to men's professional leagues as a model is not ideal, particularly when it comes to things like player agency. Trying to replicate a league like the NFL ignores the racialized way in which Black and brown athletes have had their bodies and labor exploited for the entertainment and profit of predominantly white owners and audiences, while lacking agency to speak up or make decisions for themselves. Furthermore, 70 percent of the NFL is Black, but there are only two owners of color in the league—Kim Pegula co-owns the Buffalo Bills and is of South Korean descent, and Shahid Rafiq Khan, a Pakistani-born American, is the owner of the Jacksonville Jaguars.

Women have been fighting not to be exploited by the men who own their leagues since they started playing football. As they move forward in attempting to establish their own professional leagues, it's important they don't end up replicating the same oppressive cycle for the sake of landing the kind of money, deals, or attention they hope to access—as Pam Royse once cautioned in that 1978 Troopers game program: "When, if ever, a woman crosses that line in professional football, she takes with her everything the women's football teams have fought for and won."

For now, Goodwin and the Boston Renegades and the rest of the teams in the WFA will continue pushing forward. They hope to build on some of the positive steps that have been taken so far. For example, with the recent start of NCAA and high school flag football, there's the beginnings of a possible pipeline into the professional women's football ranks. "We have to have some kind of feeder system for building teams [at the professional level]," Goodwin explained. "That helps create the athletes, coaches, referees, and helps build the overall level of play. Right now, there's still a disconnect between youth sports and actually playing full tackle."

In July 2020, the Boston Renegades appeared in a documentary by filmmaker Viridiana Lieberman called *Born to Play*, which chronicled their back-to-back championship runs over the course of the 2019 season. The documentary aired on ESPN, which was center stage for a league and a sport that doesn't receive much media attention at all. "Lack of media coverage," said Goodwin, "whether in print or online—even today on social media—is one of the biggest problems. We just don't get the same eyeballs on our sport."

There are also ethical questions around trying to launch a football league like the NFL—even if for women—given the dangers of chronic traumatic encephalopathy (CTE). Right now, society is having conversations about whether *anyone* should be playing the game as it currently exists, because of the CTE crisis that is disproportionately impacting the majority-Black men who play the game. A 2017 study from the team at Boston University School of Medicine that was published in the *Journal of the American Medical Association* found that 87 percent of the brains of men who had played American football across all levels of the game showed evidence of CTE; among NFL players it was a staggering 99 percent.

There is less research on how full-contact football affects the brains of the women who play it. Dr. Donna Duffy's Female BRAIN Project out of the University of North Carolina Greensboro is one of the only places currently studying how collision sports impact the brains of women. Duffy and her colleagues have been collecting data since 2015 on sports like football, rugby, and roller derby. And while it's true that women should be able to make decisions about assuming risk for their bodies, there are also real concerns about the ethics of continuing to play the game.

Add sexism into that; it is likely that sponsors and advertisers could use paternalistic logic to deny women's leagues the same support they provide the men's because the men's leagues are currently more profitable and they are willing to excuse the risk to players' lives and well-being in order to fill their own pockets.

Perhaps a better model is a player-centric one like Athletes Unlimited softball league, which debuted in 2020. "The league has no owners, and no coaches; instead the players coach, and have the opportunity to get equity in the league," writes Natalie Weiner for Fanbyte. "The AU base pay in 2020 was $9,000 for six weeks, and they earned bonuses based on performance for a guaranteed minimum of at least $10,000; in the [National Pro Fastpitch], in contrast, players are paid $5,000 for three months. Plus, the league matched half their bonuses in charitable donations to causes of their choice." It also merged tournament-style play with fantasy-style scoring, bringing something new that would allow players to be centered in a more explicit way.

Despite facing similar issues that have plagued women's professional football for decades, the teams, owners, leagues, and players of today have no choice but to keep going. They know that change and evolution happen over time, and believe the best thing they can do is to keep putting themselves out there like the women who came before them did so courageously—for the future of women's football and the growth of women's sports in general.

"We wouldn't be playing any of our sports without those women paving the way," Goodwin added. "It's not exclusive to football. It was a passion and they were driven. Just like the early baseball and basketball leagues, we're really lucky to have these people who had the passion and determination, and the nerve, to get out there and do it and do it in a meaningful way."

One of those NWFL women who is still connected to the leagues of today, Mitchi Collette, got a call in 2002 asking if she wanted to coach a new National Women's Football Association team, the Toledo Spitfire. Joining Collette on the coaching staff was a who's who of women's football history: former Furie Pam Whetstone was offensive coordinator and co–head coach alongside Collette; Dorothy Parma of the Troopers and the Furies coached the running backs; former Troopers and Furies coach Jerome Davis came on as the Spitfire's receiver's coach; Gloria Jimenez of the Troopers and the Furies coached defensive line; and in charge of coaching the quarterbacks was former Furies quarterback Sue Nuesmeyer.

"That team brought about the significance of Buckeye Cable Sports Network actually filming a women's professional football game," remembered Jimenez. "I never thought that would happen in my lifetime and I was pretty impressed."

But the reunion was short lived, lasting just one season. After Collette, Beth Razzoog—the marketing director and Collette's longtime partner—and the offensive coordinator, along with nineteen of the Spitfire's players walked out in May 2003, Collette and Razzoog started their own team, the Toledo Reign. Originally a member of the Women's Professional Football League, the team now plays in the WFA.

Collette, with her gray, spikey hair and no-nonsense way of talking about the game, seems aware of her place in history. The Reign's website includes a section on the history of women's football and touts Toledo as "the birthplace of women's pro football."

And it is: from the earliest days of women's football in the 1930s to today—nearly a century later—there is a thread that runs through Toledo, Ohio. Toledo, a Rust Belt town known as an industrial city, whose population has dropped drastically in the years since the Troopers took the field, is perhaps an unexpected place to be considered the mecca of women's football. And not just Toledo, but Ohio itself—it's where Sid Friedman's dream first took root, and it fielded multiple teams that participated in the NWFL. Those were some of the longest-running teams the league had. The Troopers played for nine seasons and the Furies for seven, giving Toledo a team for sixteen years. The Columbus Pacesetters were the only team that played for the entirety of the NWFL's existence, from its inception in 1974 until it folded in 1988.

"[The NWFL] would be fifty years old now. And they'd be making tremendous amounts of money had they simply just kept going. But they gave up," said David Berri, coauthor of *The Economics of the Super Bowl.* "You can't give up, you just keep it going until you get to the point where the fan base develops. Had they kept going, the people who are going to [those] games, those four thousand fans, would have had children. [Those children] would have been raised as football fans, *they* would have had children—we'd be living with the third generation here. And you would be having thirty thousand people going to these games now, and all of those women who played in those first four years would now be Hall of Fame icons."

In 2018, Rose Motil, the original quarterback for the Columbus Pacesetters, passed away. A month after her death, the Motil family received a letter from Hank Patterson, the head coach and CEO of the Columbus Comets, a team in the WFA. It was an invitation for a family member to attend a home game during the 2019 season and participate in the coin toss. "It seems to me that this is a small way that the Comets can say thank you to Rose for playing the game," Patterson wrote, "and for letting our current players have the opportunity to compete as football players.

"She helped pave the way for our current players to be able to have football as an athletic endeavor, she was a pioneer in women's sports in Central Ohio, her play and leadership set a standard of excellence for the Comets," Patterson told the family. "In our coming 2019 season, we will honor her play and are appreciative of all of her talents to have advanced the game for women."

The family, Rose's brother Joe Motil said, was "stunned." On the field the night of the coin toss, "everyone was in tears."

o———o

At first, Rose Low was hesitant to talk about her experience playing in the NWFL. She was so proud of her time on the football field and as a part of the Dandelions that she was afraid if she shared it, someone would get the story wrong, portray her and her former teammates in the wrong way and not give the NWFL the legitimacy it rightly deserved. It was a significant time in her life, as a young woman and athlete figuring out her space in the landscape of sports and Title IX and women's rights.

Low is as careful and gentle with her NWFL memories as if they were an antique vase sitting atop her dresser, that she takes down to admire and dust off now and again. They are precious to her. And even though the NWFL didn't succeed, at least not by sports leagues standards, she will always consider it a privilege to have been a part of it.

"Looking back on it now, I think we were too early," she said. "I don't know. In high school, we were taught to be ladylike. We couldn't wear pants to high school until my senior year in 1971. It was always skirts and dresses. God knows how many pairs of nylons I'd ruin in a week. I just don't think society was ready to come see women hit women [on the field]."

Society's view aside, Low also understands that there were many other things out of the players' control that led to the demise of the NWFL, such as the disorganization of the league, poor financial management, and lack of promotion and media attention. Still, she can't help feeling somewhat responsible for the NWFL's failure. "I felt horrible that we did not succeed as a league," she said. "That's why it was important for me to work very hard during that period of time because when you are the first thing, you want to do good and make it work. Things didn't work out."

The NWFL isn't the first sports league to fail and it won't be the last. But it is unique and special, not only because of the time period in which it existed but also because of the sport. Every single player, from those who were there at the start of the league to the ones who participated in only one season to the ones who stayed until the end, can revel in the fact that they were an integral part of the first professional sports league in the history of women's football. And that's something that no one can ever take away from the women who played.

The Troopers belong in the history books because they accomplished something unprecedented during the years they took the field. But the teams that never won a game, like the Tulsa Babes, or the ones that lasted a season or two, like the San Antonio Flames, deserve to be remembered, too. Even a not-so-great football team like the Detroit Demons is remarkable. The women in Detroit began as part of Sid Friedman's gimmick but wanted better for themselves and so they broke off and joined the NWFL. They rewrote their narrative, wrestled it from the hands of the man who sought to tell them who they should be, and demanded the respect they deserved.

Often the women athletes we choose to write into the history books are the ones who are extraordinary or remarkable in some way, who have broken records or beaten the odds; women have to be twice as good to even be considered for recognition. But they are all remarkable, simply because they existed at all. The women of the NWFL are worth remembering because they took the field in the first place, against all odds.

Gail Werbin, Joyce Johnson, Barbara Patton, Ann Strohecker Beebe, Rose Low, Kathy
Pearson, and Sue Davidson
Photo provided by Rose Low, LA Dandelions

EPILOGUE

Over forty years have passed since Marty Bryant was first inspired to start a football team, after seeing Linda Jefferson on the cover of *womenSports* magazine in 1975. Most of the details of how the team was formed and everything that came after are still fresh in her mind. And when the Houston Herricanes got together for their reunion in 2019, it brought everything full circle for her and so many of her former teammates. For decades, old game programs, Polaroid pictures, newspaper clippings, and ticket stubs lay stashed away in old cardboard and shoe boxes in the back of their closets or tucked high away on garage shelves. The reunion released a flood of memories with such force that sifting through all of that memorabilia after the fact was cathartic. But being there, in person, face-to-face, was the gift of a lifetime.

Three years after the Herricanes' last football game as a team, Peggy Hickman lost all of her photos, her jersey, and everything else she had collected during her time with the team in a car fire. It happened in the process of moving, and she had forgotten to turn off a map light in the back seat of her Volkswagen. Hickman has spent a good amount of time scouring the internet looking for memorabilia or anything having to do with Herricanes and the NWFL, which was hard to find. The Herricanes reunion in 2019 not only reconnected her to teammates she hadn't seen in forty years, it gave her a parting gift to hold on to. "To walk into that room and share some of those memories and see pictures, it was special. I now have one picture of me in my uniform because someone made a copy for me."

During the mideighties, Gwen Flager lost contact with most of the Herricanes as well. "People moved on," she said. "Got married, had families, changed jobs. There just wasn't that bond that we had. By the time the reunion came around, there were people I hadn't seen in forty years. With the advent of Facebook, we've reconnected and that's been nice." Brenda Cook, Janice Merritt, Rose Kelley, Jane Schulte—they were all at the reunion, too. And it felt like coming home to family, getting the gang back together, even if just for an afternoon. "It was like being outside on a cold morning and feeling the sun hit your back," said Bryant.

It was comforting for everyone at the reunion to know that despite the passage of time, they really hadn't changed at all. As for Billie Cooper, the closure she had been yearning for ever since the team had disbanded so abruptly all those years ago, never came. Instead, it was a reopening. There was a connection she hadn't realized she had been missing, a renewal of friendships and a reuniting of a sisterhood. And as she looked around at everyone's faces, at the jerseys and helmets they'd brought along, at scrapbooks filled with photos, and exchanged game memories of the highs and lows of wins and defeats, she nodded to herself.

Yeah, she thought. *We* really *did that.*

LIST OF NWFL TEAMS/ DIVISIONS/YEARS

Some teams were formed and played exhibition games before the official creation of the NWFL in 1974. This list is our best attempt to piece timelines together but is undoubtedly incomplete; many teams flew under the radar, never getting press coverage, while others played for just a season or two, and we were unable to verify information.

BATTLE CREEK RAINBOWS	Northern division	1980–1983
CALIFORNIA MUSTANGS	Western division	1974–1975
CLEVELAND BREWERS	Eastern/northern division	1979–1985/6
COLUMBUS PACESETTERS	Eastern/northern division	1974–1988
DALLAS BLUEBONNETS	Southern division	1972–1974
DALLAS–FORT WORTH SHAMROCKS	Southern division	1974–1977
DETROIT DEMONS	Eastern division	1972–1977
GRAND RAPIDS CARPENTERS	Northern division	1983–1985
HOUSTON HERRICANES	Southern division	1976–1979
LAWTON TORNADOES	Southern division	1977–1979
LOS ANGELES DANDELIONS	Western division	1973–1978
MIDDLETOWN MAVERICKS	Eastern/northern division	1975–1979
OKLAHOMA CITY DOLLS	Southern division	1976–1979
PHILADELPHIA QUEEN BEES	Eastern division	1976
SAN ANTONIO FLAMES	Southern division	1976
SAN DIEGO LOBOS	Western division	1975–1976
TOLEDO FURIES	Northern division	1983–1988
TOLEDO TROOPERS	Eastern/northern division	1971–1979
TULSA BABES	Southern division	1977–1978

ACKNOWLEDGMENTS

First and foremost, we must thank the players, coaches, and staff of the NWFL who opened their scrapbooks, closets, and memories to us. Thank you to every person involved in the NWFL who spoke with us, without whom this book would not be possible:

From the Toledo Troopers, Mitchi Collette, Gloria Jimenez, and Linda Jefferson.

From the Oklahoma City Dolls, Mary BlueJacket, Jan Hines, Charlotte Gordon, Doris Stokes, Pebble Myers, Cindee Herron, Mike Reynolds.

From the Dallas Bluebonnets, D. A. Starkey, CoCo Manson, Barbara O'Brien, Betty Young, Susie Miller, Toni Gibson, Norma Featherston, Mary Meserole.

From the Los Angeles Dandelions, Rose Low, Joyce Johnson, Ann Strohecker Beebe, Susan Hoxie.

From the Houston Herricanes, Billie Cooper, Gwen Flager, Marty Bryant, Rose Kelley, Jane Schulte, Janice Merritt, Robin Massey-Crozier, Brenda Cook, Peggy Hickman.

Joe Motil, brother of the late Columbus Pacesetters' quarterback Rose Motil. Pacesetters founding member Linda Stamps. Demons coach Dan Adair, who passed away shortly after he was interviewed in December of 2020. Cindy Turner of the Tulsa Babes and Gail Dearie of the New York Fillies. Kathy Jack, who shared her endless knowledge of the Dallas lesbian bar scene, and Karen Blazer, who shared her knowledge of Columbus, Ohio's.

Thank you to Olivia Kuan, daughter of the Herricanes' Basia Haszlakiewicz and filmmaker behind the forthcoming documentary *Brick House*, for sharing your research with us and inviting us to Houston to be part of the Herricanes reunion and appear in the film. Steve Guinan, for sharing your deep knowledge of the Toledo Troopers with us.

Thank you to Neal Rozendaal, whose 2016 *Women's Football Encyclopedia* was an invaluable resource. Andrew Linden, whose research about women's football and social movements contributed heavily to this work. And to Molly Goodwin and Odessa (OJ) Jenkins for their knowledge and candidness on where women's football and the current leagues are today.

Thank you to our fact-checker, Matt Giles, for also editing the article that would become our book proposal, without which this book would not exist. To our agent, JL Stermer, for always being our biggest cheerleader, Remy Cawley for believing in this project and taking a chance on it, and Ben Platt for making it as good as it could possibly be.

Britni would also like to thank their partner, Asher, for being a first and second and third reader, for sharing his football knowledge with them, and for supplying all the Red Bull for late-night writing sessions. Jeanna Kadlec, Austen E. Osworth, T. L. Pavlich, and Eve Ettinger for reading or consulting on various parts of this manuscript, or providing much-needed cheerleading during the writing process. Thank you to the community that held them during the writing process, which coincided with their life turning upside down: Brenda, Stacey, Rachel. Their mom for her detailed notes and close reading, their dad for instilling his love of sports, and their grandparents for always thinking they are much more impressive than they actually are. Thank you to all the queer elders in the NWFL who shared their stories with Britni, for inspiring them to divorce their husband and live the queer life of their dreams. And, of course, Lyndsey, for being the best coauthor anyone could ask for, for having strengths to complement Britni's weaknesses, and for trusting Britni's process even when it was so different from her own.

Lyndsey would also like to thank Melissa D'Arcangelo for her incredible love, support, and encouragement during the extensive research process and writing of this book, and their daughter Maggie, for providing comedic relief and inspiration. Mark D'Arcangelo for his football bond, sports-related chats, and unwavering belief that his unconventional daughter would make her writing dreams a reality. Bryan and Jason

D'Arcangelo for the endless games of tackle football at the Overlook playground, knowing full well their sister could hold her own with a bunch of boys. Tracy Fennell Hassett, Megan Schuckle Hill, and Annie Lawrence Kaftan for being the best friends a girl could ever ask for, and for always supporting Lyndsey's love of sports and writing. Hannah Withiam of Just Women's Sports for her editing prowess and friendship, and for helping to make Lyndsey a better writer. A special thanks to Rose Low for opening up and letting Lyndsey into her precious football world, without whose knowledge and information this book would have been severely incomplete. And to Britni, thank you for inviting Lyndsey along on this incredible journey, for being the yin to her writing yang, for having the courage and wherewithal to know which direction this project should take when it was still in the early stages, and for always staying true to who they are as a cowriter and individual. Lastly, a deep and heartfelt thank you to Nancy D'Arcangelo, who nurtured and cultivated Lyndsey's writing aspirations from the time she could pick up a pencil, and would have been so very proud to see this book come to fruition.

BIBLIOGRAPHY

"Action Line." *Philadelphia Inquirer*, September 28, 1970, Newspapers.com.

Allen, Samantha. *Real Queer America: LGBT Stories from Red States*. New York: Little, Brown and Company, Illustrated edition, 2019.

"Ask Them Yourself." *Family Weekly Magazine*, March 7, 1971, Newspapers.com.

Associated Press. February 22, 1978, Newspapers.com.

———. "Liberated and Footballing Football Fillies." May 15, 1972, Newspapers .com.

———. "Montrose Girls Hold Football Game, Get Muddy." *Daily Sentinel* (Grand Junction, CO), October 3, 1940, Newspapers.com.

———. "Woman's Place Is at Right Tackle?" *Odessa American*, February 19, 1974, Newspapers.com.

———. "Women's Lib Going Too Far? New York Fillies Join Football Ranks in All-Girl League." Associated Press, May 10, 1972, Newspapers.com.

Bailey, Dean. "Reynolds' Challenge: Selling the Dolls to the Public." *Daily Oklahoman*, June 27, 1976.

"Beefed up Detroit Demons Going for Broke This Season." *Detroit News*, August 9, 1977.

Bell, Debra. "U.S. News Questioned Football's Future Nearly 45 Years Ago." *US News & World Report*, February 1, 2013, www.usnews.com/news/blogs/press-past/2013/02 /01/us-news-questioned-pro-footballs-future-nearly-45-years-ago.

Bergener, John. "Troopers Establish Grid Identity." *Toledo Blade*, 1977.

Berri, David. Interview with Britni de la Cretaz, December 15, 2020.

"Big Hornet Uprising Conquers Cardinals." *Philadelphia Inquirer*, November 7, 1926, Newspapers.com.

Bill Stout picture. Toledo Lucas County Public Library Digital Collections, Toledo Troopers Football Team.

"Bluebonnets Prove Football for Chicks Too." *El Centro Conquistador*, December 6, 1972.

"Bluebonnets Will Host Shamrocks." *Dallas Morning News*, May 22, 1974.

Bosse, Paula. "Hidden in Plain Sight: A Photo History of Dallas' Gay Bars of the 1970s." Central Track, July 21, 2016, www.centraltrack.com/hidden-in-plain-sight/.

Boyle, Robert. "L.A. Gal Gridders in Debut." *Independent Press Telegram* (Long Beach, CA), July 22, 1973, Newspapers.com.

Boynton, Emily. "Menstrual Cycle Influences Concussion Outcomes." University of Rochester Medical Center, November 12, 2013, www.urmc.rochester.edu/news /story/menstrual-cycle-influences-concussion-outcomes.

Briggs, David. "Recruiting Trails Lead to Football-Crazed Ohio." *Toledo Blade*, February 3, 2013, www.toledoblade.com/sports/2013/02/03/When-it-comes-to -recruiting-football-crazed-Ohio-is-among-nation-s-best-in-producing-top -prospects/stories/20130203039.

Brislin, Tom. "Both Groups Take Negative Attitude on Football for Women in Replies to Originators." *Wilkes-Barre Times Leader*, Evening News ed., December 15, 1939, Newspapers.com.

Brower, William A. "Superstar of Women's Pro Football." *Toledo Blade*, https://www .facebook.com/TheToledoTroopers/photos/293874664145355.

Brown, Mike. "Bluejacket Has Ties to Historic Past." *Tulsa World*, October 30, 2014, https://tulsaworld.com/bluejacket-has-ties-to-historic-past/article_03341e43 -799f-5e30-bccb-ce0fc90edc60.html.

Bruder, Florence. "They Call Her Dearie, and Throw Her a Pass." *Daily Register*, August 2, 1972, Newspapers.com.

Butler, Joe. "The Sportscope." *Times Tribune* (Scranton, PA), September 26, 1967, News papers.com.

Cahn, Susan K. *Coming on Strong: Gender and Sexuality in Women's Sport*. Champaign: University of Illinois Press, 2015.

Career Trend. "NFL Salary History." Career Trend, https://careertrend.com/nfl -salary-history-13670918.html.

"Carpenters Beat Furies to Win NWFL Crown." *Battle Creek Enquirer*, October 22, 1985.

Casey, Terry. "Tribune Sports." *Tribune* (Coshocton, OH), August 30, 1967, Newspapers .com.

Casstevens, David. "HERricanes: On the Road with a Women's Pro Football Team." *Houston Post*, August 27, 1978.

"Charlotte Gordon: Dolls Confident Going Into Saturday's Opener." *Daily Oklahoman*, July 25, 1976.

Chris, Bengel. "NFL, NAIA Partnering to Launch Women's Flag Football as a Varsity Sport." CBS Sports, May 5, 2020, www.cbssports.com/nfl/news /nfl-naia-partnering-to-launch-womens-flag-football-as-a-varsity-sport/.

Collins, Bud. "Marvelous Marcella—Athlete of the Year." *Boston Globe*, December 22, 1967, Newspapers.com.

"Confident Dolls Open Grid Season Tonight." *Daily Oklahoman*, July 31, 1976.

Cooper, C. "Headless Fatties." CharlotteCooper.net, http://charlottecooper.net/fat /fat-writing/headless-fatties-01-07/.

Copley News Service. "L.A. Mother Loves Playing Professional Football." November 28, 1974, Newspapers.com.

CP. "What Will the Girls Come up with Next?" *Windsor Star* (Ontario, Canada), May 7, 1969, Newspapers.com.

Craig County Genealogical Society. "Bluejacket." The Encyclopedia of Oklahoma History and Culture, www.okhistory.org/publications/enc/entry.php?entry=BL015.

"Dallasites Calm but a Bit Startled at Gay Parade." *Fort Worth Star-Telegram*, June 25, 1972.

"Dandelions Cancel Game." *Independent Press Telegram* (Long Beach, CA), September 1, 1973.

"Dandelions' Ford Runs in High Gear, 20–0." *Los Angeles*, August 11, 1974, News papers.com.

"Dandelions Return to Long Beach Saturday." *Independent Press Telegram* (Long Beach, CA), August 12, 1973, Newspapers.com.

D'Arcangelo, Lyndsey. "PWHPA Board Member Alyssa Gagliardi on the NWHL, NHL and Boycotters' Vision for Women's Hockey." The Athletic, January 24, 2020, https://theathletic.com/1559324/2020/01/24/pwhpa-board-member-alyssa -gagliardi-on-the-nwhl-nhl-and-boycotters-vision-for-womens-hockey/.

de la Cretaz, Britni. "Almost Undefeated: The Forgotten Football Upset of 1976." Longreads, February 1, 2019, https://longreads.com/2019/02/01/toledo-troopers/.

———. "An Audience of Athletes: The Rise and Fall of Feminist Sports." Longreads, May 22, 2019, https://longreads.com/2019/05/22/an-audience-of-athletes-the -rise-and-fall-of-feminist-sports/.

———. "The Hidden Queer History Behind 'A League of Their Own.'" Narratively, May 30, 2018, https://narratively.com/the-hidden-queer-history-behind -a-league-of-their-own/.

———. "More Girls Are Playing Football. Is That Progress?" *New York Times*, February 2, 2018, www.nytimes.com/2018/02/02/well/family/football-girls-concussions .html.

———. "Tackling Patriarchy: Supporting Women's Football Leagues." Bitch Media, February 1, 2019, www.bitchmedia.org/article/support-womens-football-leagues.

———. "Maria Pepe: The New Jersey Girl Who Sued to Play Baseball with the Boys." *Guardian*, September 23, 2018, www.theguardian.com/sport/2018/sep/23 /maria-pepe-bfa-baseball-series-now.

———. "Women Play Football Professionally, Too—The Difference Is They Have to Pay to Do It." Bustle, February 1, 2019, www.bustle.com/p/women-play-football -professionally-too-the-difference-is-they-have-to-pay-to-do-it-15915293.

"Demons Rip Middletown, Even Season." *Detroit Free Press*, October 24, 1977.

"Detroit Demons vs. Toledo Troopers: Football's Answer to 'Hatfields & McCoys.'" *Macomb Daily*, 1977.

"Dirty Losers." *Longview News-Journal*, July 23, 1973.

"Dolls Breeze Past Lawton." *Daily Oklahoman*, July 15, 1979.

"Dolls Confident Going into Saturday's Opener." *Daily Oklahoman*, July 25, 1976.

"Dolls Dance Past Texans in 50–0 Rout." *Daily Oklahoman*, October 3, 1976.

"Dolls Grab 16–12 Win." *Daily Oklahoman*, 1976.

"Dolls in Dallas for a Rematch." *Daily Oklahoman*, August 14, 1976.

"Dolls Make 'Progress' as Grid Opener Nears." *Daily Oklahoman*, June 6, 1976.

"Dolls Movie in Works." *Daily Oklahoman*, May 30, 1979.

"Dolls Overpower League Foe." *Lawton Constitution*, August 8, 1977.

"Dolls Overpower League Foe." *Lawton Constitution*, August 28, 1977.

"Dolls Win 2nd Straight." *Daily Oklahoman*, 1976.

Duffy, Donna. Interview with Britni de la Cretaz, January 21, 2018.

Durslag, Melvin. "Women Make Pro Grid Rush." *Los Angeles Herald*, December 6, 1973, Newspapers.com.

"E. O. Tenison Gave Memorial Park." Dallas Gateway, February 25, 2018, https:// dallasgateway.com/e-o-tenison-gave-memorial-park/.

Ellis, Kay Crosby. "Rough 'n' Tough Female Football Not for Sisses." *Dallas Morning News*, Morning ed., June 21, 1974.

Esterly, Glenn. "Crush, Crush, Sweet Charlotte." *Local Los Angeles Magazine*.

———. "The Morning Call." Women's News Service.

"Female Football Team Invades the Gridiron." *Times* (Shreveport, LA), September 15, 1975.

Ferree, Myra Marx. "Working Class Feminism: A Consideration of the Consequences of Employment." *Sociological Quarterly* 21, no. 2 (1980): 173–184. www.jstor.org /stable/4106149?seq=1.

Fink, Janet S., et al. "The Freedom to Choose: Elite Female Athletes' Preferred Representations Within Endorsement Opportunities." *Journal of Sport Management* 28, no. 2 (2014): 207–219. https://journals.humankinetics.com/view/journals/jsm/28/2 /article-p207.xml.

Florence, Mal. "The Dandelions Are No Daisies." *Los Angeles Times*, July 23, 1973, Newspapers.com.

"Football Dolls Taking Shape." *Daily Oklahoman*, April 1, 1976.

"Football Was Dolls Game." *Daily Oklahoman*, February 14, 2000.

"Former Rainbows Aim to Find Their Pot of Gold." *Battle Creek Enquirer*, October 18, 1985.

"Four on the 50." *Dallas Morning News*, Morning ed., April 28, 1973.

Fullman, Ricki. "All-Girl Football Team Tackles a Man's Game." *New York Daily News*, April 18, 1972, Newspapers.com.

Game advertisement. *Independent* (Long Beach, CA), August 15, 1973, Newspapers .com.

Game Day Program. Lawton Tornadoes.

Game Program. Oklahoma City Dolls.

Game Program. Toledo Troopers vs. Columbus Pacesetters, 1979.

"Game Recap, Game at a Glance." *Los Angeles Times*, July 23, 1973, Newspapers.com.

Garcia, Ahiza. "These Are the Only Two Owners of Color in the NFL." CNN.com, May 18, 2018, https://money.cnn.com/2018/05/18/news/nfl-nba-mlb-owners-diversity /index.html.

"Gays March Proudly." *Dallas Morning News*, Morning ed., June 25, 1972.

Gibson, Toni. Article clipping. *Dallas Times Herald*.

"Girls' Football: These Husky Californians Play Rough, Tough Regulation Game." *Life*, November 22, 1939.

"Girls Girding for Gridiron Grappling." *Fort-Worth Star Telegram*, January 24, 1974.

"Girls on Gridiron." *Cincinnati Enquirer*, October 27, 1974.

Graham, Megan, and Jabari Young. "Women Are Watching the NFL in Record Numbers, and Super Bowl Ads Are Finally Starting to Reflect That." CNBC.com, www .cnbc.com/2020/02/01/women-nfl-fans-are-at-a-record-and-super-bowl-ads-finally -reflect-that.html.

Green, Ted. "Meanwhile, in the Other WFL (Women's Football League). . . ." *Los Angeles Times*, September 13, 1974, Newspapers.com.

Guinan, Steve. Interview with Britni de la Cretaz, January 24, 2019.

"Hall of Famers Coach Spitfire." Our Sports Central, March 26, 2003, www .oursportscentral.com/services/releases/hall-of-famers-coach-spitfire/n-1989354.

Harmon, Kimberly G., et al. "Position Statement: Concussion in Sport." *British Journal of Sports Medicine*, no. 47 (2013): 15–26. *BMJ Journals*, https://bjsm.bmj.com.

Harris, Roy J. "Wham . . . and That's No Kiss, Crazylegs." *Wall Street Journal*, December 26, 1971.

Hatz, Dave. "Coaching Job Becomes a Dream-Come-True—in Women's Football." *Chula Vista-Star News*, May 11, 1975, Newspapers.com.

Hayes, Jack. "Women's Football Queens, Toledo Troopers, For Sale." *Toledo Blade*, April 8, 1980, https://news.google.com/newspapers?id=gElPAAAAIBAJ&sjid =IwMEAAAAIBAJ&pg=7103%2C3937331.

Henry, John. "The Ingrained Roots of Texas Football." *Fort Worth Star-Telegram*, August 26, 2015, www.star-telegram.com/sports/nfl/article32437431.html.

Henry, Tom. "Remembering Toledo's Troopers: Film to Tell Story of '70s Female Football Team." *Toledo Blade*, June 16, 2013, www.toledoblade.com/Movies/2013/06/16 /Remembering-Toledo-s-Troopers.html.

———. "35 Years Later, Toledo's Furies Receive Championship Rings at Last." *Toledo Blade*, October 25, 2019, www.toledoblade.com/sports/pro/2019/10/25/national -womens-football-league-toledo-furies-getting-championship-rings-reunion /stories/20191024131.

Hirshey, Dave. "Pro Football Season Begins—with a Touch of Mascara." *Daily News* (New York), May 13, 1972, Newspapers.com.

Holtzmann, Roger. "The Lady Leatherheads of Madison." *South Dakota Magazine*, November/December 2011, Newspapers.com.

Howard, Tanner. "Development in Black and White." Belt Magazine, November 22, 2019, https://beltmag.com/manufacturing-decline-racism-development/.

Hyland, Dick. "Behind the Line with Dick Hyland." *Los Angeles Times*, October 15, 1939, Newspapers.com.

INS. "Gridiron Coach May Join Army." *Arizona Republic*, June 3, 1941, Newspapers .com.

Jayroe, Walt. "Dolls Triumph in Debut." *Daily Oklahoman*, July 31, 1976.

Jennings, Chantel. "Ladies Who Led: The Untold Story Behind Cavour (SD) High School Girls Football and the 'Female Red Grange.'" The Athletic, July 29, 2019, https://theathletic.com/1101489/2019/07/29/girls-high-school-football-1926-south -dakota-cavour-high-school/.

Jones, Charles T. "The Rise and Fall of OU Great Rod Shoate: Another Drug Casualty Makes Many Ask Why." *Oklahoman*, October 31, 1999, https://oklahoman.com /article/2673242/the-rise-and-fall-of-ou-great-rod-shoate-another-drug-casualty -makes-many-ask-why.

Kane, Mary Jo, et al. "Exploring Elite Female Athletes' Interpretations of Sport Media Images: A Window into the Construction of Social Identity and 'Selling Sex' in Women's Sports." *Journal of Communication and Sport*, 2013. University of Minnesota, www.cehd.umn.edu/tuckercenter/library/docs/research/Kane-LaVoi -Fink-2013_poster.pdf.

Kersey, Jason. "Oklahoma Football: Rod Shoate's College Football Hall of Fame Election a Blessing for His Family." *Oklahoman*, May 7, 2013, https://oklahoman .com/article/3807403/oklahoma-football-rod-shoates-college-football-hall-of-fame -election-a-blessing-for-his-family.

Kirkpatrick, Curry. "Getting into the Picture." *Sports Illustrated*, April 21, 1975, https:// vault.si.com/vault/1975/04/21/getting-into-the-picture.

The LA Dandelions. "About the NWFL" Blurb in game program. September 1974.

Leavy, James M. "Dandelions Bid for Spectators." *Independent Press Telegram* (Long Beach, CA), September 29, 1975, Newspapers.com.

Liddick, Betty. "Off with Pompoms, on with the Pads." *Los Angeles Times*, April 15, 1973.

Life Sports Editorial. "Women Grid Squat Meet on June 28." *Berwyn Life* (Illinois), June 15, 1941.

"Linda Jefferson, Athlete of the Year." *womenSports*, June 1975.

Linden, Andrew. "American Football and the 1970s Women's Movement." Sport in American History, May 29, 2014, https://ussporthistory.com/2014/05/29/american-football-and-the-1970s-womens-movement-3/.

———. Interview with Britni de la Cretaz, January 14, 2019.

Lindquist, Danille Christensen. "'Locating' the Nation: Football Game Day and American Dreams in Central Ohio." *Journal of American Folklore* 119, no. 474 (2006): 444–488. JSTOR, www.jstor.org.

Livingston, Bill. "Gals Put Best Foot Forward." *Dallas Morning News*, Morning ed., February 18, 1973, Genealogy Bank.

"Local Woman Gridder Loves Game." *Lancaster Eagle-Gazette*, October 10, 1982.

Loomis, Tom. "No Tea-Time Chatter When Troopers Play." *Toledo Blade*, October 13, 1975, https://news.google.com/newspapers?id=oD5PAAAAIBAJ&sjid=OQIEAAAAIBAJ&pg=5422%2C3906446.

Ludlum, Judy. "Purse-Toting Footballers Draw Stares." *Pittsburgh Post Gazette*, November 23, 1968, Newspapers.com.

Maher, Charles. "These Ladies Wear the Pads." *Los Angeles Times*, July 14, 1973, Newspapers.com.

Maldarelli, Claire. "Football Helmets Don't Prevent Concussions. What Can?" *Popular Science*, February 3, 2018, www.popsci.com/helmets-concussions-football/.

Maum, Emmet. "New Football Game for Girls." *St. Joseph News–Press*, October 29, 1939, Newspapers.com.

McCarriston, Shanna. "Nike Partners with NFL for New Girls High School Flag Football Initiative." CBS Sports, February 3, 2021, www.cbssports.com/general/news/nike-partners-with-nfl-for-new-girls-high-school-flag-football-initiative/.

McLeod, Paul. "Dandelions Storm Past Detroit, 25–0." *Independent Press Telegram* (Long Beach, CA), August 19, 1973, Newspapers.com.

"Media Coverage and Female Athletes: A Tucker Center/tptMN Video Documentary." University of Minnesota/Tucker Center for Research on Girls and Women in Sport, www.cehd.umn.edu/tuckercenter/projects/mediacoverage.html#:~:text=Forty%20percent%20of%20all%20sports,portrayed%20in%20sexually%20provocative%20poses.

Messina, Ignazio. "Toledo's Decline Misses Rock Bottom." *Toledo Blade*, March 25, 2013, www.toledoblade.com/local/2013/03/24/Toledo-s-decline-misses-rock-bottom/stories/20130323149.

Mez, Dr. Jesse, et al. "Clinicopathological Evaluation of Chronic Traumatic Encephalopathy in Players of American Football." *Journal of the American Medical Association* 318, no. 4 (July 25, 2017): 360–370. https://jamanetwork.com/journals/jama/article-abstract/2645104.

Morales, Carolyn. "'Bluebonnets' Prove Football for Females Too." *Denton Record-Chronicle*, January 16, 1974.

Moritz, Brian P. "The 'Problem' with Women's Sports." Sports Media Guy, www.sportsmediaguy.com/blog/2018/3/28/the-problem-with-womens-sports.

Morse, Steve. "Rainbows to Open at Home Tonight Without a Coach." *Battle Creek Enquirer*, August 20, 1983.

———. "Rainbows Team with Carpenters for Season Finale." *Battle Creek Enquirer*, October 21, 1983.

———. "Rainbows to Play Under New Coach." *Battle Creek Enquirer*, September 24, 1983.

Moses, Cat. "Queering Class: Leslie Feinberg's 'Stone Butch Blues.'" *Studies in the Novel* 31, no. 1 (1999): 74–97. *JSTOR*, www.jstor.org.

Nagel, George. "Atmore Girl Earns Post on Escambia High Eleven with Her Kicking." *Birmingham News*, November 19, 1939, Newspapers.com.

Nash, Tammye. "Honoring a Dallas Legend." *Dallas Voice*, October 14, 2016, https://dallasvoice.com/honoring-dallas-legend/.

———. "Last Call." *Dallas Voice*, July 8, 2016, https://dallasvoice.com/call-2/.

"Natalie Portman and Serena Williams' Daughter Among New NWSL Team Owners." *Guardian*, July 21, 2020, www.theguardian.com/football/2020/jul/21/natalie-portman-serena-williams-la-soccer-team-angel-city.

National Center for Education Statistics. "Title IX." National Center for Education Statistics, https://nces.ed.gov.

"National Women's Football League Championship Bowl Program, December 11, 1976." Toledo Lucas County Public Library Digital Collections, www.ohiomemory.org/digital/collection/p16007coll33/id/88793/rec/77.

NBC News. "Sports Segment." NBC News Archives, Channel Nine News (Los Angeles), September 1994.

———. "Weekend." Video footage/DVD of interviews/game play of the LA Dandelions, 1974.

NEA. "In Cleveland, Girls Are Playing the Field." *Raleigh Register*, November 11, 1969, Newspapers.com.

Negley, Cassandra. "WNBA Average Viewership Grows 68 Percent During a Season Focused on Social Justice." Yahoo Sports, October 1, 2020, https://sports.yahoo.com/wnba-average-viewership-up-68-percent-national-tv-windows-marketing-growth-210452911.html.

"The Ohio Women Who Dominated Professional Football." Ohio History Connection, www.ohiohistory.org/learn/ohio-champion-of-sports/2019-01/toledo-troopers#:~:text=Due%20to%20financial%20troubles%2C%20the,of%20Fame%20in%20Canton%2C%20Ohio.

"Oklahoma Football Twitter Account." Twitter, December 10, 2013, https://twitter.com/OU_Football/status/410429140815585280.

Patterson, Kelly L. "Rustbelt and Race." Wiley Online Library, December 30, 2015, https://onlinelibrary.wiley.com/doi/abs/10.1002/9781118663202.wberen628.

Paulsen. "Ratings: WNBA, MLB, NBA, EPL." Sports Media Watch, 2020, www.sportsmediawatch.com/2020/07/wnba-ratings-opener-hits-high-mlb-fox-nba-scrimmage-epl/.

Penn, Jean Cox. "Look." *Los Angeles Times*, March 10, 1978, Newspapers.com.

Perfect Season: The Untold Story of the Toledo Troopers. Perfect Season, www.perfectseasonthemovie.com/story.

"Perfume-Laden Tornado Ready to Descend on Lawton." *Lawton Constitution*, July 15, 2015.

"Playing Football Is Better Than Winning Miss America." *Sunday Oklahoman/Orbit Magazine*, September 12, 1976.

"The Play with Their Hearts." *Akron Beacon Journal*, November 7, 1982.

"Queens of the Gridiron: The Women and Girls of Tackle Football." Columbus Pacesetters, www.angelfire.com/sports/womenfootball/Columbus.html?fbclid

=IwAR1SM8bMZAuaw61uESpmogTb2LD3u-KS9uvQ8mVboxpPuvX6y2cek
CcA4vY.

"'Quiet' Dolls Face LA Tonight." *Daily Oklahoman*, August 28, 1976.

Rapoport, Ron. "Wham, Bam, Thank You, Ma'am." *womenSports*, November 1974.

Record, Tony. "Editorial Cartoon." *Fort Worth Star-Telegram*, May 1973, Newspapers.com.

Risinger, Elaine. "Pay Secondary to the Challenge for Women Gridders." *Long Beach Independent Telegram* (Long Beach, CA), January 5, 1975, Newspapers.com.

Rockman, Thomas, Jr. "The Role of Bars in Texas Gay and Lesbian History." *Texas Triangle*, July 17, 1997, www.houstonlgbthistory.org/Houston80s/Assorted%20Pubs/TXTriangle/TXTriangle-97-071797-bar%20history.pdf.

Rothman, Seymour. "I've Heard, 'Girls Football.'" *Toledo Blade*, September 5, 1978, Newspapers.com.

Royse, Pamela. "Football." Toledo Troopers Game Program, 1978.

Rozendaal, Neal. *The Women's Football Encyclopedia*. Rockville, MD: Rozehawk Publishing, 2016.

Rusnak, Jim. "Women Gridders Tie, but Enthusiasm Wins." *Pittsburgh Press*, November 30, 1968, Newspapers.com.

"Samuell-Grand Park." Dallas Parks and Recreation, www.dallasparks.org/Facilities/Facility/Details/SamuellGrand-Park-650#:~:text=Samuell%2DGrand%20is%20a%2080.9,community%20park%2C%20established%20in%201938.

The San Diego Lobos. "How The San Diego Lobos Got Started." 1975.

Schaefer, Matthew. "Lou Henry Hoover and Athletics for Women and Girls." *National Archives: the Blog of Herbert Hoover Library and Museum*, Hoover Heads, March 28, 2018, https://hoover.blogs.archives.gov/2018/03/28/lou-henry-hoover-and-athletics-for-women-and-girls/.

The School of Health and Human Sciences at UNC Greensboro. Program for the Advancement of Girls and Women in Sport and Physical Activity, The Female Brain Project, https://hhs.uncg.edu/pagwspa/the-female-brain-project/.

Searcy, Jay. "At QB for Dallas Barbara O'Brien." *New York Times*, September 29, 1974, www.nytimes.com/1974/09/29/archives/at-qb-for-dallasbarbara-obrien.html.

Sebo, Renee. "That's No Lady—That's Our Middle Linebacker: On the Squad of the Cleveland Daredevils, Mothers Wear Hip Pads, Broads Get Blitzed, and Nice Girls Finish Last." *Chicago Tribune*, November 16, 1969, Newspapers.com.

Shah, Diane K. "Who Says Football's a Man's Game?" *Toledo Blade*, www.facebook.com/TheToledoTroopers/photos/288907801308708.

"Shaking the Jitters, Dolls Find Football 'Is Really Fun.'" *Sunday Oklahoman*, August 1, 1976.

Shaw, Tom. "Ever Hear of 'Weight Watchers?'" *Long Beach Independent*, July 23, 1973, https://drive.google.com/file/d/15P31wf2wiuJYBriZZv6Q7XxFxOTm2-mS/view.

"She Bets and Shrieks and Pitches Away Her Muff—the Football Girl." *New York Times*, November 30, 1913, Newspapers.com.

Shefski, Bill. "Fillies Start Banging Breastplates Tonight: These Gals Forsake the Steam Iron for the Gridiron." *Philadelphia Daily News*, May 13, 1972, Newspapers.com.

Silvis, Donn. "The Quarterback Is a Lady." *Elan*, January 1976.

Smarsh, Sarah. "Working-Class Women Are Too Busy for Gender Theory—but They're Still Feminists." *Guardian*, June 25, 2017, www.theguardian.com/world/2017/jun/25/feminism-working-class-women-gender-theory-dolly-parton.

"(Special Report) Feminine Grid Team to Play in Mexico City." *Arizona Star Daily Newspaper*, December 7, 1940, Newspapers.com.

"Sports by Sikes/Speaking of Sports." *Bradford Evening Star*, December 16, 1939, Newspapers.com.

Standish, Frederick. "Rainbows Overcome Lack of Money, Rash of Injuries." The Associated Press, October 25, 1983. *Battle Creek Enquirer*, Newspapers.com.

Stein, Charles. "They Play for the Love of It: The Wild World of Women's Football." *Michigan Daily Sunday Magazine*, November 11, 1973, https://digital.bentley.umich.edu/midaily/mdp.39015071754456/583.

Stewart, D. L. "Cleveland Agent Forms Gals' Team." *Journal Herald* (Dayton, OH), September 13, 1967, Newspapers.com.

St. John, Bob. *Landry: The Legend and the Legacy*. Nashville: Word Publishing/Thomas Nelson, Inc., 2000. Google Books, www.google.com/books/edition/Landry/Q_gS6B7blfE0C?hl=en.

Strackbein, Noah. "Steelers Among Most Valuable NFL Franchises." *Sports Illustrated*, August 3, 2020, www.si.com/nfl/steelers/news/steelers-valuable-nfl-franchises.

Sun, ed. "Football Game by Girls." *Sun* (New York, NY), November 23, 1896.

Sutherland, Viv. "Without Coaches, Money or Equipment, Life for the New York Fillies Is Not One, Long Rosy Touchdown." *womenSports*, November 1974.

Taffet, David. "A Brief Herstory of Lesbians in Dallas." *Dallas Voice*, January 16, 2015, https://web.archive.org/web/20150402054042/www.dallasvoice.com/herstory-lesbians-dallas-10188119.html.

"Taft Stadium—Oklahoma City." The History Exchange, http://thehistoryexchange.com/index.php/wpa-research/taft-stadium-oklahoma-city/.

Tate, Suzy. "The Cramdown: Maintaining Respect for the Judiciary and the Integrity of Our Legal System." The Newsletter of the Tampa Bay Bankruptcy Bar Association, Spring 2014, www.tbbba.com/wp-content/uploads/2017/07/CRAMDOWN0414.pdf.

Taylor, Keeanga Yamahtta. *How We Get Free: Black Feminism and the Combahee River Collective*. Chicago: Haymarket Books, 2017.

"Thee Toledo Reign Blog." Toledo Reign, http://theetoledoreign.blogspot.com.

"These Gals Wear Cleats Not Pleats." *Detroit Free Press*, September 1, 1975.

Toledo Lucas County Public Library Digital Collections. Ohio Memory, www.ohiomemory.org/digital/collection/p16007coll33/id/88817/rec/20.

"Toledo Troopers." Toledo Troopers Facebook Page, Facebook, www.facebook.com/TheToledoTroopers.

"Toledo Troopers and Title IX." Vimeo, Perfect Season, https://vimeo.com/173462352.

"Toledo Troopers Framed Game Jersey Worn by Linda Jefferson, 1972–1979." Toledo Lucas County Public Library Digital Collections, Ohio Memory, https://ohiomemory.org/digital/collection/p16007coll33/id/88705/.

"Toledo Troopers Framed Poster, Game Scores, 1971–1978." Toledo Lucas County Public Library Digital Collections, Ohio Memory, www.ohiomemory.org/digital/collection/p16007coll33/id/88817/rec/20.

"The Toledo Troopers Women's Football Team (1971–1979): Pam Hardy Fisher." Toledo Lucas County Public Library, https://tlcpltroopers.omeka.net/exhibits/show/toledotroopers/players/pamhardyfisher.

"Toledo Troopers Yearbook, 1972." Toledo Lucas County Public Library Digital Collections, Ohio Memory, www.ohiomemory.org/digital/collection/p16007coll33/id/88587/rec/25.

"2020 Athletic Hall of Fame Inductee Spotlight: Cathie Ann Schweitzer." Springfield College Athletics, https://springfieldcollegepride.com/general/2019-20/releases/20200315xsybtn.

University of Texas. "Clipping: Those 'Ladies' of the Gridiron." University of North Texas Library Special Collections, The Portal to Texas History, https://texashistory.unt.edu/ark:/67531/metadc1635112/m1/1/?q=%22dallas%20bluebonnets%22.

———. "Flyer: Women's Professional Football Team." University of North Texas Library Special Collections, The Portal to Texas History, https://texashistory.unt.edu/ark:/67531/metadc1634931/?q=%22dallas%20bluebonnets%22.

U.P. "New Threat: Girl Gridder Can Pass as Well as Kick." *Courier* (Waterloo–Cedar Falls, IA), October 23, 1940, Newspapers.com.

UPI. "Female Bubba & Co." *Sacramento Bee*, July 24, 1973, Newspapers.com.

———. "Gals Compete with NFL." *Valley Morning Star* (Harligen, TX), January 13, 1968, Newspapers.com.

———. "Seven Teams Entered in Gals' Grid League." *Spokane Chronicle*, September 17, 1974, Newspapers.com.

———. "To Organize All-Female Grid Squad." *Sandusky Register*, August 30, 1967, Newspapers.com.

———. "Who's Gonna Guard Girdles." *Cincinnati Enquirer*, September 12, 1967, www.newspapers.com/image/104249675/.

"Weaker Sex?—My Foot: Women Take to the Gridiron in Their Own Version of National Football League." *Ebony*, 1973, 182–190, Google Books.

"Weekly League Attendance." Pro Football Reference, www.pro-football-reference.com/years/1922/attendance.htm.

Weiner, Natalie. "The Player-Centric Future of Pro Sports Looks Like this Brand New Softball League." Fanbyte, October 9, 2020, www.fanbyte.com/features/athletes-unlimited-softball/.

"What Does a Football Player Look Like?" Toledo.com, October 10, 2014, www.toledo.com/news/2014/10/10/toledo-local-features/what-does-a-football-player-look-like/.

"William (Bill) Lee Stout (1944–2012), Photograph, 1970s." Toledo Lucas County Public Library Digital Collections, Ohio Memory, www.ohiomemory.org/digital/collection/p16007coll33/id/88824/rec/45.

"Women in Sports." *Dayton Daily News*, April 4, 1979.

"Women's Football Reaction Mixed." *Ashbury Park Press*, August 13, 1984.

"Women's Football Team Purchased." *Marion Star*, May 5, 1977.

"Women's Pro Football." *SportsWoman* 1, no. 2 (Summer 1973).

"Women's Pro Football Timeline—1978, Archives." *Seattle Times*, 1978, https://archive.seattletimes.com/archive/?date=20010121&slug=time21.

Woodhull, Nancy. "Detroit Demons: A Desperate Desire To Play Ball." *Detroit Free Press*, November 1974, Newspapers.com.

INDEX